D0217864

Learning from Our Lives

Women, Research, and Autobiography in Education

Learning from Our Lives

Women, Research, and Autobiography in Education

EDITED BY

Anna Neumann and Penelope L. Peterson

FOREWORD BY MARY CATHERINE BATESON

Teachers College, Columbia University
New York and London

Published by Teachers College Press, 1234 Amsterdam Avenue, New York, NY 10027

Photograph of Penelope Peterson courtesy University Relations, Michigan State University.

Library of Congress Cataloging-in-Publication Data

Learning from our lives : women, research, and autobiography in education / edited by Anna Neumann and Penelope L. Peterson ; foreword by Mary Catherine Bateson.
p. cm.
Includes bibliographical references and index.
ISBN 0-8077-3594-9 (alk. paper). – ISBN 0-8077-3593-0 (pbk. : alk. paper)
1. Women in education–United States. 2. Women's studies–United States. 3. Education–Research–United States. 4. Women educators–United States–Biography. I. Neumann, Anna. II. Peterson, Penelope L.
LC1757.L416 1997
371.822′07′2–dc21 96-39781

ISBN 0-8077-3593-0 (paper)
ISBN 0-8077-3594-9 (cloth)

Printed on acid-free paper
Manufactured in the United States of America

04 03 02 01 00 99 98 97 8 7 6 5 4 3 2 1

Contents

Foreword

THE WOMEN WHO HAVE WRITTEN for this volume are pioneers in the familiar landscape of female roles, seeing its vistas anew as they invent themselves as researchers within it. The diversity here is not surprising, since these women, like many others of their generation, have had to work without models, each finding her own distinctive way of composing her life.

We live in a time of rapidly expanding awareness of the possible shapes of women's lives, as biographies and autobiographies of different groups become available, but this is a collection of particular importance. Here we have the stories of a group engaged in research on the field of education itself, and so especially likely to be aware of their own processes of learning and development. To function well in a society of rapid social and technological change, schools need to become teaching-learning communities through which not only children but also teachers, parents, and administrators learn and grow. This is a moving target, and pursuing it a continuous process that will never produce a perfect curriculum. Thus all participants need to be aware that new unanswered questions and unmet concerns will inevitably come to the fore. Universities and schools of education need these same characteristics, and indeed the entire society should be a place where we share an awareness of incomplete knowledge and a willingness to learn and develop.

Unfortunately, the traditional hierarchies of higher education work against this kind of openness, adhering to the obsolete notion that those in authority should already have the answers and should work only with objective fact without personal involvement. The entry of women into these hierarchies has offered real hope for change, for, although the majority of teachers in K–12 are women, this is not true of the majority of faculty in schools of education, nor is it true of administrators and policy makers in the field. Women have necessarily been feeling their way, sometimes bringing a precious quality of humility along with self-awareness. One can hope that the process of telling their stories has been educational for them individually, and that it will prove productive for their field as well.

Everydayness is a word frequently used to describe those aspects of life that are taken for granted, which have here become the context for creativity and new learning. These are stories of the evolution of curiosity and attention, for research is one of the activities through which we continue the processes of learning and exploration so crucial in childhood, transformed to offer new knowledge to the society rather than knowledge new only to the individual. It is crucial to the field of education to understand how curiosity can continue and develop in adulthood. It is also crucial to empower teachers to learn in their own classrooms. The emphasis in many of these essays on collaborative and engaged research in classrooms means that the authors are also acting as teaching-learning models to teachers. "Everyday" is, after all, where much of learning takes place.

It is a cliché that experience is the best teacher, yet experience is a teacher from whom many fail to learn. What does it take to look at the familiar and discern the assumptions and power relationships that maintain it, to go on to say, this is not the only possible way, this is not how it has to be? Under what circumstances is experience converted to wisdom and commitment, or translated to forms whereby it can be shared? Much of what we call education is concerned with passing on conclusions rather than facilitating the processes of discovery, yet each of these researchers finds, in a review of her own life experiences, the very stuff of discovery. By reflecting on their own past learning and the sources of their questions, these women have become participant observers of their own lives, exploring the meeting place of personal and social creativity.

One of the questions that is often asked about research of this kind is whether the voices we hear are "representative." This is a false question, since they offer a range of possibility, not a statistical sample. As with all personal narratives, we should not read these stories as if they were idealized courtroom testimony, the much abused "whole truth and nothing but the truth," for this is not attainable. The narratives reflect the purpose for which they have been constructed, for self-understanding always includes a dimension of justification, not only "what I did" and "what happened" but how and why I chose to understand it, and a readying of the self for the tasks that lie ahead. These processes are necessarily subjective. As such they are deeply encouraging, because they demonstrate the emergence of a cohort of researchers whose studies and conclusions are informed by their concern.

Mary Catherine Bateson
Clarence F. Robinson Professor of Anthropology and English, George Mason University

Acknowledgments

WE WOULD LIKE TO THANK the contributors to this volume for joining us in a personal and intellectual exploration of the intersection of life and work. Their courage, creativity, and energy made this project a time of learning in our own lives.

Others, most of whom were not directly involved as authors, joined us in the three-year conversation that culminated in this book. We especially want to thank Aaron M. Pallas for offering important insights on the nature of research and on life-course development–for contributing generously, in thought and time, to this exploration of the meaning of research in our own and others' lives. We are also grateful to Sari Knopp Biklen, David Labaree, and Janet Miller for providing sound reviews and advice at critical points in our work. A number of colleagues commented helpfully on the opening chapter as a frame for the volume–our thanks to Kathryn H. Au, Margaret Eisenhart, Anne Gere, Patricia J. Gumport, David Labaree, Gloria Ladson-Billings, Ellen Condliffe Lagemann, Lynn Paine, Aaron M. Pallas, Steven Weiland, and Lauren Jones Young. At Teachers College Press, Carol Chambers Collins, Brian Ellerbeck, and Lyn Grossman provided thoughtful guidance. Locally, we are indebted to Lisa Roy for helping to oversee the administrative aspects of this project and for providing essential support in manuscript preparation; completing this book would have been very hard without her.

We also wish to thank the many unnamed students whose efforts to learn educational research and become educational researchers are the center and source of this book, and who, in our classes and in our offices, fed our thoughts with stories of research emerging in their lives. This book is dedicated to them and to the stories that, looking back, they will someday write.

Finally, we are deeply grateful for our own opportunities to learn from each other and from our work together as it grew, from a small conversation more than three years ago, into this volume.

Anna Neumann and Penelope L. Peterson

* CHAPTER 1 *

Researching Lives: Women, Scholarship, and Autobiography in Education

Anna Neumann and Penelope L. Peterson

IN THIS VOLUME WE EXPLORE educational research as personal endeavor—as experiences within and expressions of a researcher's life. We also view research as relational: A researcher conducts research with, through, and in the company of others—and others around her, particularly those who are part of her life, must live with the time, thought, and energy she devotes to (but also derives from) her work. Eschewing a more traditional model in which researchers distance self from research, we see self and research as tightly intertwined—research as strivings for "objectivity" in lives and relationships that are inherently subjective. Viewed this way, research is as much a part of a researcher's life history as it is a part of her curriculum vitae.

Some educational scholars are now pursuing the idea that teachers' knowledge about teaching derives from teachers' own lives.[1] Though many scholars have yet to pursue this idea in their own lives, others, notably women, have begun to do so—for example, by reflecting on the autobiographical antecedents of their work as educators.[2] We explore this idea further, focusing explicitly on *research*, as opposed to teaching or other professional activities, in women's lives.[3]

To do this, we invited eleven women in educational research to write about the personal origins and meanings of their own research—whether quantitative or qualitative, whether empirical or not, whether situated in conventional paradigms or reflecting new research epistemologies, whether continuous or changing in substance or form throughout their lives.[4] We asked them to consider whether and how their research connects to their daily existence with and among others, including their children, spouses, partners, and friends—persons who, enmeshed in the "personal" tapestry of

Learning from Our Lives: Women, Research, and Autobiography in Education. ISBN 0-8077-3593-0 (pbk), ISBN 0-8077-3594-9 (cloth).

researchers' lives, are typically separated from their research. The authors were also to consider how their relationships with colleagues and students—as well as with study participants and influential writers—shape their research. We wanted to understand how these women's learning in everyday life related (or not) to their learning in research.[5]

Though the question of how researchers construct research in their lives applies to both women and men, we chose to focus on women, partly for practical reasons: We found numerous intellectual autobiographies of men to which we could refer our women doctoral students, but few of women. For example, in teaching the Proseminar in Educational Psychology at Michigan State University, Penelope Peterson had first-year graduate students read autobiographical chapters by Jerome Bruner. In one chapter, Bruner describes his days as a graduate student at Harvard: As a young twenty-something-year-old, he lived in a small apartment, read and studied constantly, and had wonderfully stimulating intellectual conversations about ideas with his male peers and professors.[6] Initially, Peterson thought that students would find in Bruner's account a thought-provoking perspective on becoming an academic. But she soon learned she was mistaken when several graduate students wrote journal entries such as, "Bruner's life seems like dreamy land." The students could not relate to a life like Bruner's, for he did not have to worry about anyone but himself.[7] Peterson's subsequent searches for alternative autobiographical accounts yielded little with which her students could connect. LEARNING FROM OUR LIVES represented a possible response to gaps such as this.

But there was a deeper epistemological issue we wanted to explore as well. A view of research as personal is likely to be of special concern to women whose physical and practical (and personal) labors—traditionally in homes and families—have historically been distinguished from the more abstract and intellectual (and worldly) endeavors of males, a point discussed by Dorothy Smith, Sandra Harding, and other feminist writers. Thus we asked: How do women construct research from their lives as women when these lives have not, historically, been defined as legitimate sources of intellectual thought? And how have women's personally derived intellectual endeavors, increasingly situated in the academy, contributed to the reconstruction of the field?

Though viewing these questions as beyond our immediate grasp, we wanted nonetheless to create a forum for considering how the personal elements of women's lives—formed historically and culturally—shape their scholarly endeavors. We also wanted to contemplate the proposition that rethinking women's lives as legitimate sources of intellectual thought is likely to signal a fundamental rethinking of the field itself. If research—and the knowledge it generates as the substance of a field—draws from personal lives, and if the lives that comprise a field are changing (for example, as women achieve positions of intellectual leadership traditionally held by men), then the field itself is likely to change.[8] Widely held conceptions of what counts as knowledge, whose knowledge counts, and how knowledge is pursued may change or be questioned in surprising, even disturbing ways. Thus studying diverse women's lives as sources of their research epistemologies leads us to consider how a field's previous epistemological weavings may shift and change, or simply come undone, as new and divergent lives come to spin its intellectual core.

REDEFINING RESEARCH AS PERSONAL EXPERIENCE

It is common to view research as a technical activity and to consider how various epistemologies, methods, analytical approaches, and social and political contexts contribute to the conduct of research. Though viewing these as important, we conceptualize research as a personal experience[9]–not because we wish to undo ongoing processes whereby individuals learn to do educational research, but because we want to enlarge and complicate them. Though philosophers and other scholars have traditionally separated research from the person in the researcher role, attempting to excise personal bias, emotion, and subjective knowing,[10] we go directly to that which is most personal–the lives of researchers. We wonder: What will we learn if we view research as a personal and social phenomenon–as an experience within a researcher's life? In the broadest terms, we learned that viewing research in the contexts of lives yields a richer understanding of how research evolves, and how researchers develop, than does viewing research more narrowly in the contexts of professions alone.

In creating this volume, we draw extensively from writings that portray reality as socially and personally constructed–as imagined and articulated into being by the self who knows and thinks among others, and who contemplates, in solitude, the personal content of what she has heard and learned in conversation.[11] We view "research realities" similarly–as encompassing researchers' conversations with others (authors, colleagues, study participants) and their personal contemplation of remnants of such conversation. Through such conversation and contemplation, researchers may form new thoughts, but they may re-form them as well; they may create and then re-create their subjects of study; they may rethink themselves as researchers. In sum, they may learn. But just as researchers change in what and how they know, so does their work change; sometimes, so does their field of study and, occasionally, so do their lives.

The perspective on research as personal experience and expression that frames this volume emerges at the confluence of three streams of literature, each concerned with intellectual autobiography and reflexivity: We modeled the volume initially on a literature perhaps best described as the narrative study of lives, including examinations of learning, scholarly and otherwise. Such can be found in volumes written or compiled by Bennett Berger, Jerome Bruner, Don D. Fowler and Donald L. Hardesty, Clifford Geertz, Matilda White Riley, and George C. Rosenwald and Richard L. Ochberg.[12] We also pursued a stream of literature on how self and work interrelate in the course of women's lives, as represented in works authored or collected by Mary Catherine Bateson, Ruth Behar, Carol E. Franz and Abigail J. Stewart, Ann Goetting and Sarah Fenstermaker, Carolyn G. Heilbrun, Dorinne K. Kondo, Kathryn P. Meadow Orlans and Ruth A. Wallace, Sara Ruddick and Pamela Daniels, and Michelle M. Tokarczyk and Elizabeth A. Fay. Finally, we drew on a stream of feminist studies concerned with the personal and social construction of knowledge, emphasizing contributions by Lorraine Code, Donna Haraway, Sandra Harding, Susan Krieger, Gerda Lerner, Shulamit Reinharz, and Dorothy E. Smith.

Though we learned much from these bodies of literature, we chose to depart from them: Rather than looking at the experiences of women in the academy generally, as several of these works do, we focus explicitly on women's research experiences, both in the university and outside it. This book concerns women's research as a form of learning within a field of study more than it does their experiences on university campuses. The volume authors contribute to understandings of educational research in another way: Though describing their research as embedded in their lives, they also describe their lives as embedded in particular social, historical, cultural, and economic milieux. Thus they present simultaneously personal and contextualized images of research, a perspective assumed minimally in other narrative works in education. LEARNING FROM OUR LIVES is an opportunity to glimpse how women's uniquely enculturated lives shape their research questions, epistemological stances, and methodological preferences–in short, their approaches to constructing academic knowledge within the field of education.

REFOCUSING INTELLECTUAL LEADERSHIP IN EDUCATION: THE CASE OF WOMEN, THE QUESTION OF GENDER

Historically, women have been excluded from the intellectual affairs of academic men; institutionalized intellectualism has assumed a male face, and one that, historically, has been Western and white.[13] In *The Creation of Feminist Consciousness*, Gerda Lerner describes the social institution of education, including the academy, as a construction of male minds, and she defines the slow and painful awakening of a critical feminist consciousness that has, only recently, been permitted to join the academy and to speak freely and with scholarly authority within it.

This suggests that whereas men created the meanings of institutionalized academic intellectualism, women created alternative ways to think, know, and inquire—removed from the academy that excluded them.[14] Changes in the sexual division of labor in industrialized societies have gradually opened doors to women's participation in the academy, but little scholarly attention has been given to the consequences of the clash of women's and men's ways of knowing for the production of scholarly knowledge itself. Several questions follow from this view: How have women joined an academic world they had little part in creating, and what have been their experiences in so doing? How have women situated their intellectual understandings, cares, and curiosities in the academy? How has the academy responded? How have academic women assumed intellectual authority? How have they persisted in learning authentically—without assimilating in ways that would give their selves away?

The question of how women bring their knowledge and ways of knowing to an academy originally constructed by male minds emerges uniquely in education and educational research. Over the past two centuries, women have dominated the occupational field of elementary and secondary school teaching.[15] But they have remained a minority in postsecondary academic positions bearing the responsibility for creating, extending, and preserving the core of knowledge of the academic disciplines in general and education as a field of study in particular. More than twice as many men as women work as full-time college and university faculty, and more than 50 percent more men than women hold leadership positions as campus executives, administrators, and managers (positions with the potential to provide monetary, political, and symbolic support to women's intellectual efforts).[16] Moreover, women remain in the minority in the senior leadership of the professoriate, representing only 15 percent of full professors nationally.[17] Within the academy, women have been more likely to hold temporary, part-time, and untenured positions and to work at less prestigious institutions (such as community colleges and four-year colleges) than their male colleagues.[18] As of 1987, males occupied the majority (62 percent) of full-time regular faculty positions.[19] Thus, even in education, where women have predominated as workers, positions of intellectual power and status have traditionally been beyond their reach. With few exceptions, these positions remain so even now.

Through gradual change, a critical mass of women is now assuming intellectual leadership in the traditional mainstream of women's occupations, such as education and nursing, as well as in previously male-dominated fields.[20] Though it is important to consider how women entering male-dominated fields (like the sciences) contribute, from their personal knowing, to their field's scholarship,[21] it is just as important to study how a field like education that has historically provided careers for women (though mostly in the absence of women's intellectual leadership) transforms itself to put women's thinking more explicitly at its center. Education represents an occupational field that has, historically, been *of* women; yet its intellectual foundations were authored by men writing in the contexts of men's lives.[22] This book allows us to consider how a reauthoring of the field, drawing on women's lives and women's thoughts about their lives, may be proceeding.

What makes the study of academic women in the field of education important (in contrast to women in male-dominated fields) is that in addition to charting the hurdles women encounter as they attempt to enter and shape the existing intellectual discourse, we can document their progress in doing so. Despite the continuing preponderance of men in full-time academic positions in education, the gender composition of the field's leadership has changed so rapidly in recent years that the accomplished contemporary academic in education can now easily be a woman, a circumstance uncommon in many other academic fields. Yet despite such progress, we know little about the personal experiences of such women as they crafted intellectual agendas drawing from their lives as women, though in academic contexts that have historically excluded women. We also know little about what personal content women draw upon when writing, or how this content may be contributing to their field. The chapters that follow illuminate these issues.

Finally, though we have been concerned with the public emergence of academic women's thoughts and voices in this text–as distinct from the thoughts and voices of academic men–our collective work establishes that there is not a singular woman's voice or way of knowing. We found not one overriding woman's voice but rather eleven women's voices, each unique. Moreover, we found that the authors spoke of their research in relation to their gender (or not) in distinctive ways–that they were vocal and silent on issues of gender and research in very different ways. In view of this, we are coming to regard gender less as a social construction cut sharply between internally consistent male and female imagery and voice than as a *personal construction* derived from individual experiences within multiple, shifting social discourses on gender. As Linda Nicholson explains, " . . . our claims about women are not based on some given reality but emerge from our own places within history and culture; they are political acts that reflect the contexts we emerge out of and the futures we would like to see" (p. 104).

In addition to differing in their representations of gender, the authors differ in other ways, including their personal, social, ethnic, socioeconomic, and religious backgrounds. They were born and have lived in different parts of this country, and some were born and remained attached to countries and cultures beyond it. They differ in their seniority in the field, in their ages, and in their stages of life and career. They vary in the educational topics they study and teach, the intellectual disciplines undergirding their work, their methodological interests and commitments, their epistemologies, and their stances toward the relationship between research and action. These characteristics and orientations are reflected uniquely in the research that grows from these women's lives and in the stories they tell of research in their lives.

AUTOBIOGRAPHY'S CONTRIBUTIONS TO RESEARCH IN EDUCATION

One could study women's entrance into communities of educational researchers in many different ways. Why have we chosen autobiography as method? One answer is that autobiography provides a window on life in the organizations and institutions that frame the lives of educational researchers. In her introduction to *Individual Voices, Collective Visions*, Ann Goetting, drawing on work by Gideon Sjoberg and Kathryn Kuhn, observes that, " . . . critical to the study of formal organizations, biography accesses decision-making processes of powerful actors, documents organizational secrecy, and illuminates organizational deviance. . . . Additionally, biography provides a window on informal organizational structures that infiltrate the formal order" (p. 9). That is, autobiography helps us see and understand the hurtful aspects of institutional existence in academe through the eyes of those who may have suffered in silence through subtle and overt discrimination or neglect. It also helps us see, appreciate, and support the informal structures that help people heal from and resist the hurtful features of organizational existence.

We have tried, in this volume, to extend this perspective, viewing the organization of a field of knowledge as itself an institution that frames the lives of researchers. Autobiography can help us see how long-established processes of knowledge formation in the field of education–and its multiple discourse communities–support or thwart the development and legitimation of women's epistemologies in research and teaching. It also helps us see how some women resist and redirect constraining currents of thought in the field.

Whereas this argument presents the collective benefits of autobiography, some personal benefits are clearly in store for readers and writers of autobiography as well, among them, as Ann Goetting tells us, the opportunity to "forge informed life changes" (p. 8). Drawing on the writings of C. Wright Mills, Goetting notes that the "insights into social context [provided by biography] can supply the resources necessary to not only understand one's own life but, as a result, to at least partially control its outcomes" (p. 8). "Biography," she adds, "can provide readers [and writers, we assert] with fertile ground for redirection of the life trajectory through its reconceptualization" (p. 8). In brief, the experience of reading and writing autobiography may provide the reader/writer with the reflective space necessary to reimagine her life, and her work as reflective of her life.

RESEARCHING RESEARCHERS' LIVES IN EDUCATION

Considering the unique perspectives afforded by autobiographers, we invited eleven academic women in education to write personally and autobiographically about the place, meaning, and experience of research in their lives. We asked them to look at any phase or instance of their research and to describe the webs of personal, social, and professional involvements and commitments in their lives associated with that research. Or conversely, they might draw out selected aspects of their lives, viewing these as contexts for the formation of particular research agendas, perspectives, or methods. We asked the authors to focus on the particularities of their experiences and on what and how they learned (and how they are continuing to learn) from their experiences of research in their lives.

We found it hard to craft the balances we wanted—how to help ourselves and each other speak about our professional work in personal terms, how to encourage ourselves to speak of personal matters affecting our work in a professional forum, how to balance voice and silence as text. We learned that editing autobiography often involves encouraging authors to say more about the silences in their texts, and querying them to clarify memories and thoughts. But we also learned to be silent and not to query when the silences we discerned seemed purposeful, or when we felt a writer had told us as much as she could know, about herself and others, at the time she wrote. Some of the women we invited initially turned us down; others thought long and hard before agreeing to join us; and still others joined but moderated what they said. We encouraged authors to amplify on aspects of their lives only when we felt they wanted to do so, realizing that even partial stories bear meaning; perhaps, over time, we change in what we tell and what we know, replacing one partiality with another. One author wondered aloud, "What would it be like if, five or so years from now, we all wrote our stories together again? What would we write then? What would we say that perhaps we did not dare to say before? What would we say that we simply did not know before?"

We also puzzled over how physically to organize text so as to illuminate the complex intertwining of self and work in lives. We wanted to emphasize the personal contexts within which accomplished academic women write, research, and publish. We saw their lives, initially, represented in two texts: a professional text of a "researcher self" for which each was publicly known, often through her published work, and a personal text, more simply of self, which was largely absent in representations of the more public researcher persona. Slowly we came to think of the professional texts of these authors' lives as existing in a "foreground" of public knowledge about them, and of the personal texts as invisible (though ever-present) backgrounds. We pondered how we might construct this book so as to reverse this traditional schema–first, how we might encourage these writers to place their personal lives in the foregrounds of their chapters while moving their professional activities and accomplishments to the back (but allowing them to remain visible so connections between the two might be seen). To do this, we asked our contributors to write stories within stories–to position descriptions of their scholarly efforts as internal to larger and more detailed stories of their lives–whenever this made sense. We suggested they refer to their professional work in endnotes, thereby leaving the personal material as their central text. We also asked the authors to provide brief "professional bios" capturing their public and professional personas (for the "About the Contributors" section) to contrast to the more personal images of self in their chapters. In editing the chapters, we sought to orchestrate these texts as best we could.

In doing this, we found that the popular dualism of personal and professional, though useful in designing this volume, often blurred as the writers expressed their lives and selves in texts. For some authors, the personal overlapped with the professional self in ways that could not be pulled apart; the professional was intrinsically personal, and the personal supported the professional. Other authors described not two distinct selves but multiple selves transcending the professional versus personal distinction, each changing and growing, sometimes disappearing from view, sometimes struggling to emerge and to evolve over time. We agree with the contributor who speculated that five years from now these stories might emerge in yet other forms.

As for ourselves: Though we have tried to orchestrate this project as an opportunity for us all–readers, contributing authors, ourselves–to think about the personal meaning of scholarly work in our lives, we realize that this project, about research in lives, is itself an instance of research in our own lives shaped by the unique patterns of our lives. Why did we undertake this project, and what did (and do) we hope to gain, for ourselves, through it?

In an "instrumental" sense, as the persons with responsibility for drawing the volume together, we wanted to use our own autobiographical writings (Chapters 6 and 12) as mirrors to help us reflect on what the other nine authors would tell us about the meaning of research in their lives, though realizing the inevitability of blind spots we would not be able to "see around." We also expected to use (and have used) the other authors' autobiographical writings to better understand the personal contexts and contents of our own work in our own lives. Through reflexive turns such as these, mirroring what we learn personally from one life to help us learn of another, we hope now to draw you, our reader, into reflective contemplation on the personal images that may be inscribed in your own research. We hope that, in assuming this alternative view of research–as a personal experience in and expression of a life–we may also create alternative images of education, reaching into the personal and everyday lives of our students just as they reach into our own.

RE-SEARCHING THE ORIGINS OF RESEARCH IN WOMEN'S EVERYDAY LIVES

We have sought in this volume to think of educational research, and inquiry generally, as growing from alternative sites–from women's lives as sources of questions, perspectives, and methods. But how do women inquire authentically–that is, from their lives–when the worlds in which they live and work view their questions, perspectives, and methods as antithetical to conceptions of scholarly research? To whom do they speak, and in whose company do they think, about their efforts to reimagine their own (and others') everyday lives in ways that will let them be heard, understood, and appreciated–and that will legitimate their unique efforts to learn? How might they learn about (or simply, make up) new visions of everyday life? How might they create space and time for such learning? And how might they then turn their learning into everyday life–in effect, re-presenting it?

In analyzing the diverse autobiographical accounts for this book, we learned that these authors' everyday lives–their daily existences in worlds largely predefined by others–were often punctuated by their own "times away" from the everyday. These women created what Maxine Greene calls "alternative realities" embedded within, though apart from, the realities of everyday lives. Greene read, attended lectures, and composed an alternative community beyond her everyday school and family life; Gloria Ladson-Billings committed herself to constructing an alternative cultural reality where she, and others working alongside her, would be recognized and heard; Kathryn H. Au looked to her family's past to evoke an alternative but authentic cultural identity; Ellen Condliffe Lagemann created an alternative understanding of herself and her world in her writing; Nel Noddings developed an alternative existence through her relationships with special teachers and authors; Linda F. Winfield defined the personal and professional spaces of her life as alternatives to each other. Purposefully throughout their lives, these women, and the others whose accounts are included here, worked to create personal (sometimes private) alternatives to the predefined realities of their everyday lives; these were opportunities to reflect on, question, oppose, or reimagine portions of their daily existence in the world "out there"–a world they sought to re-present to others and to themselves.

We found that a woman's everyday reality and the reality she subsequently created as an alternative to it often exist in tension with each other, at times in a struggle for power to define her life. Each writer conceived of the tension uniquely. However, each writer also went about the making of her alternative realities uniquely–by engaging in acts of reimagination, reconstruction, remembrance, re-creation, relation, or repair.[23]

Reimagining Self and Everyday Life

In Chapter 2, Maxine Greene presents the concept of "everyday life" as women's efforts to respond to inherited worlds reflecting the values and interests of (usually) the men who defined those worlds. In her youth, Greene responded to her father's and husband's expectations, cared for family and home, supported her husband's career and children's schooling, with hardly time to think for or by herself, except, as she says, "in the interstices of time" amidst tasks she performed for others. Moments she stole for herself (reading novels with a "forbidden flashlight" as a child, writing novels in scarce free moments as a wife and mother) were opportunities she created and defended. She thus began, slowly but willfully, to reimagine her life and her self–to create the beginnings of what she calls "alternative realities" that, in time, became the core of her scholarly work.

Reconstructing Self and Community

Following Maxine Greene, Concha Delgado-Gaitan and Gloria Ladson-Billings, in Chapters 3 and 4, respectively, speak to a theme of researchers creating alternative cultural realities through their research. Within the contexts of their unique lives, Delgado-Gaitan and Ladson-Billings present their scholarly endeavors as expressions of resistance to the dominant constructions of a white culture that has historically inhibited the free expression of blacks and Latinos within educational systems. Both portray their scholarship as attempts to nurture their own and others' cultural expressions within education–for example, in the creation of new knowledge in new communities that grow (in the imagery evoked by Delgado-Gaitan) from borders into borderlands.

Remembering Self and Time

In Chapters 5 and 6, Kathryn H. Au and Anna Neumann continue the discourse about self and culture in research. However, in contrast to Delgado-Gaitan and Ladson-Billings, these two writers focus less on the reconstruction of contemporary cultures and communities than on retrieval, recall, and reconstitution of past cultural existence. Au and Neumann describe what they have learned, personally and professionally, in their efforts to recollect family and community experiences–ways of knowing and being in the world–that have been suppressed and nearly lost, in their lives and in the educational settings they study.

Re-creating Self and Voice

Though acknowledging the personal and introspective powers of research, Martha Montero-Sieburth and Ellen Condliffe Lagemann, the authors of Chapters 7 and 8, respectively, describe their research–their publicly written/spoken words of academic discovery–as forms of power. They describe how the power of their scholarship led them to re-create their lives, and how, slowly, they are turning that power toward the re-creation of the educational communities within which they work, each in her own way.

Relating to Self and Others

Research, however, is about more than garnering power in public domains, for as Nel Noddings and Patricia J. Gumport show in Chapters 9 and 10, there is power to be claimed more privately as well, from within personal relationships and, concomitantly, from within oneself. Noddings and Gumport speak, each in unique ways, to a common theme–their learning over the years to create alternatives to everydayness (often defined by the social routines of family and school life) by allowing themselves to trust the power of personal relationships (for example, with teachers and authors) and the learning that may grow from and within such relationships.

Repairing Self and Contexts

Linda F. Winfield in Chapter 11 and Penelope L. Peterson in Chapter 12 portray their struggles to develop and integrate disparate commitments to profession on the one hand and to themselves and their families on the other–for example, as they strive to mesh learning in one context with learning in the other. Winfield's and Peterson's efforts to repair the splits in their lives grow from desires for integration–and integrity–in their own and others' lives.

Collectively, these diverse accounts reflect a common idea: When the everyday world fails to accept or support women's attempts to inquire from their lives–to explore and learn authentically–women create alternative opportunities to do so. In effect, they work at re-presenting their everyday lives. In this way, they may, over time, re-present their own (and others') lives–for example, as the "alternatives" they compose, initially *away* from their everyday lives, *become* their lives. This may occur as women commit themselves to educational research as a vocation that frames (and, to some degree, legitimates) researchers' efforts to re-present both worlds and lives.

But this kind of re-presentation through research is often contentious, proceeding slowly, sometimes painfully, through the full course of a life. It also proceeds uniquely for each woman at different times in her life. The following chapters illuminate women's personal efforts to re-present their worlds and their lives through their research in education.

NOTES

1. For studies of teaching in lives, see Goodson, 1992, and Middleton, 1993.

2. See Bateson, 1994, and Lightfoot, 1988.

3. We note, however, that contemporary distinctions between research and teaching are often artificial, especially when viewed from within scholars' lives (see Wilson, 1995).

4. We view the word *research* as having multiple meanings and researchers as often disagreeing about what constitutes research. We invited authors whose views of research differ, whose educational research is recognized in their scholarly communities though raising important questions about the nature of knowledge, and whose commitment to educational research is central to their lives.

5. For discussion of the epistemology of women's everyday lives, see Smith, 1974, 1987.

6. See Chapter 3, "Graduate School at Harvard," in Bruner, 1983.

7. These graduate students' lives were very different from Bruner's. Most were adults with spouses and children; many worked; several commuted an hour each day to the university and their only "reflective" time was in the car. Many were women and people of color to whom the life of a white, male intellectual and aesthete seemed foreign and undesirable. Though some students responded by deeming the reading irrelevant to their lives, others experienced a crisis of confidence: If Bruner's story was true, they should give up now because they would never make it. These students worried Peterson because as mature adults with rich knowledge and experiences, they had much to offer the field. She was loath to hear that in their first semester, they already believed they would not succeed in graduate school or in academic careers.

8. We concur in this regard with Geertz's (1995) observation that "it has become harder and harder to separate what comes into science from the side of the investigator from what comes into it from the side of the investigated" (p. 135). Geertz's considerations of his life in the context of developments in the field of anthropology – and anthropological developments in the context of his life – point to a need to theorize further relationships between lives and fields of knowledge.

9. Although our aim resonates with others' efforts to illuminate the social and political contexts of research (see Hammond, 1967; Walford, 1991), our concern differs: We focus on the researcher's life as the context of her research, though acknowledging that her life is embedded in other contexts.

In defining research as personal, we do not urge researchers to adopt autobiographical methods but rather to consider the autobiographical origins of their research (independent of choice of method).

10. See Kerlinger, 1991.

11. For social constructivism, we rely on Berger and Luckmann, 1967, and Rabinow and Sullivan, 1987, though we frame constructivism in light of feminist standpoint epistemologies as discussed by Smith, 1974, 1987, and Harding, 1986, 1991. For phenomenological and interpretive social science perspectives on individual experience constructed among others, we rely on Kondo, 1990; Krieger, 1991; and Schutz, 1970.

12. For discussion of this genre in studies of academic lives, see Weiland, 1994.

13. See Harding, 1986, 1991; Rich, 1979; and Aisenberg and Harrington, 1988.

14. See Harding, 1986, 1991, and Lerner, 1993.

15. See Clifford, 1983.

16. U.S. Department of Education, 1990.

17. Fox, 1995, p. 231.

18. See Aisenberg and Harrington, 1988, and Moore and Sagaria, 1991.

19. N.C.E.S., 1990.

20. See Moore and Sagaria, 1991.

21. A good example is Keller, 1985.

22. Martin (1982) observes that "although throughout history women have reared and taught the young and have themselves been educated, they are excluded both as the subjects and objects of educational thought from the standard texts and anthologies . . . " (p. 134).

23. We derived these terms, and the overall theme of alternative realities in everyday life, by analyzing the completed eleven accounts rather than by stipulating the terms in advance. To appreciate each author's unique approach to creating alternatives in everyday life, we identified prominent themes in each chapter, then clustered chapters whose themes connected substantively. We were particularly influenced by Maxine Greene's conception of "alternative realities" as an organizing rubric.

BIBLIOGRAPHY

Aisenberg, Nadya, and Mona Harrington. 1988. *Women of Academe: Outsiders in the Sacred Grove*. Amherst: University of Massachusetts Press.

Bateson, Mary Catherine. 1990. *Composing a Life*. New York: Plume.

Bateson, Mary Catherine. 1994. *Peripheral Visions: Learning Along the Way*. New York: HarperCollins.

Behar, Ruth. 1993. *Translated Woman: Crossing the Border with Esperanza's Story*. Boston: Beacon.

Berger, Bennett M., ed. 1990. *Authors of Their Own Lives: Intellectual Autobiographies by Twenty American Sociologists*. Berkeley: University of California Press.

Berger, Peter L., and Thomas Luckmann. 1967. *The Social Construction of Reality: A Treatise in the Sociology of Knowledge*. New York: Anchor/Doubleday.

Bruner, Jerome. 1983. *In Search of Mind: Essays in Autobiography*. New York: Harper Colophon.

Bruner, Jerome. 1990. *Acts of Meaning*. Cambridge, MA: Harvard University Press.

Clifford, Geraldine J. 1983. "'Shaking Dangerous Questions from the Crease': Gender and American Higher Education." *Feminist Issues* 3(2):3–62 (Fall).

Code, Lorraine. 1991. *What Can She Know? Feminist Theory and the Construction of Knowledge*. Ithaca, NY: Cornell University Press.

Fowler, Don D., and Donald L. Hardesty, eds. 1994. *Others Knowing Others: Perspectives on Ethnographic Careers*. Washington: Smithsonian Institution Press.

Fox, Mary Frank. 1995. "Women and Higher Education: Gender Differences in the Status of Students and Scholars." In *Women: A Feminist Perspective*, 5th ed. Jo Freeman, ed. Mountain View, CA: Mayfield, 220–237.

Franz, Carol E., and Abigail J. Stewart, eds. 1994. *Women Creating Lives: Identities, Resilience, and Resistance*. Boulder, CO: Westview.

Geertz, Clifford. 1995. *After the Fact: Two Countries, Four Decades, One Anthropologist*. Cambridge, MA: Harvard University Press.

Goetting, Ann, and Sarah Fenstermaker, eds. 1995. *Individual Voices, Collective Visions: Fifty Years of Women in Sociology*. Philadelphia: Temple University Press.

Goodson, Ivor F., ed. 1992. *Studying Teachers' Lives*. New York: Teachers College Press.

Hammond, Phillip E., ed. 1967. *Sociologists at Work: The Craft of Social Research*. Garden City, NY: Anchor/Doubleday.

Haraway, Donna. 1988. "Situated Knowledges: The Science Question in Feminism and the Privilege of Partial Perspective." *Feminist Studies* 14(3):575–599.

Harding, Sandra. 1986. *The Science Question in Feminism*. Ithaca, NY: Cornell University Press.

Harding, Sandra. 1991. *Whose Science? Whose Knowledge? Thinking from Women's Lives*. Ithaca, NY: Cornell University Press.

Heilbrun, Carolyn G. 1979. *Reinventing Womanhood*. New York: W. W. Norton.

Heilbrun, Carolyn G. 1988. *Writing a Woman's Life*. New York: Ballantine.

Keller, Evelyn Fox. 1985. *Reflections on Gender and Science*. New Haven, CT: Yale University Press.

Kerlinger, Fred N. 1991. "Science and Behavioral Research." In *Knowledge for Policy: Improving Education Through Research*, Don S. Anderson and Bruce J. Biddle, eds. New York: Falmer, 87–102.

Kondo, Dorinne K. 1990. *Crafting Selves: Power, Gender, and Discourses in a Japanese Workplace*. Chicago: University of Chicago Press.

Krieger, Susan. 1991. *Social Science and the Self: Personal Essays on an Art Form*. New Brunswick, NJ: Rutgers University Press.

Lerner, Gerda. 1993. *The Creation of Feminist Consciousness: From the Middle Ages to Eighteen-Seventy*. New York: Oxford University Press.

Lightfoot, Sara Lawrence. 1988. *Balm in Gilead: Journey of a Healer*. Reading, MA: Addison-Wesley.

Martin, Jane Roland. 1982. "Excluding Women from the Educational Realm." *Harvard Educational Review* 52(2):133–148 (May).

Middleton, Sue. 1993. *Educating Feminists: Life Histories and Pedagogy*. New York: Teachers College Press.

Mills, C. Wright. 1959. *The Sociological Imagination*. New York: Oxford University Press.

Moore, Kathryn, and Mary Ann C. Sagaria. 1991. "The Situation of Women in Research Universities in the United States: Within the Circles of Academic Power." In *Women and Higher Education in Comparative Perspective*, Gail P. Kelly and Sheila Slaughter, eds. Dordrecht/Boston/London: Kluwer Academic, 185–200.

National Center for Education Statistics (N.C.E.S.). 1990. "Percentage Distribution of Full- and Part-Time Regular Faculty, by Gender, Type and Control of Institution, and Department Program Area: Fall 1987." Table reported in *Survey Report, 1988 National Survey of Postsecondary Faculty (NSOPF-88), Faculty in Higher Education Institutions, 1988, Contractor Report*. Washington, DC: U.S. Department of Education, Office of Educational Research and Improvement, p. 13.

Nicholson, Linda. 1994. "Interpreting Gender." *Signs: Journal of Women in Culture and Society* 20(1):79–106.

Orlans, Kathryn P. Meadow, and Ruth A. Wallace, eds. 1994. *Gender and the Academic Experience: Berkeley Women Sociologists*. Lincoln: University of Nebraska Press.

Rabinow, Paul, and William M. Sullivan, eds. 1987. *Interpretive Social Science: A Second Look*. Berkeley: University of California Press.

Reinharz, Shulamit. 1991. *On Becoming a Social Scientist: From Survey Research and Participant Observation to Experiential Analysis*. New Brunswick, NJ: Transaction.

Rich, Adrienne. 1979. *On Lies, Secrets, and Silence: Selected Prose, 1966–1978*. New York: W. W. Norton.

Riley, Matilda White, ed. 1988. *Sociological Lives*. Newbury Park, CA: Sage.

Rosenwald, George C., and Richard L. Ochberg, eds. 1992. *Storied Lives*. New Haven, CT: Yale University Press.

Ruddick, Sara, and Pamela Daniels, eds. 1977. *Working It Out: 23 Women Writers, Artists, Scientists, and Scholars Talk About Their Lives and Work*. New York: Pantheon.

Schutz, Alfred. 1970. *On Phenomenology and Social Relations*, ed. Helmut R. Wagner. Chicago: University of Chicago Press.

Sjoberg, Gideon, and Kathryn Kuhn. 1989. "Autobiography and Organizations: Theoretical and Methodological Issues." *Journal of Applied Behavioral Science* 25(4): 309–326.

Smith, Dorothy E. 1974. "Women's Perspective as a Radical Critique of Sociology." *Sociological Inquiry* 44(1):7–13.

Smith, Dorothy E. 1987. *The Everyday World as Problematic: A Feminist Sociology*. Boston: Northeastern University Press.

Tokarczyk, Michelle M., and Elizabeth A. Fay, eds. 1993. *Working-Class Women in the Academy: Laborers in the Knowledge Factory*. Amherst: University of Massachusetts Press.

U.S. Department of Education. 1990. "Distribution of Full-Time Faculty Members by Age and Discipline at Four-Year Institutions, 1987." Table reprinted in *The Chronicle of Higher Education Almanac* (September 5):22.

Walford, Geoffrey, ed. 1991. *Doing Educational Research*. New York: Routledge.

Weiland, Steven. 1994. "Writing the Academic Life: Faculty Careers in Narrative Perspective." *The Review of Higher Education* 17(4):395–422.

Wilson, Suzanne M. 1995. "Not Tension but Intention: A Response to Wong's Analysis of the Researcher–Teacher." *Educational Researcher* 24(8):19.

* *CHAPTER 2* *

Exclusions and Awakenings

Maxine Greene

THINKING BACK FROM THIS TIME of acknowledged cultural diversity and of new (if often grudging) regard for "difference," I find something poignant in my father's decision to send me to an Episcopalian school as a very young child. He hoped I might "assimilate" and somehow merge with what he thought of as the majority. I learned to take for granted the daily chapel service at Berkeley Institute; I was only faintly surprised when the school offered a scholarship because my father could no longer afford private school tuition. For some years, I was a token Jew in that school; and, even now, I am astonished by my passive acceptance of the exclusion I experienced. My best friend could not invite me to her house because her grandma did not like Jews; many of my classmates belonged to a riding club that did not allow Jews in the door. (For a long time, I thought one sign of being a real American was to have blue, red, and yellow ribbons hanging over one's fireplace, evidence of having been a first-class horsewoman.) When, years later, the principal said regretfully that she could have gotten me a scholarship to Mount Holyoke if only I were not Jewish, I remember apologizing. I went to Barnard College largely because the quota there was large enough, and because my family did not want to send me out of town.

Many of my discoveries were private ones, I now realize: I thought I was strange in what I chose to like, usually what my family spurned. Perhaps most significant for me was the free Sunday concert in the Sculpture Court at the Brooklyn Museum. It opened doors to some alternative reality; my experiences there were like those I had under the bedsheet when I read novels with a forbidden flashlight and transported myself to the Hebrides, to Pamplona in Spain, to Paris cafés. Just when I was finishing high school, I discovered a lecture series at a public school near the museum; and the topic had to do with freedom of speech. Not only was the significance of the issue a surprise to me; feeling myself to be a part of an eager, committed audience fascinated

Learning from Our Lives: Women, Research, and Autobiography in Education. ISBN 0-8077-3593-0 (pbk), ISBN 0-8077-3594-9 (cloth).

me and expanded what I had thought of as a secret, private garden. Also, I was startled to find many of the people who attended the lectures also attended "my" Sunday concerts. I was beginning to find my alternative reality.

I remember picketing in Bedford-Stuyvesant in Brooklyn because the stores there had never hired black cashiers, and I had joined a neighborhood group working for equal opportunity. I remember joining a march to protest when the German ship, the *Bremen*, docked in New York. I wanted desperately to be part of the group who tried to climb up and pull down the swastika banner–and feeling totally useless because I could not. Moments like those, however, were high moments and memorable ones, distanced from the banal and the everyday. Everydayness meant taking dutiful notes in my Barnard classes, working in the library there, helping a fellow student who had had polio, selling dresses in Altmann's on Saturdays (or, when really lucky, selling Modern Library books at Macy's), riding the subway back and forth from Brooklyn to Barnard.

At the end of my junior year, my father let me go to Europe with a classmate, ostensibly to do some business for him (which, for all his carefully listed instructions, I never understood). It was the time of the Spanish Civil War; and there were volunteers on the ship en route to joining the Abraham Lincoln Brigade to fight for the Spanish Republic. Falling wholly in love with one of the volunteers (or thinking I was in love), I begged to go to Spain along with him and his comrades and had to be persuaded by a group of them that I had none of the required skills (firing a gun, I suppose, nursing, spying, marching in step). In Paris, later, I went to work for the embassy of Loyalist Spain, translating, doing errands, staring at the famous people enlisted in the cause. I wanted to stay as long as the war lasted; but a few stern cablegrams from my father brought me home. I came laden with Spanish Civil War literature and posters, not to speak of notes for the speeches I began giving in odd meeting places around New York. I suppose that was when I learned how to lecture and to connect lecturing with having a cause.

MARRIAGE, MOTHERHOOD, AND NOVEL-WRITING

I did go back to Barnard; but, when the term ended, I suddenly found I had accumulated enough honor points to graduate, and I announced that fact to the college officials. No one suggested, even indirectly, that I go on to graduate school, or law school, or Teachers College. Presumably, they had done the requisite job of preparation, and I simply left. I eloped immediately with a socially conscious physician and found myself desperately trying to combine housekeeping, medical assisting, and proper partnering with courses at the New School for Social Research and some vaguely political, antifascist activity.

But that did not seem at all sufficient, what with all my fantasies of living in the "Manhattan of the world."

Unable even to conceptualize what it meant to be sentenced to so much housework, I thought I could manage to keep things clean and write a book at the same time. I had majored in American history at Barnard; and I suppose I thought I could make my own what had only been memorized in school by writing a historical novel. Eager to incorporate some of my particular passions and concerns, I chose the pre-Jeffersonian period and the persecutions of those who supported the French Revolution, those who formed Democratic Societies in opposition to Hamiltonianism, and the rest. The hero of my book was a folk singer who nailed his songs to trees during the Revolution (like Tom Paine and the poet Philip Freneau). It strikes me now that I could not have conceived placing a woman at the center of a story in the 1940s, although I would seriously consider doing so now. In any case, I remember taking the train to Philadelphia every few weeks and poring over the actual notes of the Democratic Societies and the Junto without any realization that this was legitimate historical research or that anyone besides myself might be interested. (I can see myself now cleaning my husband's medical office at night, or doing the dishes, unable to get my mind off those men in the late eighteenth century trying to build a free society.)

At length I finished a 700-page novel, which turned out to be an "almost." Little, Brown and Company in New York was interested and sent the manuscript to its Boston office. Suddenly, however, a book on the same period was reviewed in the *New York Times*; and, although the Little, Brown people said some nice things when they returned the novel, I was desolated, put it away, and never looked at it again. No one explained to me that many writers sent their work to as many as nineteen publishers before finding one willing to take a chance. I doubt now that I was adult enough to have written a decent novel; but, adult or not, I could not deal with rejection; and that, for a while, was that.

Soon after, my little girl was born. We lived in back of my husband's office; and my life became a test of women's "ways of knowing" and feminist ethics, what with an infant to care for, cardiographs to give, x-rays to administer, phone messages to take, food to prepare. In the interstices of time, however, I wrote one and a half new novels: one having to do with a woman pianist and the WPA Arts Project (which I researched with enormous care); the other with the daughter of a John Dewey–like character who may or may not have betrayed a friend before an un-American Activities Committee. One publisher was interested enough in the one about the pianist to ask me to rewrite it in the first person, which I did, but unsuccessfully. The other had to do with whether the father did or did not commit suicide. Then my own father committed suicide, and I could not write fiction any longer.

WORLD WAR II AND NEW BEGINNINGS

Soon after Pearl Harbor, my husband enlisted in the medical corps. Linda and I followed him to various army camps. In Carlisle, Pennsylvania, where there was a training center for medical officers, I made a discovery which led to my first publication. The name "Molly Pitcher" was visible throughout the city–on the door of the leading hotel, on the bread, on a hardware store; and I became curious. The Molly Pitcher I knew was a character in what I thought was a child's version of the American Revolution. She was the woman who accompanied her husband to the battlefield and kept refilling a water pitcher to keep his musket properly damp. I went to the Carlisle library and discovered some tattered relics in a library drawer, along with a piece of paper saying, "Molly McCartney Debit: Six Shillings for Cleaning the Courthouse Steps." Fascinated, I started to write about her and then enlarged my story into one about women in war. I was lucky enough to publish it in the magazine *Mademoiselle*, probably in 1942. (It never occurred to me, I must say, that I was launching an effort in women's studies or that I was or might be a feminist!)

When my husband went overseas to the European Theater, as it was called, I worked at various writing jobs, legislative research jobs, canteens, and the like. I was the legislative director for the American Labor Party in Brooklyn, edited a newsletter, began making speeches on price control, the beginnings of the United Nations, and the like. When the war ended, my husband decided to go into psychiatry and had, almost immediately, a conversion experience, certainly where gender was concerned. He kept asking (with reference to his nonplussed wife), "What do women want?" Because his newfound orthodox Freudian beliefs did not allow for an ambitious wife with ideas of her own, we were divorced after about two years.

STILL ANOTHER FRESH START

I remarried fairly soon after that–this time to a patent attorney who had been a friend of my family. It meant moving away from Brooklyn to Queens, where my new husband's first family lived; and my young daughter suffered greatly in her efforts to readjust. It was her difficulty, in fact, that occasioned my career. Late to school, nauseated, upset by all the changes in her life, she needed special attention; but when I explained all that to her second-grade teacher, the teacher suggested taking a baseball bat to the child; and that opened my path to becoming an academic, although I could not have suspected it at the time.

In any case, I decided to drive Linda back to her old school in Brooklyn every day; and, not having to work for a living any longer, I considered going back to school as well. I wrote to every university in the city to find out where I could register as a special student. I had one principal criterion: The class had to meet from 10:00 A.M. to 2:00 P.M., or between those hours. As an existentialist, I find it hard to realize how little choice had to do with it; but I was lucky enough to find an eight-point class at New York University in philosophy and history of education, meeting twice a week from 10:00 to 2:00. There were three professors–Adolphe Meyer, Theodore Brameld, George Axtelle–and I was plunged into what now seems like a far-ranging, pragmatically oriented history of ideas with educational concepts vaguely fixed at the center. I had never thought of myself as a teacher or writer in education; but all this fascinated me, and I managed (in my part-time devotion to my studies) to do well. I was asked to assist the next term; and, suddenly, I was made an instructor and presented with a large class in history of education to teach on my own. It abruptly occurred to me that I could pursue graduate degrees without asking my husband to pay tuition. For a number of reasons, that was as important as anything else. Guaranteed an adjunct's salary, I thought I would be left free.

In the midst of the general and required courses, Dr. Brameld decided to offer a seminar in analytic philosophy and existentialism; this was a watershed experience for me. Granted, it was necessary to read A. J. Ayers, Gilbert Ryle, and (especially) Ludwig Wittgenstein and to learn something about playing what was then the dominant philosophic game. But Soren Kierkegaard and Jean-Paul Sartre represented quite another thing to me. My courses in philosophy at NYU had centered around John Dewey's work (totally ignored in the philosophy courses I had taken at Barnard); and I was excited by it, involved with it, particularly (I recall) with his *Art as Experience*. My problem with Dewey (and I did not quite have the courage to admit it, even to myself) was that he lacked a tragic sense of life, that awareness of contradiction and paradox and absurdity that spoke to me so directly in existential literature. Indeed, I recall writing a paper on the "philosopher as existing person," emphasizing what we now call the "situatedness" and the biography of the knower, and having it returned to me as "trivial." I rather suppressed my new interest, after writing a piece on Sartrean existentialism as a member of the seminar at Dr. Brameld's request. I recall its being published in *Educational Theory*, in the early 1950s, under Brameld's name.

My second child, Timothy, was born by then; and I especially remember (after a long siege due to my illness and his prematurity) the apologies I was forever uttering at having to rush from a class to go home between assignments, at having to confine so much of my schedule to evening classes when my husband could be home. I am amazed, looking back, at the intense guilt feelings I experienced for having a child who made altogether natural demands. (I was not helped by reading in *The Second Sex* that Simone de Beauvoir associated playing with a child with infantilism.) I do have a rather sweet recollection, though, of having to leave a philosophy seminar with a careful explanation that the babysitter was leaving–and seeing the aged and dignified William Heard Kilpatrick get up as well, calling, "Take me with you!" In any case, among the dominant memories of my initial studies for my doctoral thesis is one of propping up a huge book on eighteenth-century philosophy while feeding Tiny Tim from a bottle.

THE DOCTORATE AND BEYOND

George Axtelle, my sponsor, treated me (and he announced this to many people) as a good daughter, a kind of humble heiress, and asked me to do a thesis on "Henry Fielding as Humanist." This was because he was an active member of the American Humanist Association, which I felt compelled to join. I often spoke for the association and, for a time, was literary editor of the journal called *The Humanist*–generally in my daughterly role. (I am not sure if there was any connection between that and an editorial I once wrote calling many of the humanists "Karamasovs," eager to kill off their fathers, or whatever their churches signified.) It turned out that I could not, would not do precisely what Dr. Axtelle requested of me; but I could not reject his suggestion totally. So I decided on a huge, interdisciplinary thesis: "Naturalist-Humanism in 18th Century England from 1750 to 1780: An Essay in the Sociology of Knowledge." The topic was grand enough to encompass Fielding and other literary figures; but it included Locke, Hume, Priestly, and other philosophers and writers. In addition, it extended outward to a consideration of the parliamentary, social, and industrial history of the time. Oddly (and I certainly realize it now) the eighteenth century never appealed to my temperament (which finds pleasure in the nineteenth century). I can understand very well a critique undertaken by postmodernists and critical theorists of what is more or less sardonically called "the Enlightenment Project." It may be that my guilt at my unwomanly scholarship was somewhat allayed by my dislike of what I was writing about. What stands out most from my eventual defense was Professor Louise Rosenblatt (now celebrated for "reader response theory" in literary theory) asking me to define and discuss Coleridge's theory of imagination. That question drove me into all sorts of further reading after I received my degree; and I often think that the question and the reading fed into my persistent interest in interdisciplinary teaching, my long engagement with aesthetic education, my present efforts to establish a Center for Social Imagination at Teachers College, and my most recent book, *Releasing Imagination*.

PUBLISHING AND FAMILY LIFE

There I was, finally, with a Ph.D. in philosophy of education with no possibility of securing a job in either philosophy or philosophy of education. Dr. Axtelle, my sponsor, had just offered an instructorship in philosophy of education to a male fellow student who did not yet have a doctorate; and Axtelle benevolently explained that the poor fellow had no one to support him, whereas I had a husband. I realized abruptly that there were practically no women in the field, and I began to see why. Dr. Louise Antz, at NYU, was a rare exception; but I recall her saying that, having to choose between being a philosopher and being a wife and mother, she chose to be a philosopher. She could not be a role model for me, in consequence; and discouraged as I was, I applied to the Columbia Graduate School of Arts and Sciences to see if I could win a Ph.D. in "real" philosophy. A kindly admissions director there talked me out of it, suggesting that few people like me needed two doctorates in order to live their lives.

Fortunately, I had been fairly aggressive in my graduate-student days and had suggested to Professor William Brickman, a colleague who was editing a journal called *School & Society*, that I write some articles on educational leaders on the model of the "profiles" appearing in the *New Yorker*. He published several interviews–with Robert M. Hutchins; Nathan M. Pusey, President of Harvard; and James R. Killian, Jr., President of MIT; and, years later, when I was at Teachers College, with Harold Howe, U.S. Commissioner of Education. All this helped me do some similar things in the *Saturday Review of Literature*, which in 1959 had published a feature article of mine called "A Return to Heroic Man." The *Saturday Review* also published, in 1960, pieces on Francis Keppel, John Gardner, and Alvin Johnson; and there were a number of book reviews as well. In the same period, I wrote prefaces for Collier Book editions of *Silas Marner*, *The Mill on the Floss*, and *The Nigger of the "Narcissus."*

All this helped me secure an unlikely appointment for which I was wholly unprepared: an instructorship in world literature and semantics at Montclair State College in New Jersey. Taking this job meant a 1½-hour commute each way every day, a heavy load of guilt at leaving the children for so long, traffic nightmares, and the rest. Fortunately, a Swedish woman who had lost her husband and had a child about Linda's age came to live on our third floor and be available to greet the children after school, watch out for them, feed them when necessary; and we managed to manage. But I never stopped murmuring "mea culpa" until years of psychotherapy later on. (I never recall asking my husband to babysit or pick up the children or prepare dinner, even for himself.)

IN SEARCH OF A DISCIPLINE

There was a state curriculum at Montclair; and we were required to teach a world literature course beginning with the Scriptures and going on to Homer's epics. The course was to end before Shakespeare. I have never had a year richer in self-study; and it confirmed my passion for literature, even as it almost laid me low because of the critical and other texts I had to read to gain some mastery over what I did not yet think of as "the canon." I even had to teach the Douay Bible as well as the King James version to accommodate the Catholic students. I was so troubled by the requirement that we stop before Shakespeare that (not yet a conscious feminist) I invented a "theme of the hero" and had my students read *Hamlet* and *Moby Dick*. I still would like to write an essay on "A Feminist's Moby Dick" or "My Love Affair with Herman Melville." I still wonder about that essay, "A Return to Heroic Man," and recognize that a concern for the tragic element in life haunted me from the beginning–to such an extent that the need to give it articulation (yes, as a woman) overrode a consideration of gender differences ("white men in power" and the rest), at least for a while. In any event, I had to leave Montclair after a year because of the long trip and because our plans to move to Montclair were nipped in the bud when we discovered that the golf club and a number of housing developments still would not accept Jews.

For two or three years, I was back at NYU doing part-time teaching. Desperate for courses, I went on the road in a "field program," teaching courses like "World Perspectives on Philosophy and Literature," "Literature and the American School," "Community Histories and the Arts." A positivist philosopher, who had studied under Rudolph Carnap in Vienna, took on the chairmanship of the History and Philosophy of Education Department at the time; and he soon informed me that I was no longer welcome in the department because I was "too literary." He may well have meant that I was too "female" or "too soft": I am not sure. Be that as it may, the English Education Department took me in. There were good things, of course. Louise Rosenblatt was a colleague; she helped me ponder the relations between values and the literary experience, between the aesthetic and the literary. I cannot say that our philosophies of art are identical today; but I certainly must affirm the power of her influence and her (often unintentional) support. It seems somehow to be in the nature of things that our sons came to know each other without realizing their mothers had been colleagues; and Timothy and Jonathan are still good friends.

At NYU, also, I was permitted to teach a large course called "Literature and Philosophy," so that I could keep at least one hand in my field. Meanwhile, of course, I kept teaching composition, introductory literature classes, and the other required courses (most of which I was still teaching myself). At that time, too, I was beginning to have papers accepted at the Philosophy of Education Society. I particularly remember "Philosophy of Education and the 'Pseudo-Question'" and "The Enlightenment Faith and the Public School." I believe that, about that time also, I published two papers, "The Uses of Literature," in *Educational Theory*, and "The Teacher and the Negro Child: 'Invisibility' in the School," in an edited volume entitled *The Disadvantaged Learner*. Looking back now, I paraphrase Robert Frost and say, "I took the road less traveled by, and that made all the difference." I do want to stress, however, that throughout I kept feeling marginal in all my fields.

My interdisciplinary concern helped get me an invitation from the University of Hawaii to lecture and teach for two summer sessions, in 1962 and 1964. It also enabled me to meet Professor Harold Rugg, one of the famed "foundations" people from Teachers College, a man particularly concerned for the arts, for imagination, and for those he called "force" rather than "thing" people. He called me because he had seen one of my articles; and there followed unexpected hours of talk–and a chance to tap the lore of Teachers College, of which I knew hardly anything.

BECOMING AN EDUCATIONAL PHILOSOPHER

Hawaii meant a whole range of new colleagues, encounters with thus far unfamiliar "voices," and a new sensitivity to what we now call "otherness." I saw exclusion and discrimination masked by palm trees and leis; I saw what I thought of as a genocide when I perceived the plight of the Native Hawaiians (so similar to that of Native Americans on the mainland); and it all left a mark. It is hard to grasp the impact of these abrupt insights on my academic work; but I choose to believe they made a difference in the courses I was beginning to invent.

I had been struck since returning to college by the relative blandness of the educational discourse dominant at different periods of time. There seemed to be an absence of recognition or a denial when it came to obvious contradictions in the "promise" of public education–ambiguities, blurred places, even a degree of absurdity. I was struck most of all by the absence of a tragic sense of life in the public speech about the schools. Of course, I recognized that Horace Mann, Henry Barnard, and the other great spokespersons for public education felt obligated to create a polemic or the kind of rhetoric that would sway a whole spectrum of minds, especially when it came to tax support of something intended to "equalize the conditions of men." Still, I was much affected by the glaring contrast in consciousness between, say, a reformer like Mann and his brother-in-law Nathaniel Hawthorne, living in the same place, caught up in the same currents of change. And, certainly, it astonishes even today to probe the very depths of things with Herman Melville and then attend to the self-confident claims of those administering schools.

The seminars I was enabled to teach at the University of Hawaii gave me an opportunity to explore differing, sometimes conflicting perspectives on the culture at various times in history. Also, they gave me opportunities to examine the relationships between different kinds of communication–fiction, for instance, painting, and the discursive prose of educational argument when it came to the construction of meanings. I was trying to tap, I soon realized, the historical record and various vantage points with respect to what might be taken to be the record. I was trying to make somehow audible silenced voices; I was trying to make visible invisible faces. I need only summon up Melville's Bartleby, saying "I prefer not to," and ask whether history has a place for the one who prefers not to, important as the negation has come to be. I need only summon up Ellison's "invisible man," who can be seen only in terms of a category, never as a distinctive existent, a human being in process of creating his visibility. It is Ellison's narrator who ends by speaking of "the mind, the mind," the mind creating patterns against chaos, something I still see philosophy and the arts doing in collaboration.

Still teaching a course based on those old seminars, I repeatedly find that students pose more and more probing questions when they are enabled to look from a number of vantage points at the same phenomena. Moreover, because engagement with works of art tends to confront people with the shapes and nuances of their own lived experiences, the questions posed become *situated* questions with specific reference to moments of practice. Since the Hawaii seminars were composed of as many Asian students as "mainland" students, I think I was introduced to what we now conceive of as cultural diversity with all its complications. Like many other academics, I am still working through the problems of opening the American tradition to those we view as newcomers.

Returning from the second Hawaii summer, I had a position teaching educational philosophy in the Foundations program at Brooklyn College, where I spent three challenging years. Members of the faculty there felt as allied to the working class as did our students, most of them the children of taxi drivers, tailors, garment workers, store owners. My memories of them are studded by recollections of remarkable classrooms in Brooklyn's high schools, where I often had the feeling of light breaking and discoveries being made. But I also recall how few of our Brooklyn College students had ever journeyed on their own across the river to Manhattan. The provincialism was remarkable, even among the gifted. When I reach back to those days, I also recapture memories of the 1963 March on Washington in which I participated (in awe and invisibility), a variety of "teach-ins" with regard to the war in Vietnam, a number of peace demonstrations and marches.

Once a week, the second year at Brooklyn, I traveled by subway to Teachers College to teach 150 graduate students in a philosophy of education class at Professor Lawrence Cremin's invitation. Although he never committed himself, I wanted to believe it was prefatory to an appointment at Teachers College; but it turned out that I was understudying for a new professor who had not yet arrived. Still, there were benefits: Not only did I come to know Larry Cremin; he suggested that I write a book based on my seminars in Hawaii. I did, rather quickly, and he found a contact for me at Random House. The book was *The Public School and the Private Vision*, part of a paperback series in education. (Another book in that series was one on work and leisure by Thomas F. Green of Syracuse University, who later became my cherished comrade, adviser, and–when I was president of the Philosophy of Education Society and The American Educational Research Association–my program chairman.)

I was, at last, beginning to feel like a philosopher of education, in part because of the courses I could teach and develop at Brooklyn College, in part because more and more of my papers were being accepted at the Philosophy of Education Society. Many of them were existential in emphasis; and, later, when I began realizing the overly personalist dimension of some of the philosophies I was expounding, I turned as well to social phenomenologies. (There was Alfred Schutz with his approach to the social construction of reality, his idea of "multiple realities," of "making music with others," and his idea of the "stranger," which I later adapted for my own book, *Teacher as Stranger*. There was the wonderful, luminous existential phenomenologist, Maurice Merleau-Ponty, with his notion of the "primordial landscape," of consciousness "opening to the common," of the "primacy of perception," and his fascination with painting, film, and "the prose of the world." I may have come to Schutz and Merleau-Ponty by means of a somewhat star-struck journey among existentialists beginning with Kierkegaard, Nietzsche, Dostoievsky, and others, published as *Existential Encounters for Teachers* in the Random House series to which I had first contributed a year or so before.)

Just as I was leaving Brooklyn College to go to Teachers College, I was elected (startlingly) to the presidency of the Philosophy of Education Society. I was publishing papers on values, then, on what the Vietnam War was asking of academics. One article, "Real Toads in Imaginary Gardens," published in the *Teachers College Record*, led the departing editor of the journal (Dr. J. Edward Shoben) to invite me to take over the editorship. That, of course, demanded a faculty appointment; and I suspect the phone calls that followed Dr. Shoben's suggestion were what made the appointment possible. I remember being at the Columbia Men's Faculty Club (where women visitors were expected to wait in the ladies' room until their male colleagues arrived) and finding myself confronting representatives from the Department of English Education. They interviewed me in a rather cursory fashion, quite obviously feeling compelled to do so. Having believed I was at last a recognized philosopher of education, I hustled angrily back to Brooklyn College, only to be reassured over the phone that I was indeed "wanted" on Morningside Heights, that I should take what was offered, and all would eventually be repaired. That was Larry Cremin on the phone, and I trusted him; but he did not announce the subtext, which was that the Department of Philosophy and the Social Sciences had never hired a woman. This was in 1966, before Dr. Donna Shalala arrived, trailing clouds of glory, grants, and political efficacy.

COMBINING TEACHING AND ACTIVISM

I was appointed an associate professor of English education and became the editor of the *Record* at a particularly dramatic moment in history. I could write editorials on peace and war; I could attend to ghetto children (and even print a special issue on the "children of welfare"); I could remind readers of the civil rights struggle in the south. And, yes, I could ride buses to Washington early in the morning with student activists. For a while (especially in the memorable year 1968), I was a professor and a wishful recruit to Norman Mailer's "armies of the night." At the time of the Ocean Hill–Brownsville struggle (ostensibly for decentralization of the schools), I was the so-called principal of a "liberation school" in Harlem during the teachers' strike that year. I have a feeling that I spent more time buttoning sweaters and teaching little ones "We Shall Overcome" than engaging in curriculum building or serious teaching.

Along with Patricia Graham (former dean at the Harvard Graduate School of Education, former director of the National Institute for Education, presently president of the Spencer Foundation), who was a history professor at Barnard College at the time, I was permitted to teach one class in the Department of Philosophy and Social Sciences and to attend their meetings. We also were to feel free to come to the once-a-semester dinners at Luchow's, where we were treated with awkward formality, offered cigars, presented with old-fashioned gestures of courtesy. The one course I taught then (in addition to my English courses) was an interdisciplinary one called "The Arts and American Education"; and we read (as we still do) Hawthorne, Thoreau, Emerson, Melville, Mark Twain, Henry James, F. Scott Fitzgerald, and, gradually, Kate Chopin, Frederick Douglass, Ralph Ellison, Zora Neale Hurston, Edith Wharton, Ntozake Shange, Gloria Naylor, Alice Walker, Maya Angelou, Jamaica Kincaid, Maxine Hong Kingston, Amy Tang, and (climactically) Toni Morrison.

At this point, I am still teaching that course, remaking it as I go, and rewriting the original book so as to come to terms with critiques of the canon, with contextualism, with gender and class and ethnic concerns. In Toni Morrison's Nobel address, she argues against a monolithic language and for the wonders of the Tower of Babel and multiplicity. There is a kind of hubris in my turning to Toni Morrison to try to explicate what is important to me. But she is essential to my work and thinking in a hundred ways. I have taught over and over *The Bluest Eye*, *Sula*, *Beloved*, and (most recently) *Jazz*, although I am sure I do not fully understand any one. That may be part of it. The questions, the sense of incompleteness: Those seem to be among the themes of my attempt to compose a life.

In the English department, meanwhile, I was allowed to choose a course of my own in addition to what I was assigned to teach. I decided to regenerate my old course, "Literature and Philosophy," or, more accurately, "Philosophy and Literature." The department chair whimsically asked, "Philosophy *and* or philosophy *of*?" "Oh, well," I replied, responding so some *daimon* or ministering angel, "philosophy *of*." That catapulted me into the field of aesthetics, where I had never been. A rather hectic course of research and self-study followed; "aesthetics of literature" led me to study theories of aesthetics with regard to other art forms. I began publishing a bit in that field; I started to teach (and still do) "Aesthetics and Education," the classes getting larger and larger over the years. Also, my interest and my self-study led to what is now a two-decade engagement with the Lincoln Center Institute for the Arts in Education, invented by a number of Lincoln Center Institute colleagues and myself. It is a project involving public school teachers from New York City and its suburbs (sometimes to the number of 1000) who meet at the Juilliard School (which the institute uses as its site, along with the Museum of Modern Art and a number of galleries) for three weeks in July each year. The teachers work in workshops with professional artists who serve as their teachers of the different "languages" of art (dance, music, drama, painting) and initiate them into the "speaking" of those languages. They view and listen to performances in the various domains; they "read" paintings; some do a workshop in "literature as art" with me. Also, the entire group of teachers gather at intervals to hear me in my role as "philosopher-in-residence" speak about imagination, perception, the achievement of meanings, and their connection with teaching and learning in contemporary schools. I have drawn, in this long process of "inventing" aesthetic education, from John Dewey, Jean-Paul Sartre, Mikel Dufrenne, Maurice Merleau-Ponty, Louis Arnaud Reid, Mary Warnock, Cynthia Ozick, Susanne Langer,

Arthur Danto, Helene Cixous, and many others. Perhaps most of all, I have drawn from my precious experiences with the teaching artists at Lincoln Center, rare and driven and gifted beings who have often become my beloved friends. And so it goes on.

DIALOGUE AND ORGANIZATION

And so do the social concerns persist. When I was president of the Philosophy of Education Society, my presidential address had to do with philosophy and action. I called it "Morals, Ideology and the Schools: A Foray Into the Politics of Education." (We broke with many precedents that year, 1967, in New Orleans. Traditionally, the presidential address was part of a formal dinner affair. I gave the address as part of the regular sequence and hired some musicians from the Preservation Hall jazz band to play at our hotel. That too was an interdisciplinary undertaking.) There have been moments of shared dialogue outside professional conventions and seminars–conversations with Paulo Freire, Henry Giroux, Philip Wexler, William Pinar, Ira Shor, Myles Horton (a very old and dear friend), Bayard Rustin, Jervis Anderson (former student, author, *New Yorker* staff writer), Deborah Meier, and (later) Michelle Fine, Herb Kohl, Colin Greer, Bill Ayers. And yes, after five or six years, I was admitted into the Philosophy and Social Sciences Department full time; and I have been teaching "Social Philosophy," "Philosophies of Education," "Changing Styles in Philosophy, Literature, and the Visual Arts," as well as the aesthetics course and "The Arts and American Education" since. Now and then, there have been colloquia; there have been courses in women's studies and in health ethics. Obviously, my interests (and my course materials) have expanded as I have tried to enter into contemporary dialogues on identity, difference, situatedness, the subject.

Feeling myself to be lucky and remaining incredulous, I was appointed in 1975 to the William F. Russell Chair in the Foundations of Education. (It was endowed explicitly to promote the value of freedom.) For a long time, I felt as if I were standing on the shoulders of giants, until the clear recognition struck: The "giants" were all grave white men, wearing suits, vests, and ties. (The late Dr. Francis Keppel, long my good friend, told me he could imagine William F. Russell agitating in his grave at the thought of a woman, a Jewish woman, holding a chair with his name.) The books began to appear, and I have felt increasingly fortunate and still hope to live long enough to finish two now "in progress." Following the two works mentioned earlier were *Teacher as Stranger*, *Landscapes of Learning*, *The Dialectic of Freedom*, and *Releasing Imagination*. There have been many articles in the many fields where I have gone adventuring, as well, and chapters in books, and essays in anthologies. Again, I wonder at my own *hubris*, writing as I have, speaking as I have on ethical issues, feminist issues, curriculum, youth problems, literature and literary theory, civil rights, pluralism and multiculturalism, the arts and aesthetics, postmodernism, the new epistemologies, existentialism and phenomenology. Much of this has been due, strangely enough, to my experiences of exclusion: Were it not for my being excluded from the inner circles of philosophy, or even from the department at Teachers College, I would not have had to reach out on my own. I often speculate on what would have happened had I joined a liberal arts institution, where specialties are taken really seriously. It was only in teacher education that I could play (that others could play) so many intellectual games. I wonder what it says about teacher education; I wonder what it says about research with an orientation to *praxis*.

THE REALITIES OF RESEARCH

A seriocomic moment for me came when the Nominating Committee of the American Educational Research Association called me some years ago and told me I had been nominated for president of AERA. (The only reasons I can think of now have to do with the many papers I had given there, my five-year editorship of the *Record*, presence on so many journal boards, my peripatetic existence as wandering lecturer and consultant at campuses across the country, my occasional talks at conferences overseas, or simply name familiarity.) In any case, the person who called told me not to worry, that I would never be elected. I was running against a statistician; and that (a decade or so ago) was before the days of diversity, attempts at equity, qualitative research. Then I received several phone calls from some women colleagues, eager for my election, but worried that my odd humanities credential would do me in. One asked whether I could do some "real research" by that December. Ruffled, I suggested that someone take my place; and the response was that I had spoiled it for the women in AERA. I felt the way I did as a child in the face of an anti-Semitic principal. I wanted to apologize for my intellectual frivolity.

I was, surprisingly, elected. I am aware of voter percentages; I realized that women, after all, did gather and vote for me. But I do not choose to undervalue it. I still feel greatly honored, surprised, put to the test. Those were the difficult Republican days, with research underfunded, with equity issues thrust aside, with a care-less attitude governing much of Capitol Hill. As president-elect and then as president, I did a great deal of lobbying and testifying, abruptly discovering an astonishing commitment to educational research in myself. I remember Senator Paul Simon asking me once how someone like me, who had never even applied for a grant, could argue as I was doing for funding in domains of which I knew nothing. Some of my enthusiasm came from a sense of obligation; a good deal of it came from my association with memorable and wonderful people like Marianne Amarel (good, admired, glowing friend), Courtney Cazden, Carol Tittle, Geraldine Clifford, Nancy Cole, and others, even men, far too numerous to name. Realizing this sounds like ritual talk, I still have to say that survival in that presidential role would have been impossible without William Russell, the executive secretary, one of the most intuitive, gracious, insightful of men, and my colleague Thomas Green, program chair, co-schemer, co-creator, co-thinker.

We built "our" annual program around the idea of what Dewey had called an "articulate public"; my presidential address (much influenced by the work of Hannah Arendt) focused on "Public Education and the Public Space." In addition, however, a separate section of the program was dedicated to the arts. We had an actual enactment of a play by David Mamet, *Duck Variations*, involving two old men musing by a river. We had talks by Elliot Eisner, Merl Wittrock, Robert Stake, Michael Parsons, opening diverse perspectives on the arts in human life. We had a special section allotted to Louise Rosenblatt, ignored for so long by the world of literary criticism because she wrote out of the field of teacher education rather than out of one of the traditional specialties.

Then, as now, I was obsessive about connecting the domains of imagination, the arts, social commitment, and cultural transformation. My present preoccupation is with the founding of a Center for Social Imagination, the Arts, and Education at Teachers College. We have just completed our second annual conference and are hoping to open spaces for teachers to work with artists and scholars, to initiate dialogues, to network, to create curriculums, to find their own voices, to compose what Dewey called an "articulate public" able to look at things "as if they could be otherwise." The Center, in some manner, is an expression of a desire to play some part in breaking through the rigid structures, the exclusions, the constraints that prevent people from envisaging possibility.

I wanted (and I still want) people to become "wide awake" in Virginia Woolf's sense and Henry David Thoreau's and Albert Camus's and John Dewey's and Michel Foucault's–to refuse passivity, to refuse to be mere clerks or functionaries. It is all too apparent, as Christa Wolf's narrator says in the novel *Accident: A Day's News*, that most people have a desire for "a comfortable life, a tendency to believe the speakers on raised platforms and the men in white coats: an addiction to harmony and a fear of contradiction of the many seem to correspond to the arrogance and hunger for power, the dedication to profit, unscrupulous inquisitiveness, and self-infatuation of the few. So what was it that didn't add up in this equation?" (p. 17). It is the day of the nuclear accident at Chernobyl, and she is wondering about the kinds of men–the men of science and technology–who insisted in the face of protest on going ahead with the "peaceful" production of nuclear energy. She thinks of the activities that such men might consider a waste of time if they were forced to perform them: "Changing a baby's diapers. Cooking, shopping with a child on one's arm or in the baby carriage. Doing the laundry, hanging it up to dry, taking it down, folding it, ironing it, darning it. Sweeping the floor, mopping it, polishing it, vacuuming it. Dusting. Sewing. Knitting. Crocheting. Embroidering. Doing the dishes. Doing the dishes. Doing the dishes. Taking care of a sick child. Thinking up stories to tell. Singing songs. And how many of these activities do I myself consider a waste of time?" (p. 31).

Looking back, I think of those dishes. I think of the guilt and the apologies and of the balancing of values. I came to the presidency of AERA at a moment when the tides were changing–when the doors were opening to our participation, to an acknowledgment of vantage point and of situatedness, to a recognition of the importance of particularity and, yes, of materiality (and, to go further, even of maternality). We can think together about story telling, about shaping our lives in terms of narrative and about how much that enables us to begin to understand. And, yes, as philosophers like Alasdair MacIntyre are telling us, to discover our moral purpose, our orientation to the good. Perhaps I have never done any "real research"; but I have worked to compose a life, in the full knowledge that the work can never be complete, that the losses can never be recovered. There have been professional losses; there have been personal losses. For me, the loss of my daughter to cancer, not so many years ago, is one that leaves a hole in the center of what I am still trying to compose. It leaves a hole that cries out to be filled; and it may be this loss that keeps me moving in search of myself, my woman-self, that makes me sure now it was not a "waste of time."

I want to end by referring to another novel, Whitney Otto's *How to Make an American Quilt*, because I believe that is what we are doing in this text. The most common kind of quilt is called the Crazy Quilt; like others, it is made by a circle of women:

> The women in your circle must contribute odds and ends to the project. They must sit in their places around the large wooden frame, piercing their fabric to the base cloth and cotton batting. As I mentioned earlier, some women enjoy the freedom of form afforded by the Crazy Quilt, while others prefer the discipline and predictability of an established pattern. (p. 233)

And finally:

> Remember, you do not need to tell anyone what your contributions mean and it is more than likely they will hold meaning for you alone anyway. Do not explain. This is your right. (p. 179)

Still, we have come together, and images have emerged along with meanings. As Otto suggests, "You will find this work to be most revealing, not only in the material contributions to the quilt, but in who enjoys sewing them and who does not. This random piecing together" (p. 236). And so we choose our lives.

BIBLIOGRAPHY

Brameld, Theodore, and others. 1952. "Existentialism and Education." *Educational Theory* 2(2):80–91 (April).

de Beauvoir, Simone. 1968. *The Second Sex*, ed. H. M. Parshley. New York: Modern Library.

Dewey, John. 1934. *Art as Experience*. New York: Minton, Balch.

Ellison, Ralph. 1952. *The Invisible Man*. New York: Modern Library.

Green, Thomas F. 1968. *Work, Leisure, and the American Schools*. New York: Random House.

Greene, Maxine. 1955. "Naturalist-Humanism in 18th Century England, From 1750 to 1780: An Essay in the Sociology of Knowledge." Ph.D. diss., New York University.

Greene, Maxine. 1956. "Robert Maynard Hutchins, Crusading Metaphysician." *School & Society* 83 (May 12):162–166.

Greene, Maxine. 1957a. "Especially the Faith: Nathan M. Pusey." *School & Society* 85 (April 27):142–145.

Greene, Maxine. 1957b. "The Uses of Literature." *Educational Theory* 7:143–149.

Greene, Maxine. 1958. "James R. Killian, Jr.: Humanistic Missleman." *School & Society* 86 (March 15):131–134.

Greene, Maxine. 1959. "A Return to Heroic Man." *The Saturday Review of Literature* 42 (August 22):10–11.

Greene, Maxine. 1960a. "John W. Gardner." *Saturday Review of Literature* 43 (December):58–59.

Greene, Maxine. 1960b. "Keppel of Harvard." *Saturday Review of Literature* 43 (November):68–69.

Greene, Maxine. 1960c. "Learning for Those Deeply Involved in Life." *Saturday Review of Literature* 43 (January):12–13.

Greene, Maxine. 1960d. "Philosophy of Education and the 'Pseudo-Question.'" *Proceedings of the Sixteenth Annual Meeting of the Philosophy of Education Society* 16 (April):56–61.

Greene, Maxine. 1962. "The Enlightenment Faith and the Public School." *Proceedings of the Eighteenth Annual Meeting of the Philosophy of Education Society* 18 (April):80–89.

Greene, Maxine. 1965a. *The Public School and the Private Vision: A Search for America in Education and Literature*. New York: Random House.

Greene, Maxine. 1965b. "Real Toads and Imaginary Gardens." *Teachers College Record* 66(5):416–424.

Greene, Maxine. 1966. "The Teacher and the Negro Child: 'Invisibility' in the School." In *The Disadvantaged Learner: Knowing, Understanding, Educating*, Staten W. Webster, ed. San Francisco: Chandler, 447–453.

Greene, Maxine. 1967a. *Existential Encounters for Teachers*. New York: Random House.

Greene, Maxine. 1967b. "Morals, Ideology, and the Schools: A Foray Into the Politics of Education" (Presidential Address, Philosophy of Education Society). *Educational Theory* 17(4):271–288 (October). *Proceedings of the Twenty-third Annual Meeting of the Philosophy of Education Society* 23:141–161.

Greene, Maxine. 1967c. "The Visibility of Harold Howe: Some Notes Towards a Profile." *School & Society* 95 (January 21):45–48.

Greene, Maxine. 1973. *Teacher as Stranger: Educational Philosophy for the Modern Age*. Belmont, CA: Wadsworth.

Greene, Maxine. 1978. *Landscapes of Learning*. New York: Teachers College Press.

Greene, Maxine. 1982. "Public Education and the Public Space" (Presidential Address, American Educational Research Association). *Educational Researcher* 11(6): 4–9 (June–July).

Greene, Maxine. 1988. *The Dialectic of Freedom*. New York: Teachers College Press.

Greene, Maxine. 1995. *Releasing Imagination: Essays on Education, Art, and Social Change*. San Francisco: Jossey-Bass.

Hawthorne, Nathaniel. 1970a. "The Maypole of Merrymount." In *Hawthorne: Selected Tales and Sketches*, 3rd ed. New York: Holt, Rinehart and Winston, 198–210.

Hawthorne, Nathaniel. 1970b. "Young Goodman Brown." In *Hawthorne: Selected Tales and Sketches*, 3rd ed. New York: Holt, Rinehart and Winston, 149–163.

Hawthorne, Nathaniel. 1972. *The Scarlet Letter*. New York: Pocket Books.

Mamet, David. 1978. *Sexual Perversity in Chicago and the Duck Variations: Two Plays*. New York: Grove.

Melville, Herman. 1956a. "Bartleby the Scrivener." In *The Shorter Novels of Herman Melville*, Raymond Weaver, ed. New York: Fawcett Premier.

Melville, Herman. 1956b. "Billy Budd." In *The Shorter Novels of Herman Melville*, Raymond Weaver, ed. New York: Fawcett Premier.

Melville, Herman. 1988. *Moby Dick, or The Whale*. Evanston, IL: Northwestern University Press.

Morrison, Toni. 1970. *The Bluest Eye*. New York: Holt, Rinehart and Winston.

Morrison, Toni. 1987. *Beloved: A Novel*. New York: Knopf.

Morrison, Toni. 1992. *Jazz*. New York: Knopf.

Morrison, Toni. 1993. *Sula*. New York: Knopf.

Morrison, Toni. 1994. *Lecture and Speech of Acceptance, Upon the Award of the Nobel Prize for Literature, Delivered in Stockholm on the Seventh of December, Nineteen Hundred and Ninety-Three*. London: Chatto & Windus.

Otto, Whitney. 1991. *How to Make an American Quilt*. New York: Villard.

Shakespeare, William. 1992. *Hamlet*. New York: St. Martin's.

Wolf, Christa. 1989. *Accident: A Day's News*. New York: Farrar, Straus, Giroux.

* *CHAPTER 3* *

Dismantling Borders

Concha Delgado-Gaitan

MY LIFE HAS BEEN A "TINKLING" dance in which I have hopped between two clanking bamboo sticks, skillfully avoiding getting a foot severed as I jumped in and out. I have searched to find the space that is a synthesis of my worlds. I have sought to reconcile living in varied settings, to discover the "borderland"[1] or meeting ground that synthesizes my identity, experience, feelings, beliefs, and dreams. In this chapter, I reflect on various borderlands of my life beginning with my early childhood learning and socialization. I then comment on my formal and informal education, informed by the sociopolitical and historical context. That led me into a third major borderland, my research in culturally diverse communities. I conclude my chapter with reflections of continued personal and professional challenges as both domains braid, and I'm once more propelled into borderlands to unfold a new identity.

BUILDING A SOLID FOUNDATION

The concept of borderlands helps me to visualize an arena for questioning, reflecting, and transforming. Borderland suggests a space where multiple cultures, multiple consciousnesses, and multiple possibilities exist–where a border is dissolved. Rigid walls fall and make room for borderlands to configure. By remaining flexible, my psyche stretches, and I'm tolerant of ambiguity to understand my multiple identities and those of others. It seems in retrospect that since my early childhood, I was unconsciously shaping my agenda for a later day as a researcher.

We spoke only Spanish in my family. My parents expected my sisters and me to learn English at school and become bilingual. Learning everything I could in English and Spanish intrigued me, but it wasn't always easy to do so

Learning from Our Lives: Women, Research, and Autobiography in Education. ISBN 0-8077-3593-0 (pbk), ISBN 0-8077-3594-9 (cloth).

in English because it was my second language since the age of eight. Bilingualism wasn't something that seemed useful until much later. According to my mother, my being bilingual was an asset because the ability to communicate in two languages would give me twice the opportunity for employment. We spoke only Spanish at home but read English texts that we brought from school. Mother adamantly promoted education, I believe, because her own schooling was aborted as a result of her family's occupation as international migrant workers. Very early in my childhood my mother helped me find my freedom by insisting that I read rather than watch television or fight with my sisters. I turned to books and stories, and they became my intimate friends. Although my mother spoke very little English, she always got involved in our schooling–from being a room-mother to monitoring our daily homework and quarterly report card grades. We accepted her authority unquestioningly because she was fair. She trusted my sister and me enough to make us accountable for our school-related actions. I remember that she did not mind when I insisted on staying home from school because she knew that I would never miss an important class or test. I had the freedom to make my own decisions based on my assessment of my responsibilities.

My mind is flooded with warm memories when I recall my absorption in the world of literature as a child. Stories of far-away lands fascinated me: Excitement, intrigue, and new worlds opened as I mentally marched off to unknown realms with characters in *The Island of the Blue Dolphins*. Other stories like *Charlotte's Web*, *Helen Keller*, *A Wrinkle in Time*, or *Eve's Diary* took me to closer geographic destinations but stretched my imagination beyond its limits with new characters that marked my growing-up years.

I associate learning with joy and pleasure and school with dread and stress, even now. School has usually meant fear, anxiety, and demands, although, generally, I was rewarded with outstanding grades throughout most of my school years. One particular event that comes to mind occurred during the first weeks of high school in September. An Indian summer heat settled into the stifling air of our English classroom with twelve windows pushed open, making the teacher's normally boring routine even more insufferable. The scene was familiar. The teacher stood in front of the room to drill us in vocabulary words such as *truck*, *sharp*, and *settle*. I looked around and noticed that most of my classmates were asleep. At first, I thought it was the warm weather that lulled us, but then I realized that I had never before seen my classmates with their heads on their desks in English literature classes, even during extremely hot weather. Therefore, the only culprit reasonable to blame was the teacher, who was boring us with vocabulary drills.

In my freshman year in high school, I had received A's in my English and American literature classes. However, in my sophomore year, I was placed in the "dummy" English class because of my low Iowa Standardized test scores.

I was angry that the school would place me in such a class–confident that I could do better work because of my previous success in college preparatory classes. Unlike most of my classmates, I complained. When I complained to my mother, I remember that she encouraged me to advocate for myself. I was able to do something about my situation, but at the same time I couldn't help wondering why my classmates, who I believed were equally intelligent, did not also protest about the class curriculum and their placement. Maybe they did not know how to navigate themselves through the school system. The infantile curriculum and the students' inability to advocate for themselves made them prisoners in these classes where boredom was the only outcome. These classes acted as fences, holding Chicano students back from the opportunities they might have had to cross the border to advanced academic tracks.[2]

Shifting from home to school, from school to home, from Spanish to English and English to Spanish, from advanced to slow and slow to advanced classes kept me busy figuring out where I belonged. Ethnic identity, however, was never a question. My family made it clear that I was Mexican, and that was something to be proud of.

I witnessed other forms of educational neglect involving Chicano students in other classes. Home economics was one such. Yes, it was that era before girls were allowed to take carpentry. Mrs. Moore, the teacher, had assigned us a sewing project, a gym bag for carrying our physical education clothes. We had to buy materials including cloth, thread, and other paraphernalia.

Regina, a classmate with a towering beehive hair-do almost as high as she was tall, wearing a miniskirt the length of a wide belt, approached Mrs. Moore at the beginning of class. In a voice only slightly higher than a whisper, she said, "My mother can't get the material for me this week but she says she can get it next weekend." Mrs. Moore grabbed her spiral notebook from the top of her desk, opened it, and said to Regina, "Well, that's another F and if you get another one, you'll be out of this class. You shouldn't take classes that require you to buy things if you can't afford them." I cringed with humiliation and shame for Regina. I was also appalled that a teacher would be so callous because I well knew the sacrifice involved in such expenses. Most Mexican parents worked in construction and other seasonal jobs, rendering unemployment the norm for those families for almost half the year. Those families, usually Chicanos, were poor, under- or unemployed, and had a difficult time making even the monthly rent.

During my high school years, I worked at several part-time jobs after school and on weekends. A great many part-time jobs were available to me in our community, as Head Start projects, part of the War on Poverty, abounded. I wanted to do what I could to abate the pain for children and families around me. As a translator for Spanish-speaking families at a Head Start program, I listened to doctors ask parents about their children's diet, teeth, and vaccinations. After the parents left the office, the doctors laughed with the nurses about the families and speculated how many tortillas made them fat. I felt a soul-piercing pain that left me hopeless. I was invisible to them, or maybe they were just callous! "Will I ever be able to achieve anything?" I asked myself. Could I ever help the people who needed help?

My political consciousness was shaped by my own experience as well as my father's frequent reminders that the system "couldn't be trusted." Sometimes my older sister and I interpreted for my father at the construction labor union when he felt the organization discriminated against him. I stood on my toes in front of the clerk so I could see her face. Her desk was inside a cagelike office with bars in front. My father stood at my right, facing me, and, in his familiar gruff manner, complained,

> Díles que se vallan a la chingada, que porque ḿe siguen pasando. Mi numero es 5 y me ubieran llamado hace tres días y les han llamado a otros con numeros mas grandes. Creen que me pueden hacer pendejo porque no se hablar inglés, pero no saben que yo sé más que ellos. [Tell them to go to hell because they keep passing me up. My number is 5, and they should have called me three days ago, and they've called other larger numbers. They think that they can make a fool of me because I don't speak English, but they don't know that I know more than they do.]

I tried to convey my father's concern without the angry words, but I was left with his rage in my heart because I knew that what they were doing was wrong and that my father's worth as a bricklayer was devalued because he did not speak English well. How could I convince them that he really did know how to work hard? He had had a successful contractor's business in Chihuahua, and I had seen his artistic perfectionist talent in the work he did for family and friends. If they could only understand that he hadn't had a chance for a formal education because he got tired of stepping over dead bodies on his way to school during the revolution, and after first grade, he went to work as a sheepherder with his uncle. Even without formal schooling he tutored me in trigonometry and geometry when I needed help in high school.

That people should have a voice was a notion I derived from my observations of injustice around me. I believe that my parents were wise and knowledgeable in spite of their limited formal schooling–if for no other reason than that they guided my sisters and me to books and learning, which allowed us to have some choices in our lives. The household struggles due to poverty pained me such that I embraced education as a means of obtaining other options for myself. I genuinely wanted to share with others my fervor for learning through books, as it had given me a sense of personal freedom and the key to extend my boundaries.

REFLECTING THE TIMES

College activities in the late 1960s meant total involvement for many of us committed to justice. The sixties' political climate focused on racial and cultural issues that demanded a critical consciousness and made action its logical extension. In my college community, the University of the Pacific, a student was expected to belong to the Chicano Estudiantil (CHE), United Farm Workers (UFW), Brown Berets, Mexican American Political Association (MAPA), or Students for a Democratic Society (SDS). We could count on at least one protest march per week. Anger against the war in Vietnam as well as concern about local issues such as desegregation motivated these protests. I refused to be excluded from the action; I participated wholeheartedly in the activities of these organizations. I was driven by the political consciousness that emanated from the grass roots and national movements.

The idea that people should be provided with the tools to cultivate their own voices took shape from my early participation in Cesar Chavez's United Farmworkers union and other community organizations. During my work with the UFW, I met intellectually and politically astute activists who introduced me to readings by political leaders. Equally influential were writings by Paulo Freire, Saul Alinski, Miles Horton, and Antonio Gramsci.[3] Their theoretical positions resonated with my political beliefs. Beliefs in the ability of "others" superseded thinking about the individual. At last I had found an area where there was a confluence between ideas and actions.

My work in the community matured with my subsequent affiliation with organizations like the Third World Women's Alliance (TWWA). Self-critique as well as consciousness-raising activities with communities of color enhanced my appreciation and knowledge of the diversity in my local and international community.

Teaching was an extension of my political work. I was driven by a desire to "make a difference" and help poor families. Some now refer to this as missionary work, but in actuality I was inspired by a more profound desire—to work for justice. I entered the first national undergraduate Teacher Corps training project, which emphasized the teacher's role as an agent of change in the community. Through rigorous marathon sessions we were forced to confront our racism and all the other "isms" that pervaded our thinking and practices. These sessions were precursors to teacher preparation courses at the university. We had to live in the community where we taught. We wanted to teach the "whole child," which meant involving family and community in the classroom as part of the curriculum.

My training as an educator during this period in history taught me that *literacy* meant reading for a purpose, and that purpose was the liberation of poor communities. Learning to read meant reaching beyond the textbooks. My mornings and evenings, therefore, were taken up with trips to the public library, where I selected works of literature for all my students, taking into account their individual reading levels and topics that interested them. My personal experience had convinced me that people learn best when motivated by what is important to them. Thus I concluded that students in my third-grade class who could not read at all could be challenged by books about topics of interest to them rather than humiliated by struggling to read pre-primers designed for five-year-olds.

Teaching forced me to blur the boundary between theory and practice. Parents and children who had novice literacy skills were my central concern, but critical literacy skills dominated the curriculum. I found myself at the center of community activities involving tutoring programs for what were then termed *disadvantaged* children. I held English and literacy tutoring sessions for families in people's homes, community centers, and schools. Many of the children were students in my third-grade class during the day. In fact, weeks before I saw the students in my class, I met them in their homes when I visited the parents to present my classroom curriculum and to solicit their support.

During the War on Poverty, everyone who wasn't from the white middle class was considered disadvantaged. I abhor the pejorative implications of such labels. Although this word is used less frequently now, and we're more politically correct in our references to children who underachieve, the underlying beliefs from past years remain with us. We use terms like *minority*, *culturally different*, *racially different*, *ethnically different*, and *linguistically different*; and we seldom hear the term *educationally disadvantaged* because more white middle-class children are dropping out of school now, giving rise to *dropout* and *high risk* as more encompassing descriptions. Nonetheless, these currently popular terms continue to promote separation and exclusion by holding people who are poor, of color, ethnically different, linguistically different, or female–the "other"–at a distance. The "other" is always an outsider, which renders the person a victim, incapable of becoming part of the "insider" group.

In the 1960s and early to mid-1970s, prevailing politics greatly influenced my work as an elementary school teacher and principal. It was unpopular to think of "me." Political trends focused on the War on Poverty, national critique, community activism, ethnic identity, cultural awareness, and resistance movements. For me, being a principal in the mid-1970s meant being the first woman and the youngest administrator in the school district. I found becoming a principal an extension of being a teacher, with one great experience: Instead of 32 students from diverse ethnic backgrounds, I now had 850 students, 27 teachers, and a total of 96 people on my staff.

Teaching at that time meant something quite different to innovative educators and communities interested in social change. Today, too many teachers have become laborers controlled by the clock and paperwork. I believe that as educators, we must remain cognizant of the political forces that influence our work, both positively and negatively, for democratic ideals. As a teacher and principal, I was driven by the political ideas of that time as well as by a total love for children and a firm conviction that everyone could learn beyond his or her perceived limits.

NEGOTIATING IN THE BORDERLANDS

Gloria Anzaldua writes that, "To live in the Borderlands means that one is neither *Hispana india negra española ni gabacha, eres mestiza, mulata*, half breed caught in the crossfire between camps while carrying all five races on your back not knowing which side to turn to, run from. . . . To survive the Borderlands you must live *sin fronteras*–be a crossroads" (pp. 194–195). Negotiating two worlds takes a great deal of effort. Compelled by academic theory and an ardent belief that literacy is a powerful tool for personal and political liberation, I have focused my research on ethnographic studies in four communities: Carpinteria, Commerce City, Redwood City, and West Sacramento. Several articles in research journals and a book detail specific findings from research conducted in Commerce City, Redwood City, and West Sacramento. I could easily write lengthy reports on all the communities I've examined, because I have special memories of my work peppered with great stories of the wonderful people whom I have studied and with whom I have developed a mutual trust.[4] However, given the scope of this chapter, I focus on Carpinteria because my work there best illustrates my active participation as an ethnographer who has successfully crossed personal and political borders through negotiations between researchers and participants.

Carpinteria, in particular, has provided me an immense opportunity to understand and reconcile ethnic, intellectual, and political borders. This extended research project has been my borderland, providing me with the "time" to work through academic, interpersonal, and political problems in a protracted way. I have had the chance to observe the changes in which I participated, which has given me an appreciation of their significance. Just as time has led me to a deeper understanding of these problems, it has also helped me learn to deal with such problems in more empowering ways than was my practice in the past. All of this has stretched my consciousness theoretically, politically, and personally. The unity of ideas and praxis afforded me by my work in Carpinteria constitutes a borderland for me. It has been the community where I have conducted the major part of my academic work. As a researcher, I have participated in the growth and development of Latino families and they, in turn, have influenced my understanding of literacy, family relationships, and sociocultural change in the Latino community.[5]

I began to work in Carpinteria nine years ago. At that time Carpinteria School District administrators were concerned that some Spanish-speaking children were not achieving to their potential and that the schools did not have much contact with the families. Teachers, principals, and other administrators became an integral part of the Carpinteria research. These teachers often face overt discrimination and scorn from others in their ranks who reject the notion of bilingual education.

As an ethnographer interested in family and community literacy, I studied literacy activities in families and in classrooms. After collecting more than thirty case studies, I met with large groups of Spanish-speaking parents from the same community to get feedback in order to verify, confirm, clarify, or modify what I had learned in the case studies. Through close contact with many people in the community, I won their trust and respect.

Initially, I did not intend to participate as actively in the ethnographic study as I eventually did. However, I became curious about the organization I observed in the community meetings. Little did I know that my involvement would be so edifying. I learned things that I will carry with me not only into future research but also into my personal life;[6] my work with Latino families reaffirmed my appreciation for patience, respect, and collectivity as virtues. The qualities displayed by these people in their interactions with the people being studied in the field demonstrated a strength born of what could only be love.

In their initial discussions, this parent group focused on their feelings of fear, confusion, despair, frustration, and isolation in not knowing what was expected of them or whether they were behaving appropriately. Soon came the recognition that they could not continue just sharing complaints about their feelings. They confronted and dispelled stereotypes about themselves that had prevented them from becoming more visible in the schools. Some of these were that they spoke only Spanish; that they did not have extensive formal schooling; and that Mexicans had a reputation for being unmotivated. I felt tremendous excitement in watching the scope of their ideas expand. The parents now focused on working together to open up more opportunities for their children's education. Through critical reflection they learned about their relationship to social forces.

From the outset, the focus of the parent organization, called COPLA, has been their children's welfare. These parents have reached out to other Latino families in the school district and supported one another as they learned to be advocates for their children. Another major goal was to work cooperatively with school personnel to resolve concerns pertaining to children both in and out of school. Parents often credited me for much of the organization's success. However, I made it clear that they, not I, should receive recognition for what they created. This was a border I should not cross. My stance as a researcher derived from my interpretation of critical ethnography, which locates the researcher in interaction with research collaborators in the community, not in a privileged position to them. Thus I could not assume leadership in Carpinteria because it was not my residential community. They knew best what they needed, and how the organization evolved would depend on their strengths and vision. I have been both an outsider and an insider throughout this research project, and in this case I drew the line because I believed that the community needed to recognize their own efforts, not mine. So I tried to applaud their progress and accomplishments from a distance. One could argue that my credit is recognized through the research I publish about the community.

From my work in Carpinteria I have come to understand the significance of learning through interaction with others. I have observed how empowerment occurs through collective sharing and reflection. I have witnessed parents and children in many Carpinteria families discard the shame of not understanding the educational and social systems around them. This confirmed my belief that people, in general, are not "bad" or somehow inferior because they lack knowledge; rather, the system in place produces and reproduces knowledge and controls the access to this knowledge. Tormented during my childhood by fears of not knowing enough and of being punished because I did not speak English, I again confronted those feelings as they surfaced in my study. In the second grade, I seldom saw the playground at recess because I was kept in the classroom with my head down on the desk for not speaking or reading English. Parents in Carpinteria have been my teachers, and their connection to each other and the schools has been a constant reminder that knowledge is much more than language. I have seen that regardless of how desperate the situation appears, by joining with others one can overcome seemingly insurmountable obstacles. My research is as much a statement of my action in the world as was my teaching and leadership work.

Applied anthropology research has taught me that empowering relationships between people can be forged through critical interaction. In this case, families and school personnel enlightened each other through self-reflection, self-critique, and a common language that unified them in a vision.

Some people define empowerment as just "any change" or "outcome" benefiting an oppressed group. Unfortunately, such trivialization of the concept has diminished its explanatory power. To me, the most disturbing use of the word *empowerment* is one that reduces the concept to a simplistic notion of people's "feeling good" about themselves. By limiting the idea of empowerment to a strictly psychological state, such a definition disregards the perception of self that is influenced by sociocultural and sociopolitical conditions.

The concept of power has been a central spirit in my academic and personal life. I have surrendered the notion that empowerment is something that one does for another to raise him or her from a lower to a higher status. Nor can a researcher or any other professional empower someone else.[7] I have learned, and now maintain, that empowerment is not something I can do or give someone else; it is a potential within all of us and is developed in our life's journey. Fundamentally, empowerment is not a commodity to be exchanged; it's who we are. Every time we unite with others to deal with common issues, it is an opportunity to empower ourselves. We are empowered when we feel in control of our lives.

Empowerment rarely conforms to our timeline and expectations and frequently eludes us. Events in my personal life testify to this. About three years ago, I reveled in successes in all areas of my life. Then on a Saturday night, the last thing I remember was feeling a bit tired. I went to bed only to be awakened at 4:00 A.M., burning with fever, unable to breathe, with screaming pain from shoulders to toes and my heart doing jumping jacks. After grueling in-hospital tests and endless speculation, I was diagnosed with systemic lupus erythematosus (SLE). For a period of time, I tried dealing with it the same way I had approached every other problem, wanting to control the disease while I kept right on moving as fast as I could. But I accomplished little, since I neither healed nor advanced in my professional work as much as I expected. My health worsened; and after nearly crossing the final border, I was forced to acknowledge that I was seriously ill. Enraged by my inability to cure myself, I have had to reassess the way I do everything in my life. Painfully, I have learned that the border I had delineated between my work and my personal life must fade to make possible an integration of self and profession. In order to survive this disabling and deadly disease, I must remain conscious of my activity and environments on a moment-to-moment basis. Daily, from the time I awaken, it's a continuous inventory of all my activities and decisions. Every action bears consequences, even when I feel strong. I have learned to doubt science and research that have no answers for me; even hope has betrayed me.

Without a doubt, my daily healing course requires the attention equivalent of a full-time job to accommodate all of the necessary therapies from chemo to holistic, physical to metaphysical. The magnitude of SLE has made it one of my toughest life curriculums, surpassed only by the death of my daughter. It has been a sobering barometer of reconciliations between my work and personal borders. Only by befriending the shadows in my life am I able to remain open to learning what I need, and even then I still sometimes foolishly question why it's necessary to learn those particular lessons. Above all, the concept of moment has gained new significance in my life. Although I've always rejected the cliché "one moment at a time," now it applies all too appropriately to the way that my life, in the past three years, has become unpredictable from moment to moment.

Introspection about my healing process has caused me to draw parallels to my approach as a researcher. I would prefer well-defined formulas and predictable patterns. Theories, however, offer only limited and partial explanations. The realization is that, oftentimes, no answers exist in the conventional places. Whether in research or in my personal life, I am inevitably distressed when I believe that I've failed to solve a problem. In these borderlands I am learning to join with others and shift my perception, thereby creating new imaginative possibilities–a feat I witnessed many Latinos accomplish in Carpinteria.

A RELATIONAL SELF

My greatest challenge has been to live in multiple cultures while maintaining a sense of integrity. I have spent over twenty-five years immersed in issues of literacy as an applied anthropologist, critical ethnographer, educator, community activist, and advocate for children and family rights. My need to challenge perceived personal limits has fueled my research, as has the rigorous exploration of the concept of empowerment.

I attempt to locate my research in settings where people are interested in changing the plight that creates obstacles to their advancement. This entails supporting people in self-critique as they empower themselves.

Borderlands replace the tinkling dance more each day. That is, creating borders between myself and others is less frequently the case now as I more often confront ambiguity, uncertainty, and complexity in borderlands. Yet, just as in the tinkling dance, the need for a delicate balance persists, and I must continuously remain alert not to erect barriers when I should cooperate with others to better understand and resolve issues. Inner thoughts about knowledge and politics and external expressions of my love preoccupy me in my ceaseless appraisal of the past with careful attention to the now. Mary Catherine Bateson says it elegantly: "Composing a life involves a continual reimagining of the future and reinterpretation of the past to give meaning to the present" (p. 29).[8] Transcending boundaries extends our conscious selves;

and in my life, tribulations have been transformed through the unconditional support and love of those who have made it possible for me to locate my borderlands.

Stories about ourselves teach us much about women's lives and life in general. Many stories come from travail; theirs, ours, mine, yours, someone's we know, someone's we do not know far away in time and place. Close to home, the case of Carpinteria as well as my own case unites us through our sense of empowerment. Some stories clearly come about as a result of one person's or a group's compelling suffering—because women share a history of oppression, we easily relate to one another's stories.[9] Stories help us cross borders and connect us. As Dorthy Lee acknowledges, "The experience of value occurs when there is uninterrupted relatedness. We are open to the experience of the other" (p. 5).[10] To transcend the us/other binary becomes the challenge of the academic discourses that have privileged some and disempowered others.[11] Borders between women's personal and work life are blurred when we learn the influence of one in the other.[12] When we share our stories with each other, we learn that the borders we created to differentiate between "us" and "the other" become not a barrier but a zone in which we are all neither/nor. Borderlands offer endless possibilities for being and acting.

Borderlands are not confined by time and space, nor are they a one-time synthesis that endures. The notion of borderlands defies borders, empowering us to experiment with our protean selves where we do not have to run from who we are or from our potential. By ethnicity, I'm Mexican; by profession, I'm an applied anthropologist; by occupation, I'm a professor; by political identity, I'm Chicana; and my praxis is in education. All these identities are defined by borders needing to be crossed and reconciled in a given space to represent my totality, not as an "other." My particular borderland incorporates my personhood in the remaking of my ideas through cross-ethnic, cross-generational, cross-cultural, and cross-racial discourses.

NOTES

Thank you to my editors, Anna Neumann and Penelope Peterson, in addition to Lubna Chaudhry, Judy Berzon, and Martha Montero-Sieburth for their insightful feedback on earlier versions of this chapter.

1. In *Borderlands—la Frontera: The New Mestiza*, Gloria Anzaldua constructs the notion of borderlands/*la frontera* as a meeting ground for people of diverse cultures to join in dialogue and create new traditions.

2. In this chapter, I use labels like *Chicano/a*, *Latino/a*, *Mexican*, and *Mexican American* to refer to ethnic badges of different groups within the Latino/a community at large. My choice of term also represents how my cultural identity label changes

across my particular contexts. These labels change as groups identify differently with one another in different regional, political, and social contexts. For example, *Latino/a* is used by Mexican families in Carpinteria, California–the community where I have spent nine years conducting ethnographic research–as a title that includes all families of Spanish-speaking Chicanos/as who are of Mexican descent but do not speak Spanish. In other Latino/a communities, such as San Francisco, people from diverse homelands may identify as Latinos/as. Central Americans, South Americans, Mexicans, and even immigrants from parts of Western Europe use *Latino/a* as a more general cultural label.

3. Paulo Freire's (1970) work on indigenous populations in Brazil influenced my thinking, as did Saul Alinski's (1968) writing on organizational communities and Myles Horton's (1970) work in the Highlander Research Center and his literacy development campaigns with rural workers in Tennessee. Antonio Gramsci's (1957) notion of hegemony had a great deal of impact on my life as I attempted to understand the persistent oppression of people of color. The notion refers to an organized assemblage of meanings and practices, the central, effective, and dominant system of meanings, values, and actions that are lived, determined by one class's imposition on another. Educational institutions act in the process of saturation. Before reading these works, I became quite familiar with Cesar Chavez's work through my involvement with the United Farm Workers union. These people's unselfish and humane commitment to social justice spoke loudly to me.

4. See Delgado-Gaitan, 1987a, 1987b, 1988, 1991, 1992, 1994; also Delgado-Gaitan and Trueba, 1991.

5. Although both the community (research participants) and I have influenced each other as we've worked together in Carpinteria, the task has involved dealing with unsuspected tensions stemming from our preconceived ideas about each other. In some of my work (1993), I consider the question of studying communities where we believe that we have an advantage because of our cultural commonalities. My analyses, however, revealed that the researcher is highly influenced by the institutional culture, which makes the boundaries (between ethnographer and community) difficult to permeate.

6. Some of my work (e.g., Delgado-Gaitan, 1993) discusses the value of collaborative research and critical ethnography in underrepresented communities.

7. Elizabeth Ellsworth (1989) asked, "Why doesn't this feel empowering?" in her article by the same title, which raises issues of the meaning of empowerment.

8. In *Composing a Life*, Mary Catherine Bateson presents the lives of five women; her honest portrayal affirms our continuity over the generations.

9. In *The Gift of Story: A Wise Tale About What Is Enough*, Clarissa Pinkola Estes calls stories powerful medicine because they come from people's experience and can provide potent remedies for past, present, and even future ills.

10. An anthropologist of Greek heritage, Dorthy Lee evoked a spirit of caring. She believed that if we value ourselves, we can reach out to others and form community. In *Valuing the Self: What We Can Learn from Other Cultures*, Lee promotes a kind of anthropology that vitalizes a dialogue between the communities in which she worked.

11. Anthropologists who have addressed theoretical issues of "the other" include

Marcus Clifford and George E. Marcus in *Writing Culture: The Poetics and Politics of Ethnography* and Smadar Lavie in *The Poetics of Military Occupation*. Essentially, conventional anthropological perspectives have regarded "other" cultures from a position of cultural superiority. They have described cultures other than their own as "exotic" or "inferior"–defined as primitive, or non-Western, or preliterate, or nonhistorical. Recent years have seen a more critical theoretic approach to culture; anthropologists have attempted to be more careful in their depiction of cultural groups. Actually, much earlier than any current theorist, Margaret Mead wrote in *Culture and Commitment* about this conflict between the mentality of the Western researchers and our responsibility to represent the "other." Mead asserted that the Western view of the world is not reality per se but only one vision of a number of possible realities. She explicitly stated, "It is not only participation in the material gains and freedoms which are being demanded by the world's people but also the dignity of sharing in all decisions that affect a person's own life and that of his or her kin and neighbors, descendants and successors" (p. 155). The "us" and "them" dichotomy is less rigid in social science research. Now, ethnography encounters "others" in relation to itself, while seeing itself as other. The science of the exotic is being "repatriated" (see Clifford and Marcus, 1986).

12. Writings about women's lives include Mary Catherine Bateson's *Composing a Life*, Kathleen Casey's *I Answer With My Life: Life Histories of Women Teachers Working for Social Change*, Gwendolyn Etter-Lewis's *My Soul Is My Own: Oral Narratives of African-American Women in the Profession*, and Sara Ruddick and Pamela Daniels's edited volume, *Working It Out: 23 Women Writers, Artists, Scientists, and Scholars Talk About Their Lives and Work*.

BIBLIOGRAPHY

Alinski, Saul. 1968. *Organizing Communities*. Berkeley, CA: Unpublished pamphlet.

Anzaldua, Gloria. 1987. *Borderlands-la Frontera: The New Mestiza*. San Francisco: spinsters/aunt lute.

Bateson, Mary Catherine. 1990. *Composing a Life*. New York: Plume.

Casey, Kathleen. 1993. *I Answer With My Life: Life Histories of Women Teachers Working for Social Change*. New York: Routledge.

Clifford, Marcus, and George E. Marcus. 1986. *Writing Culture: The Poetics and Politics of Ethnography*. Berkeley: University of California Press.

Delgado-Gaitan, Concha. 1987a. "Compassion and Concern: Mentoring Students Through High School." *Urban Education* 8:93–102.

Delgado-Gaitan, Concha. 1987b. "Traditions and Transitions in the Learning Process of Mexican American Children: An Ethnographic View." In *Interpretive Ethnography of Education*, George and Louise Spindler, eds. Hillsdale, NJ: Lawrence Erlbaum, 332–362.

Delgado-Gaitan, Concha. 1988. "The Value of Conformity: Learning to Stay in School." *Anthropology and Education Quarterly* 19:354–382.

Delgado-Gaitan, Concha. 1991. "Linkages Between Home and School: A Process of Change for Involving Parents." *American Journal of Education* 100:20–46.

Delgado-Gaitan, Concha. 1992. "School Matters in the Mexican-American Home: Socializing Children to Education." *American Educational Research Journal* 29: 495–513.

Delgado-Gaitan, Concha. 1993. "Researching Change and Changing the Researcher." *Harvard Educational Review* 63:389–411.

Delgado-Gaitan, Concha. 1994. "Russian Refugee Families: Accommodating Aspirations Through Education." *Anthropology and Education Quarterly* 25:137–155.

Delgado-Gaitan, Concha, and Henry T. Trueba. 1991. *Crossing Cultural Borders: Education for Immigrant Families in America*. London: Falmer.

Ellsworth, Elizabeth. 1989. "Why Doesn't This Feel 'Empowering'?" *Harvard Educational Review* 59:297–324.

Estes, Clarissa Pinkola. 1993. *The Gift of Story—A Wise Tale About What Is Enough*. New York: Ballantine.

Etter-Lewis, Gwendolyn. 1993. *My Soul Is My Own: Oral Narratives of African-American Women in the Profession*. New York: Routledge.

Freire, Paulo. 1970. *Pedagogy of the Oppressed*. New York: Seabury.

Gramsci, Antonio. 1957. *The Modern Prince*. New York: International.

Horton, Myles. 1970. *Teaching Appalachia*. Lexington, KY: Unpublished booklet.

Lavie, Smadar. 1990. *The Poetics of Military Occupation*. Berkeley: University of California Press.

Lee, Dorthy. 1976. *Valuing the Self: What We Can Learn from Other Cultures*. Prospect Height, IL: Waveland.

Mead, Margaret. 1970. *Culture and Commitment*. Garden City, NY: Anchor.

Ruddick, Sara, and Pamela Daniels, eds. 1977. *Working It Out: 23 Women Writers, Artists, Scientists, and Scholars Talk About Their Lives and Work*. New York: Pantheon.

CHILDREN'S LITERATURE CITED

Keller, Helen. 1967. *Helen Keller, Her Socialist Years; Writings and Speeches*. New York: International.

L'Engle, Madeline. 1976. *A Wrinkle in Time*. New York: Dell.

O'Dell, Scott. 1960. *Island of the Blue Dolphins*. Boston: Houghton Mifflin.

Twain, Mark. 1906. *Eve's Diary*. New York: Harper & Brothers.

White, E.B. 1981. *Charlotte's Web*. London: Macmillan Education.

* *CHAPTER 4* *

For colored girls who have considered suicide when the academy's not enough: Reflections of an African American Woman Scholar

Gloria Ladson-Billings

[We] deal intimately with the White power structure and cultural apparatus, and the inner realities of the Black world at one and the same time.
—Harold Cruse, *The Crisis of the Negro Intellectual*

And ain't I a woman?
—Sojourner Truth

I BEGIN THIS CHAPTER with apologies to Ntozake Shange.[1] However, the power and urgency of her language best speak to me when I think about my position as an African American woman in the predominantly white, male world of the academy. Certainly, I have not seriously considered suicide because of professional challenges and difficulties. My working-class, African American family background assures me that no "job" is worth dying for. And it is just this attitude of blurring the distinction between "job" and "career" that has sustained me in the rigors of academic life. I attempt to write this chapter somewhere within the nexus of my life as an African American woman and an African American woman scholar. I deliberately write this narrative within and outside of my personal life because I believe that my personal life (or who I am as a person) informs and shapes who I am as a scholar. I resist notions of myself as an "objective" researcher when what I research is so intricately linked to the life I have lived and continue to live.

In this chapter, the reader has the opportunity to hear whispers of my "inner voice" that are self-reflective about the cultural and educational world

Learning from Our Lives: Women, Research, and Autobiography in Education. ISBN 0-8077-3593-0 (pbk), ISBN 0-8077-3594-9 (cloth).

that has shaped me. Without these "voices from within" the story is woefully incomplete. Even with my selective sharing of the narrative that is my life, the story still is partial. The reader is privy only to that which I choose to share, but that I would share it at all represents a break with much of traditional academic writing.

GOING TO SCHOOL

> "Now remember, when we go downtown people will be staring at us," said Mrs. Gray, the accelerated reading teacher. "They'll be staring at us because they're not used to seeing groups of Negro children walking in and out of the best downtown stores." I had been in downtown stores many times but this was a special Christmas visit for a group of "special" readers. At my segregated elementary school, it never occurred to me that African American students weren't as smart as other children. We were told so often and in many ways. But, this special visit to watch the dancing fountain in John Wanamaker's Department Store Christmas Show was a public declaration that we were special–we were smart.

Except for a brief period in junior high school, I remember enjoying school. I reveled in the life of the mind. Books and the world of words brought me great comfort (most of the time). But the luxury of spending one's life reading and thinking seemed far beyond my grasp. I had to "make a living" and making a living meant having a secure and stable *job*!

Life in the academy was not one I selected for myself, consciously. I entered college without any idea about what I wanted to do. I knew I enjoyed history and writing. In my secret life I was a writer, but just thinking about saying that aloud made me laugh. I could see it all clearly. After earning a bachelor's degree I would return to the solitude of my room (in my parents' home) to think and write. Never mind that most of my family's resources had gone to secure my education. Never mind that there was an expectation that I would both take care of myself (financially) and contribute to the family.[2] I merely would announce that I had returned home a "writer" and each morning while other family members marched off to work, I would retreat to my "study" and "write." The entire imagined scene was ludicrous.

What was more imaginable was the "sensible" (and understandable) profession of teaching. Everyone knew that teaching was a "good job" (almost as secure as working at the post office). I would have job security, good benefits, summers "off," and a "short" work day. Best of all, I could continue living in the world of intellectual activity.

Although I enjoyed teaching and supervising for ten years in a large urban school district, there was less intellectual activity and more work involved than I imagined. I taught middle grades (7–8) and intermediate (4–6) students for eight of those ten years. For two years I served as a social studies/ science collaborator (or consultant) for one of the city's eight geographic area districts. My area consisted of forty-four schools with approximately four thousand teachers. My job was to respond to the teachers' curriculum and instructional needs as requested. In actuality I spent too much time observing struggling teachers for principals who wanted documentation they could use to fire them. By 1978 I could not resist the lure of graduate school. Still I lacked a clear notion of what I would "do" as a result of graduate study. I just knew that graduate school would be a place to once again read and study.

However, the difference between the "me" who attended undergraduate school and the "me" who attended graduate school was dramatic. One month after I entered undergraduate school (in mid year), Malcom X was assassinated and my hope for strong, militant, black leadership filled with righteous indignation was dashed. Throughout my collegiate years the Vietnam War raged on while many of the male students at my historically black college campus struggled to maintain a high enough grade point average to keep them from being drafted. Too many of them lost that battle and found themselves in Southeast Asia fighting a war they did not understand.

By the time I graduated in 1968, Martin Luther King, Jr., had been assassinated and once again a void in black leadership was apparent. Robert Kennedy would be slain before I turned in my first professional employment application. It was a time of death and dying, protests and riots. My own coming of age was inextricably linked to the larger changing consciousness of African Americans who were challenging the existing social order in new ways. Rather than a cry of "let us in," which had seemed to shape the discourse of the early civil rights struggle for school desegregation and public accommodation, there were increasing calls for self-definition and self-determination among African Americans and other people of color. This confluence of social change, my interests in intellectual and political activity, and my reawakened sense of myself as an African American woman, all pointed me toward finding ways to make a closer fit between my "work life" and my "real life."

YOU CAN'T GET THERE FROM HERE

It is the summer of 1993 and I am meeting with a group of African American and Latino undergraduate students who are a part of a special program aimed at mentoring them into graduate school. During the course of the meeting one student asks, "How did you make it through

> graduate school, all the way to a Ph.D.? What should we be doing?" I remember laughing aloud and saying to the student, "Do you realize how much farther ahead you are then I was as an undergraduate? I didn't even know there was any such thing as graduate school!" I was not lying to them.

In my family, the term "doctor" was reserved for someone who could write you a prescription or preach fire and brimstone. After I received my doctorate my father would explain to friends and family that I wasn't a "healing doctor, just a *writing* doctor." While there was no overt opposition to my returning to school, there was no real support. I was a parent with responsibilities. Why would I give up my job–my good job–to go back to school? I could not expect my family to support what they did not understand. I especially could not expect them to support what I, myself, could not explain.

My first weeks in graduate school had me rethinking why I had given up my secure teaching job. The whole experience seemed surreal. People were speaking an alien language and arguing over seemingly meaningless problems at the same time *real* people were struggling with *real* problems. I was reminded that for many children, school is not a *real* place. My solace in those first weeks of graduate school came as a result of a decision I had made to not take advantage of campus housing. I felt the need to live in a "familiar" community. Thus I found housing in a nearby African American community.

While my days were spent in the "unreal" world of graduate school, my nights and evenings were spent in the real world of a struggling, largely African American and Latino school district geographically located near a prestigious university and alongside a predominantly white school system that was reputedly among the best in the state. The parents of the African American and Latino school system's "town-gown" issues were not the typical ones of zoning permits and fraternity raucousness. Sitting in the shadow of a "great" university, they wondered why the fact that their children were failing at unprecedented rates seemed not to be an issue for scholarly inquiry. Their questions were my questions and became the principal way for me to merge my personal interests and community politics with my professional goals. Their struggles helped me articulate the meaning that education and educational research could have in the lives of African American people.

That commitment–to make what I got from graduate school meaningful–was more of a challenge than I anticipated. My graduate school had one African American faculty member (not in my area) who was preparing to leave. Other African American graduate students who expressed an interest in the African American community were either discouraged or struggling with little faculty mentorship or support. The general pattern of successful graduate study meant attaching oneself to a faculty member via a research project or teaching assistantship. But there were no research projects focused on African American education.

My years of teaching and supervision in a large urban school district meant that I was qualified for a teaching assistantship in the school of education's relatively small (thirty to forty students) teacher education program.

> My job as a supervisor would be a snap. I was required to supervise eight social studies interns. After all, I had recently had the responsibility of "supervising" 4,000 teachers in 44 separate school sites–44,000 students, and that was just my geographic region. Sometimes I had to respond to supervisory requests systemwide–280 schools, 13,000 teachers, more than a quarter of a million students. I didn't kid myself about what I did. I was a firefighter. I did damage control. Working with eight eager beaver student teachers was something I could do in my sleep.

Even though I regarded my work as relatively easy, I was not prepared for the sense of alienation I would feel as an African American woman.

> "Aren't there any other black supervisors in the teacher education program?" I asked. "You mean there is one?" came the reply from a third-year African American doctoral student. "Yeah, I'm supervising," I said. "How'd you pull that off?" she asked.

In many ways graduate school was a pleasant divergence from the cares of the world. I found the work enjoyable, if not inspiring. The first years of course work seemed a lot like having a day at an amusement park. There were so many different rides and attractions from which to sample, and yet you knew you could never do it all.

Graduate school did not get "hard" for me until I had to declare a research interest. The closer I got to having to make that declaration, the more arduous just getting up and going to campus became.

> My course work is winding down. I am supervising four students and teaching the methods course for my advisor while he is on sabbatical. I have a part-time job at a local middle school. At home, I am parenting a pre-teen son and serve as chairperson of his school's advisory committee. I wake up each morning with a headache. It plagues me throughout the day and accompanies me to bed every night. Not prone to headaches, I go to an optometrist to have my eyes examined. Two prescriptions and two pairs of eyeglasses later I am still suffering with a nonstop headache. I drag myself to the campus health center. The doctor can find nothing

wrong with me. "No, you don't have a brain tumor." "No, your sinuses look fine." "Do you have a history of migraines?" The quarter is ending and we are returning home for Christmas. As the plane touches down at Philadelphia International Airport, I notice that my headache has disappeared. For the next three weeks I am headache free. Ten minutes after we return to San Francisco, I feel like my head is going to explode.

Members of my graduate school cohort are busy "collecting data." They want to know how to "improve students' memory," or how to "determine young children's understanding of chronology," or do "analyses of social problems in elementary social studies textbooks." I did not even have a question and could not imagine being interested in the things they were busy researching.

Someone who was a dissertator during my first year told me that this phase of graduate school was akin to the "loneliness of the long-distance runner." And, while the sports metaphor made sense to me, my perception of what I was experiencing seemed more like the solitary and isolated picture of a James Meredith walking swiftly to and from classes at "Ole Miss" or the little girl marching up the steps of a school accompanied by two National Guardsmen.

Now, lest I be misunderstood, I must make clear that my graduate school experience was never one of overt racism or discrimination. I think I was relatively well liked and had little or no trouble getting along with classmates and professors. My loneliness resulted from "intellectual segregation," not social segregation. I had no mentors who were interested in the issues of race and racism in the same way I was. I found some intellectual stimulation in my minor department–anthropology. Culture was a real thing in the anthro department. My challenge was to transpose the notions of "exotic" culture to investigations of a marginalized culture like my own.

My "salvation" came in the form of the Afro-American Studies Program.[3] After attending a lecture given by the chair of the program, I talked my way into her undergraduate course, entitled "The Afro-American in Fact and Fiction." As I surveyed the syllabus and required readings, I smiled to myself. I had read almost every book listed, Ellison's *The Invisible Man*, Chinua Achebe's *Things Fall Apart*, Camara Laye's *The Dark Child*, Harriet Beecher Stowe's *Uncle Tom's Cabin*, Frederick Douglass's narrative. This would be a snap. Here I was a "mature" student sitting in a class with younger African American students with a reading list filled with texts I already knew. I was just happy to know that for a little over an hour, three times a week, I would be in an all-black intellectual space. It was a comforting feeling.

To my surprise, this class on texts that I "knew" was one of the most difficult and challenging I had encountered at this prestigious institution. It was an Afro-Am course, but the professor, an Afro-Caribbean female (a black woman!) was talking to us about Foucault and Bourdieu–"regimes of truth" and "prescriptive modes of rationality." We would do "multiple readings" of texts. We would "interrogate meaning." We would wrestle with the "imaginary social significations" of race, class, and gender. A few students dropped out after the first two weeks. Many seemed lost throughout the quarter. I was as excited and invigorated as I had ever been in school. I was spending "way too much time" reading for my "undergraduate" class. Although there were obvious differences in the curriculum and the teaching styles, this course reminded me of my sophomore humanities course. For me, the common denominator was a strong black woman academician, confident in her persona, well-grounded in her subject area–a rarity in my college career:

> "Don't take Dr. Jones's humanities section, she's too hard!" That was sound advice from juniors and seniors who had learned the hard way. I didn't need a course that was too hard. I was already taking nineteen units in an attempt to graduate early. I couldn't be sabotaged by a required humanities course. I had to stay on the dean's list to keep my scholarship. My eyes were tearing as I kept turning the pages of the timetable trying to find a humanities section that would fit my schedule. As it stood, the only one that fit was Dr. Jones's and I didn't need that kind of grief. Unsuccessful in my quest for the most desirable schedule, I find myself sitting in Dr. Jones's classroom. She walks in dressed in black from head to toe, wearing makeup that looked as if it had been applied by an undertaker. She could be a slightly darker version of the Addams Family mother, Morticia. She begins right away rattling off information about Dante, Greek and Roman myths, Chaucer, Milton. I am terrified and at the same time intrigued. She is both mesmerizing and brilliant. Throughout the semester I never miss a class. I read and study constantly and emerge with the grade of A. More importantly, I understand that the arena of the academy is *not* off limits to black women.

My time in the undergraduate Afro-Am course was less a respite from the all-encompassing "whiteness" of the ed school than it was an opportunity to rethink and reenvision the relationships between and among race, culture, and education. If I could read Ellison and Douglass in a new way, perhaps I could read education and anthropology in new ways. In what ways were these disciplines "socially constructed" and how did these social constructions intersect with race and gender? What were the implications of these constructions for the educational lives of African American children?

In my circuitous route from the ed school to the anthropology department, to Afro-Am, I was beginning to formulate a question–a question I do not think I would have gotten to in the narrow confines of the School of Education. Taking the long way around may have saved my (intellectual) life.

LIVING THE LIFE OF A "PUBLIC INTELLECTUAL"[4]

Space constraints do not allow me to tell the entire story of my graduate school career. Suffice it to say I "found" a question, researched it, wrote a dissertation, and defended it. But in this section I attempt to discuss the integration of personal, public (sociocultural/civic), and intellectual interests.

Like most academics I gave serious thought to the rigors of the academy–teaching, service, and above all else, scholarship. But I believe I was less interested in the proliferation of my work than whether or not the work had meaning for those whom I intended to serve. Thus in this section of the chapter I move away from my personal narrative toward a theory of African American female intellectual life. I feel compelled to make this switch because African American and other scholars of color rarely have the luxury of considering only their personal sojourns. Rather, our position in the academy is typically the result of collective struggle and support. Thus our understanding of our roles includes an intertwining of the personal and the public–the intellectual and the emotional–the scholarly and the political.

I approach this theory of African American female intellectual life as theory-in-the-making–unfinished and open-ended. I begin contemplation of this theory with a historical glance back to those who have previously pondered and theorized the dilemmas of African American intellectual life.

W. E. B. DuBois declared it at the turn of the century. Carter G. Woodson refined it in the 1930s. Harold Cruse named it in the 1960s. Jacqueline Mitchell restated it in the 1980s, and Cornel West reframed it in the 1990s. The "it" is what Cruse termed "the crisis of the Negro intellectual."

In *Keeping Faith*, West asserts that "[T]he choice of becoming a black intellectual is an act of self-imposed marginality" (p. 67) and in charting options for African American intellectuals, he suggests four possible models: the bourgeois, the Marxist, the Foucaultian, and the insurgency. Below I attempt to summarize each of these models.

The bourgeois model is characterized by its quest for legitimation. In West's terms, this model "sets intellectual limits, in that one is prone to adopt uncritically prevailing paradigms predominant in the bourgeois academy" (p. 76). An African American scholar who adopts this model might ask, "What are the rules of the academy? What must I do to achieve and be rewarded by the existing structure? Rather than commitment to scholarship or community, this model reflects commitment to self in a personal, self-aggrandizing manner that never questions the legitimacy of the academy. Indeed, in an attempt to curry favor the bourgeois black intellectual seeks conformity within the institution and conducts "safe" scholarship or seeks "safe" positions within a scholarly discourse.[5] The second model, West argues, is the Marxist model, a model that allows access to the "least xenophobic white intellectual subculture available to black intellectuals" (p. 78). However, its early liberatory benefits are lessened because it "tends to stifle the further development of black critical consciousness and attitudes" (p. 79). Thus, an African American scholar who adheres to this model may enjoy the opportunity to engage in intellectual pursuits that challenge the dominant paradigms, but those challenges will rarely, if ever, be linked to the everyday circumstances of people outside of the academy.

The Foucaultian model constitutes the black intellectual as a postmodern skeptic. By interrogating the "regimes of truth" that are constructed by discursive practices and institutional power, black intellectuals in this model participate in a reconception of what it means to be an intellectual. Rather than struggle, in West's terms, "on behalf" (p. 81) of the truth, African American intellectuals in this tradition struggle over the status of the truth. Thus the work of the black intellectual as postmodern skeptic becomes that of uncovering myths of representation and challenging so-called universals.[6] However, its shortcoming lies in its provision of "ideological and social distance from insurgent black movements for liberation" (p. 81). In African American parlance it allows the intellectual to "talk the talk without walking the walk." Finally, the insurgency model calls for a melding of the positive aspects of the preceding models. From the bourgeois model it lifts the determination and will but reshapes it for collective rather than individual benefit. From the Marxist model it acknowledges the structural constraints without becoming enmeshed in an economic determinism. From the Foucaultian model it maintains a worldly skepticism about power relations but speaks directly to the specificity of African American life, history, and culture.

However, for all of the theoretical rigor and intellectual seductiveness of West's formulations, his model fails to acknowledge a salient feature of my intellectual life–gender. Thus, while white women can and have written persuasively about the challenges of women in the academy[7] and African American men have done likewise around issues of race, it is only the African American female who can speak to the specificity of coping with this "dual otherness."[8]

In *Theorizing Black Feminisms*, Stanlie James says that, "[A]lthough Black women are often characterized as victims, theorizing is a form of agency that provides them with opportunities to 'learn, think, imagine, judge, listen, speak, write, and act'–which transforms not only the individual (from victim to activist, for example) but the community, and the society as well" (p. 2). This act of theorizing from an African American woman's perspective, although marginalized in the literature, is not new. As far back as the late 1800s, Anna Julia Cooper, in *A Voice from the South by a Black Woman of the South*, conceived the black woman's intellectual and political position thusly: "She is confronted by a woman question and a race problem, and is as yet an unknown or unacknowledged factor in both" (p. 27).

Rose Brewer argues that "Black feminist theorizing places African American women at the center of the analyses" (p. 15). For too long critiques of academic life have been one-dimensional along either race or gender lines. However, in 1982, three black women scholars, Gloria Hull, Patricia Bell-Scott, and B. Smith, initiated scholarly work in "Black Women's Studies" in which they summarized the shortcomings of both black studies and women's studies:

> Women's studies courses . . . focused almost exclusively upon the lives of White women. Black studies, which was much too often male-dominated, also ignored Black women. . . . Because of White women's racism and Black men's sexism, there was no room in either area for serious consideration of the lives of Black women. And even when they have considered Black women, White women usually have not had the capacity to analyze racial politics and Black culture, and Black men have remained blind or resistant to the implications of sexual politics in Black women's lives. (pp. xx–xxi)

So entrenched are the notions of either black studies or women's studies that even on one historically black women's college campus there was debate about the legitimacy of a black women's studies program.[9] However, black women's epistemology revolves around notions of "the simultaneity of oppression."[10] Therefore, no study of black women is complete without an understanding of the intersections and interactions of race, class, and gender. These intersections/interactions apply both within and outside of the academy.

MAKING SENSE AND SCHOLARSHIP ON MY OWN TERMS

As an African American female, public intellectual, I struggle to do intellectual work that is politically significant and culturally grounded. I struggle to do this work as a way to acknowledge and revere those who have gone before me and as a way to pave the path for those who must come after. This struggle is grounded both in what I choose to study and how I choose to study it. Study of African American life and culture has been legitimated even when situated in a deficit model.[11] Problems faced by African Americans in schooling are almost legendary. From school desegregation to resegregation, scholars of various races and ethnicities have attempted to unravel the knotty complexities of African Americans' failed schooling experiences. Thus my research interest is not perceived as "alien" in the academy.

However, my academic struggle primarily has been one of methodology and theoretical grounding. Indeed, while the academy may be more tolerant of what scholars choose to study, it can sometimes be rigidly dogmatic about how research is to be conducted. Thus theoretical frameworks must be precisely explicated to support the work–particularly that work done in unconventional ways.

Patricia Hill Collins's work on black feminist epistemology provides a theoretical and conceptual platform on which to rest my methodology. Collins's notion of a black feminist epistemology is based on the propositions of (1) concrete experience as a criterion of meaning, (2) the use of dialogue in assessing knowledge claims, (3) the ethic of caring, and (4) the ethic of personal accountability.

Concrete Experiences as a Criterion of Meaning

This dimension suggests that only black women can truly know what it is to be a black woman. As straightforward as this sounds, its import should not be minimized. It underscores the significance of what Patricia Hill Collins refers to as "two types of knowing–knowledge and wisdom" (p. 209). Thus "individuals who have lived through the experiences about which they claim to be experts are more believable and credible than those who have merely read or thought about such experience" (p. 209). This particular stance means the life of an academic often is treated with skepticism unless it can be supplemented with real life experiences.

In my own work, I have attempted to work with people in settings with which I have had some familiarity. Thus my work with successful teachers of African American children was conducted in a community with schools very similar to ones where I have worked and lived. My experiences, although unique to my life, lend credibility to my work. I, too, have struggled to be a successful teacher of African American students. I have confronted some of the same bureaucratic, institutional, and structural challenges that the teachers in my research do. Our shared experience as teachers with analogous situations made entree into this setting, with these participants, easier and faster.

The Use of Dialogue in Assessing Knowledge Claims

In this dimension, Collins points to the importance of creating equal status relationships via dialogue. "Dialogue implies talk between two subjects, not the speech of subject and object. It is a humanizing speech, one that challenges and resists domination" (p. 212).[12] By "talking with" rather than "talking to" other black women, African American women have the opportunity to deconstruct the specificity of their own experiences and make connections between and among those that are more representative of collective experiences of black women. This give and take of dialogue makes struggling together to make meaning a powerful experience of self-definition and self-discovery (recovery).[13] Dialogue was the hallmark of my investigation with successful teachers of African American students. Initially, my conversations with parents to locate the teachers meant I had to talk "with" the parents to get their candid impressions of which teachers were most successful with African American students. Subsequently, I entered into dialogue with each teacher as a part of the ethnographic interviews,[14] and later in our conversations about her teaching, and finally as we met together to view videotaped examples of each teacher's teaching. In our full group meetings–the research collective–we participated in lively discussions and dialogue that reflected African American linguistic style. Our talk was filled with overlapping speech, interruptions, Black English Vernacular (BEV) expressions and syntax. Unlike a recitation where the teacher (or leader) "lobs" a question and the student fires back an answer–something like a tennis match–we participated in a more diffuse, collective questioning and answering. Perhaps the best metaphor would be, more like a volleyball game. Someone might "serve" up a question and it got "batted around" several times before another question emerged. Question asking and answering were a shared responsibility. The researcher was not privileged to pose and determine the questions while the "researched" answered.

The Ethic of Caring

Although some white feminists have identified the ethic of caring[15] as an aspect of women's scholarship, Collins reiterates its centrality to black women's lives (and scholarship): "[T]he ethic of caring suggests that personal expressiveness, emotions, and empathy are central to the knowledge validation process" (p. 215). Collins further points out that these convergent notions of white and black women about caring do not negate its importance in developing and understanding an Afrocentric feminist epistemology.

In my research with successful teachers of African American students, I needed to demonstrate a level of caring for and about the teachers. I was asking them for unlimited access to their classrooms as well as posing hard questions about their practice. Because their community often had been under the scholarly gaze of the research community, I had to demonstrate genuine caring to guarantee their continued participation. Several ways that I attempted to demonstrate an ethic of caring were by listening to the teachers throughout the process, sharing every aspect of the process and documentation, and religiously guarding their identities and their privacy.

The Ethic of Personal Accountability

The final dimension of Patricia Hill Collins's theoretical position suggests that knowledge claims must be grounded in individual character, values, and ethics. While the dispassionate, "objective," white, masculinist discourse allows people with radically differing public positions to socialize and mingle in private, a black feminist epistemology argues that private qualities have bearing on public standpoints. Thus not only what was said but who said it gives meaning and interpretation to knowledge claims.

How then do I, an African American female scholar, meld the disparate pieces of my own schooling experiences with the persistent crises of black intellectuals and the particular dilemmas of black women scholars? For the most part, my work has been an attempt to explain myself. Despite the wide acceptance (or at least recognition) of the cultural ecological model[16] which posits an explanation of African American school failure, my own life is testimony to alternative explanations for African American school achievement. Thus my work has been an attempt to reorient the thinking about African American school performance away from failure and deficit to a proactive pragmatism grounded in the successful practices of exemplary teachers of African American students.[17] I am compelled to engage in this work for personal and well as public reasons. As a parent who has had to help her children negotiate the uneven and precarious terrain of public schooling, I am dismayed to see how regularly African American children are assumed to lack the "appropriate tools" (read intelligence).

> "Oh, don't tell me you've got Kevin in your class," remarked a teacher in the teachers' lounge. "What's wrong with him, is he a problem?" "Oh, no, he's actually a very nice kid, but that mother!" My information comes from a friend who was listening in on that conversation. Yes, I am that mother, a title I wear with distinction because it tells people not to "mess over" my children. Unfortunately, I cannot be that mother for every child and the specialized treatment I am able to broker for my own children never impacts the children of those parents who are too tired, too intimidated, or too unfamiliar with school procedures to challenge the negative perceptions held by too many teachers.

I need to do the kind of research that will help make the system more equitable and just. Thus one of the earliest questions the decision to conduct this kind of research evoked was, "How do you capture 'pedagogical excellence'?"[18] A meta-question within a black women's epistemology was, "How do you capture it in ways that are consistent with the cultural values and ethos of a particular community?" As a member of the African American community[19] I felt comfortable about the nature of my research, but I treaded carefully regarding the way I conducted it.[20]

Initially I began talking with African American parents about who they thought were excellent teachers for their children. I chose African American churches as the places where I might find numbers of African American parents who might be willing to talk with me. While the parents were used to and comfortable with the idea of talking about teachers, several seemed surprised that their suggestions were to be taken seriously. However, my recollections about parents, in general, and African American parents, in particular, were that they had keen insights about teachers and teaching. Even when parents were unaware of pedagogical and curriculum innovations, their ability to talk about the interpersonal and subtle aspects of school–home relations helped them make evaluations that served their purposes.

The parents took their role as assessors of teacher "goodness" very seriously. They offered examples of teacher behaviors and interactions, comparative data (for example, comparing siblings' and other relatives' experiences), and levels of improved student achievement as evidence for the kinds of recommendations they made. Some common threads among the teachers they recommended were teachers who "respected them" and believed that they knew something about what was best for their children. They reported that when their children were in these "good" teachers' classrooms, they demonstrated an enthusiasm for school and what the parents termed a "good attitude" toward school and learning.

By the time I was able to meet with and talk to the identified teachers, I had rethought the way I was to conduct this research several times.[21] How could I learn about teachers' expertise without the teachers' participating in the project beyond the data collection and into the analysis and interpretation? I realized that I could not. Now, instead of a project where I interviewed, observed, and videotaped teachers and, subsequently, retreated to the solitude of my office where I would reconstruct the teachers' experiences and say for them what they were doing and why, I was now considering a different tack.

At the analysis stage of the project, I convened the teachers to create a "research collaborative." Instead of my telling teachers what they were doing (and, perhaps, why they were doing it), I employed a modified version of the group conversation method[22] designed, in Joyce King and Carolyn Mitchell's words, to "reduce social tension . . . and help participants identify shared experiences and to facilitate the discussion of highly personal or deeply felt emotional issues" (p. 3).

Over the next two years I listened and learned from expert teachers whose practice I had observed, videotaped, and discussed with them on an individual basis. But here in this intimate group setting, teachers talked, agreed, disagreed, laughed, and almost cried. Even though they were not all African American teachers (five of the eight participants were African American, three were white), the African American teachers took a leadership role in the discussion. The form, pace, and style of their conversations were similar to African American informal speech. Throughout the conversations participants talked in an overlapping style–interrupting, completing each other's sentences. Their conversational pattern reminded me of a novice white teacher who had worked in their district and indicated that she could not organize her students into cooperative groups because "they just talk too much." She went on to say, "I guess it's cultural, because the black teachers talk all the time too!" Despite her pejorative way of expressing it, this white teacher had observed that oral expression was valued in this community. Their "talking all the time" was, for me, a research heaven.

As I listened, both during their conversations and during transcription, I marveled at the ways they melded their lives as teachers and as vital members of their communities. I was reminded of my own teachers who seemed also to work in ways that were consistent with the lives they led. Their ability to "make sense" of the two worlds in which they lived reminded me of disjunctures in my own life. I wanted to do academic work and be a committed advocate for my community. Would that advocacy compromise my research? Would my biases mean that I would not have the capacity to recognize the problems as well as the strengths of my community? Would my work gain acceptance in the academy if I pursued my work in this way? Why was I even asking myself these questions?

The academy is shaped by many social forces. More women of color are defining and redefining their roles within it. New ways of thinking about teaching and research have provided spaces for women scholars to challenge old assumptions about what it means to be in the academy.[23] While both the women's movement and the black studies movement have helped increase the parameters of academic work, new paradigms emerging from black women's scholarship provide me with a liberatory lens through which to view and construct my scholarly life. The academy and my scholarly life need not be in conflict with the community and cultural work I do (and intend to do).

In some ways my coming to terms with my scholarly life and my personal/cultural life is not unlike coming to terms with the dual identity of African American-ness. Growing up in the segregated 1950s and early 1960s, one could not escape the derogation and denigration of Africa (and blackness). That was not an identity many embraced with ease. Even though my fifth-grade teacher had worked to correct the prevalent images, still I was assaulted by images of Africa as a "dark" continent and its inhabitants as "primitive" and "uncivilized." It was not until the pride-filled civil rights era that I, like many others, began to understand the ways Africa's reality had been systematically denied and distorted. To affirm our newfound heritage we wore our hair in huge natural crowns and adorned our bodies with African fabrics. We declared that black was beautiful and made peace with the history and heritage that had been stolen by others and hidden by our own. We were Africans, but were we Americans?

Coming to terms with my American-ness was another matter. How could one feel a civic (or even personal) commitment to a nation that rejected you? You were not wanted in its schools, could not sit at its dime-store lunch counters, and could not try on a hat in its department stores. How could you "pledge allegiance" when you had seen the men in your life serve in the armed services, only to be subjected to various and sundry humiliations at the hands of local police officers? How could you think "my country, 'tis of thee" when there were no representations of you (particularly of you as a black female) in any aspect of public life? But to think that I led a miserable life, horribly scarred by racism, would be a mistake. My life was perhaps more safe, secure, and nurturing than my own children's. My sense of belonging within my community was apparent. I did not lament not being accepted by America. I imagine the feeling was mutual.

However, with time and maturity I began to understand that without the profound impact of Africans (and African Americans) on this nation, there may not have been an America as we know it. My claim to this country is as legitimate as anyone's. But we are in an era when contestation over what it means to be an American is at the center of our public debate. I have come to understand that my African-ness does not diminish my American-ness and vice versa. My identity is not an either/or proposition. Rather, it is both/and. In the same way my scholarship and my personal/cultural life are not either/or propositions. I do scholarly work that both challenges and enhances my personal/cultural life. I live a personal/cultural life that challenges and enhances my scholarly work. I am a "colored girl" who has attempted to make life in the academy satisfying and meaningful "enuf."

NOTES

1. Ntozake Shange's "choreopoem," *For colored girls who have considered suicide when the rainbow's not enuf*, brought the African American woman's experiences and perspectives to life for the theater-going public.

2. The notion of "mutuality"–a reciprocal relationship in a network of social obligation–is discussed by Joyce Elaine King and Carolyn Ann Mitchell in *Black Mothers to Sons: Juxtaposing African American Literature With Social Practice* as a key feature of African American cultural values and by Patricia Hill Collins in *Black Feminist Thought: Knowledge, Consciousness, and the Politics of Empowerment.*

3. The currently accepted term *African American* was not in use during my graduate school years. The term *Afro-American*, or *Afro-Am*, was commonly used on many campuses.

4. I borrow the term *public intellectual*, its use and meaning, from my colleague and friend, Joyce E. King.

5. Ishmael Reed, in his novel *Japanese by Spring*, has a black character, Professor Puttbutt, who exemplifies this bourgeois model.

6. For a discussion of the current debate about African American scholars and postmodernism, see *The Black Scholar* (October–November 1993), which contains a special section on the "multicultural debate."

7. See, for example, Code, 1991; Arnot, 1982; and Martin, 1982.

8. For a discussion of "dual otherness," see Dubois, [1903] 1989.

9. Guy-Sheftall, 1993.

10. Brewer, 1993.

11. See, for example, Bettleheim, 1968; Bloom, Davis, and Hess, 1965; and Ornstein, 1971.

12. hooks, cited in Collins, 1990.

13. hooks, 1993.

14. Spradley, 1979.

15. Noddings, 1984.

16. Ogbu, 1978, 1987.

17. Ladson-Billings, 1994.

18. Ladson-Billings, 1990.

19. I do not want to suggest that there is one monolithic African American community. By identifying myself as a "member" I am suggesting that I see African Americans as my primary cultural group and believe there are a number of values, beliefs, attitudes, linguistic styles, expressive styles, etc., that we hold in common.

20. This concern over methodology emanated from my awareness that many African American communities have participated in research (both willingly and unwittingly) that has ill-served them. Thus research that is designed allegedly to help African Americans has been constructed to maintain stereotypes and distortions about the nature of the community. I was decidedly conscious of the need to be respectful and in a "learner mode" throughout the research process.

21. After talking with the parents, I also talked with school principals. Teachers whose names appeared on both the parents' and principals' lists were invited to participate in the study.

22. DuBois and Li, 1971.

23. Examples include Weiler, 1988, and Lather, 1986.

BIBLIOGRAPHY

Achebe, Chinua. 1958. *Things Fall Apart*. London: Heinemann.

Arnot, Madeleine. 1982. "Male Hegemony, Social Class, and Women's Education." *Journal of Education* 164:64–89.

Bettleheim, Bruno. 1968. "Teaching the Disadvantaged." *National Educational Association Journal* 54:8–12.

Bloom, Benjamin, Allison Davis, and Robert Hess. 1965. *Compensatory Education for Cultural Deprivation*. New York: Holt, Rinehart and Winston.

Brewer, Rose. 1993. "Theorizing Race, Class, and Gender: The New Scholarship of Black Feminist Intellectuals and Black Women's Labor." In *Theorizing Black Feminisms*, Stanlie M. James and Abena P. A. Busia, eds. New York: Routledge, 13–30.

Code, Lorraine Code. 1991. *What Can She Know? Feminist Theory and the Construction of Knowledge*. Ithaca, NY: Cornell University Press.

Collins, Patricia Hill. 1991. *Black Feminist Thought: Knowledge, Consciousness, and the Politics of Empowerment*. New York: Routledge.

Cooper, Anna Julia. 1892. *A Voice from the South by a Black Woman of the South*. Ohio: Aldine.

Cruse, Harold. 1967. *The Crisis of the Negro Intellectual: From Its Origins to the Present*. New York: William Morrow.

Douglass, Frederick. [1845] 1973. *Narrative of the Life of Frederick Douglass, an American Slave*. New York: Anchor.

DuBois, Rachel Davis, and Mew-soong Li. 1971. *Reducing Social Tension and Conflict: The Group Conversation Method*. New York: Association.

DuBois, W.E.B. [1903] 1989. *The Souls of Black Folks*. New York: Penguin.

Ellison, Ralph. 1952. *The Invisible Man*. New York: Modern Library.

Fauset, Arthur. 1938. *Sojourner Truth, God's Faithful Pilgrim*. Chapel Hill: University of North Carolina Press.

Guy-Sheftall, Beverly. 1993. "A Black Feminist Perspective on Transforming the Academy: The Case of Spelman College." In *Theorizing Black Feminism*, Stanlie M. James and Abena P.A. Busia, eds. New York: Routledge, 77–89.

hooks, bell. 1989. *Talking Back: Thinking Feminist, Thinking Black*. Boston: South End.

hooks, bell. 1993. *Sisters of the Yam: Black Women and Self-Recovery*. Boston: South End.

Hull, Gloria T., Patricia Bell-Scott, and Barbara Smith, eds. 1982. *All the Women Are White, All the Blacks Are Men, but Some of Us Are Brave*. Old Westbury, NY: Feminist.

James, Stanlie. 1993. Introduction to *Theorizing Black Feminisms: The Visionary Pragmatism of Black Women*, Stanlie M. James and Abena P. A. Busia, eds. New York: Routledge.

King, Joyce Elaine, and Carolyn Ann Mitchell. 1990. *Black Mothers to Sons: Juxtaposing African American Literature With Social Practice*. New York: Peter Lang.

Ladson-Billings, Gloria. 1990. "Like Lightning in a Bottle: Attempting to Capture the Pedagogical Excellence of Successful Teachers of Black Students." *International Journal of Qualitative Studies in Education* 3:335–344.

Ladson-Billings, Gloria. 1994. *The Dreamkeepers: Successful Teachers for African American Students*. San Francisco: Jossey-Bass.

Lather, Patti. 1986. "Research as Praxis." *Harvard Educational Review* 56:257–277.

Laye, Camara. 1954. *The Dark Child*, trans. James Kirkup, Ernest Jones, and Elaine Gottlieb. New York: Noonday.

Martin, Jane Roland. 1982. "Excluding Women From the Educational Realm." *Harvard Educational Review* 52:133–148.

Mitchell, Jacqueline. 1982. "Reflections of a Black Social Scientist: Some Struggles, Some Doubts, Some Hopes." *Harvard Educational Review* 52:27–44.

"The Multicultural Debate." 1993. *The Black Scholar* 23 (3–4):48–80.

Noddings, Nel. 1984. *Caring: A Feminine Approach to Ethics and Moral Education*. Berkeley: University of California Press.

Ogbu, John. 1978. *Minority Education and Caste: The American System in Cross-Cultural Perspective*. New York: Academic.

Ogbu, John. 1987. "Variability in Minority School Performance: A Problem in Search of an Explanation." *Anthropology and Educational Quarterly* 18:312–334.

Ornstein, Alan. 1971. "The Need for Research on Teaching the Disadvantaged." *The Journal of Negro Education* 40:133–139.

Reed, Ishmael. 1993. *Japanese by Spring*. New York: Atheneum.

Shange, Ntozake. *For colored girls who have considered suicide when the rainbow's not enuf: A Choreopoem*. New York: Macmillan, 1977.

Spradley, James P. 1979. *The Ethnographic Interview*. New York: Holt, Rinehart and Winston.

Stowe, Harriet Beecher. 1938. *Uncle Tom's Cabin: Or, Life Among the Lowly*. Garden City, NY: Nelson Doubleday.

Weiler, Kathleen. 1988. *Women Teaching for Change*. New York: Bergin and Garvey.

West, Cornel. 1993. *Keeping Faith*. New York: Routledge.

Woodson, Carter G. 1993. *The Miseducation of the Negro*. Washington, DC: Association.

* CHAPTER 5 *

Schooling, Literacy, and Cultural Diversity in Research and Personal Experience

Kathryn H. Au

MY RESEARCH STANCE HAS BEEN characterized as that of a reformer, which is an accurate description of my intentions. I hope my research will contribute to the improvement of literacy instruction in classrooms with students of diverse cultural backgrounds.

Of the studies I have conducted, those on talk-story–like reading lessons are probably the most cited. In these studies I showed that teachers effective in teaching reading to young Native Hawaiian students did not conduct discussion following the pattern for classroom recitation observed in mainstream classrooms.[1] Rather, they conducted discussions following rules similar to those for talk story, a Hawaiian community speech event. Furthermore, when Hawaiian students participated in talk-story–like lessons, as opposed to mainstream recitation lessons, they showed higher rates of academic behaviors related to learning to read: They spent more time focused on the reading task, discussed more story ideas, and made more logical inferences about the story.[2] These studies were among the first to verify the possibility of improving the academic learning of students of diverse backgrounds through the use of culturally responsive instruction, that is, instruction reflecting values and practices similar to those of the home culture. These studies, and others that I have conducted, highlight the themes of schooling, literacy, and cultural diversity.

SCHOOLING AND FAMILY HISTORY

I cannot remember a time when I did not think of schooling as a precious commodity, so family members must have instilled this notion in me at an

Learning from Our Lives: Women, Research, and Autobiography in Education. ISBN 0-8077-3593-0 (pbk), ISBN 0-8077-3594-9 (cloth).

early age. Although I did not always like going to school, I never doubted the goodness of the abstract idea of school. Because I grew up believing that education would be the key to my own success in life, it was easy for me to come to believe as a professional that education would be the key to helping students of diverse backgrounds achieve a better life.

I am a Chinese American and in the fourth generation of my family to live in Hawaii. I have always had an interest in family history, particularly in the lives of my grandmothers, and have been consciously gathering information about my family's past for about fifteen years. My maternal grandmother died in 1985 at the age of 103, and my paternal grandmother is now 96, forgetful of recent events but with clear memories of the distant past.

Grandmother Hew

Many generations of men in my family have had the chance to attend school and to learn to read and write. However, only in the past two or three generations have women had this opportunity. My maternal grandmother, Hew Ngim Moi, could not read or write in either Chinese or English, a fact she regretted all her life. Grandmother Hew was born in the Hakka village of Nam Wai, in the New Territories near Hong Kong, in 1883. Her father, Shinn Sam Shing, left for Hawaii that same year. As the third son in a poor village family, he went in search of a brighter future. He worked as a bookkeeper for a Chinese merchant and also earned money by writing letters for his acquaintances who wished to communicate with their families back in China. Thirteen years passed before he was able to send for his wife and daughter.

While growing up in the village, Grandmother Hew did not go to school because only boys could attend. But she wanted to go to school and was very curious about what went on there. One day she climbed a tree so she could get a better look. I have that image of my grandmother as a young girl, on the outside looking in.

When Grandmother Hew came to Hawaii, she and her parents lived in Kula on the island of Maui. Quite a few Chinese families lived in the area at the time, most earning their living as farmers. My grandmother lived with her parents in a shed originally built to store corn. She walked across the hilly countryside to gather firewood for cooking and to draw water from a stream. She and her mother found life more difficult than in the village, where they had been surrounded by family and the work could be shared. Although the neighbors in Kula were generous, they were not close at hand.

In theory, Grandmother Hew could have attended the public school in Kula. However, her parents, like others of their generation, believed that education was important for boys but not for girls; since a Chinese woman became part of her husband's family after she married, her parents' investment in her education was considered to be wasted. Also, my grandmother's help was needed to run the household and the farm and, later, to care for the younger children. I once asked my grandmother whether there were truant officers who could have required her parents to send her to school. She laughed. When the truant officers came around, she said, the families simply hid the girls. At any rate, by the time she had been in Kula a few years, she was considered too old to go to school.

Although Grandmother Hew never had the chance to go to school, she supported the education of her brothers and sister. Grandmother Hew's four younger siblings were all born in Kula. They attended public school, and after that school let out for the day, they went to classes at the community-sponsored Chinese school. Her first brother, Tenn Sung Shinn, attended St. Anthony, a Catholic high school, where he could study business. While at St. Anthony, Tenn Sung lived at my grandmother's house. He worked at a store after school and gave my grandmother everything he earned in return for his room and board. Although she had a growing family of her own, my grandmother never spent any of his money. When he graduated, she returned the full amount to him, and he in turn gave the money to his parents.

Mun Fook Shinn, Grandmother Hew's second brother, attended St. Anthony for a year but then contracted tuberculosis and went to the Kula sanitarium where he learned to be a laboratory technician. According to Great-Uncle Mun Fook, the expectations for education changed rapidly among the Chinese families in Kula in the early 1900s. Men his age thought themselves lucky to continue past the eighth grade, but those only a few years younger were among the first to graduate from college. As the educational expectations for boys rose, the families also began to send girls to school, and this practice had become common by about 1906.

Mabel Shinn Liu, my grandmother's sister, benefited from the changing views of women's education. She completed grade school in Kula and then spent a year at Maunaolu Seminary, a girls' high school. Her education came to an end when she too contracted tuberculosis. Barring illness, she might have become a teacher like the other Chinese women who attended Maunaolu.

Grandmother Hew married at the age of nineteen, and my mother is the youngest of her eight children. Following the customs of the time, she did not see her new husband, Hew Sing Cha, until the day of the wedding. My grandfather became a cook and baker serving the Chinese laborers on the sugar plantation in Paia. Later, the family ran a store and restaurant in Paia. They spoke Chinese at home, and my mother (and probably her brothers and sisters as well) did not speak any English before entering school. Grandmother Hew walked her children to and from school and took a great interest in their education.

My oldest uncle, Chong Meo Hew, graduated from St. Anthony and then went to work, making it possible for his seven younger brothers and sisters to continue their education. In his generation, he took the role my grandmother had taken in hers, of caring for and supporting the younger children. All graduated from Maui High School, and all but one went on for higher education. Poor health prevented Richard, the youngest son, from moving to Oahu to attend the university.

Grandmother Hew wanted her daughters, as well as her sons, to be well educated. My mother, aunts, and uncles all speak of this fact with pride. In the 1920s and 1930s my grandmother's views about the education of women ran counter to those of most members of Paia's Chinese community. One day my grandmother got into a heated argument with a Mr. Wong. He contended that girls should not go on to higher education, that they should just be married off. Mr. Wong's remarks upset my grandmother. Eventually one of my aunts, Ah Kewn, called him a troublemaker and chased him out of the house. The story of my grandmother's argument with the peanut man (Mr. Wong earned his living by selling boiled peanuts) is part of the lore of our family, and over the years I have heard it repeated many times.

As Grandmother Hew hoped, my mother and her three sisters all went on for higher education. Two of my mother's sisters had careers that in some ways prefigured my own. My first aunt, Ah Lun Hew Zane, went to the Territorial Normal School and later received a bachelor's degree in education from the University of Hawaii. She taught first on Maui, then on Oahu. My second aunt, Ah Kewn Hew, received a certificate (the equivalent of a master's degree today) from the New York School of Social Work in 1940, an unusual achievement at the time. When she returned to Maui, she was one of only two social workers on the island.

Until I was a teenager, I spent all of my summer vacations at the house in Paia. After dinner, Grandmother Hew and the adult relatives often "talked story," reminiscing and gossiping in a mixture of Hakka and English. My grandmother was a skillful storyteller with an excellent memory, and others in the circle often turned to her with questions. As a child I did not participate in these discussions, but I developed an appreciation for uses of language and literacy that did not necessarily involve English or a printed text.

Grandmother Hew had a lively intelligence and quick wit and took an active interest in everything around her. Sometimes she and I would sit on the sofa downstairs and look at photographs in the pages of *Life*, *Look*, and other magazines. She always spoke to me in English, and I did not learn to speak Hakka, although I could understand a few common phrases. I do not recall when I became aware that my grandmother could not read. I know that by the time I was about eight or nine, I was reading captions to her or scanning the text so I could answer her questions about the photographs.

When I was an adult and thought to question my grandmother about her literacy, I learned that she could read a calendar and prices and recognize a few words in English and in Chinese. If she saw the words often enough, she said, after a while she could figure out what they were. I discovered that she had learned some Hawaiian, Ilokano, and Japanese through working in the store and other contacts with people in the community. Late in life, she learned to sign her name in English.

Grandmother Au

My paternal grandmother, Katherine Choy Kan Ahana Au, was born in Hawaii on the island of Kauai in 1898. She was the sixth of the twelve children of Chun Lin Hung and Jay Shee. His Chinese acquaintances called my great-grandfather Ah Hung, a name the Hawaiians pronounced as Ahana, and for this reason Ahana replaced Chun as the family surname. My grandmother and her siblings grew up in Huleia, where my great-grandfather had a rice mill and plantation.

When she was nine or ten years old, Grandmother Au began to attend the one-room school in Huleia. Her brothers and sisters had already taught her to read and write in English, and when she got to school, she discovered that the teacher knew less than some of his pupils. One day, she and a couple of other students gave their teacher a little test. They wrote out the word *bouquet* and asked him to pronounce it. As they had predicted, he told them the word was "bo-ket."

At the age of about twelve, Grandmother Au began to attend Lihue School, taking a horse-drawn cart to town and back every day. She liked to study and was eager to learn, and she and a Japanese boy became the best students in their class. She did not think that most of the teachers knew how to help the students learn. The exception was a Mrs. Burke, who went step-by-step through the lessons so that everyone understood, instead of rushing through as the other teachers did.

Grandmother Au wanted to continue past the eighth grade, but her father did not think his daughters should get any more education than that. At the time, my grandmother said, a girl considered herself lucky to be able to go even that far in school. Still, my grandmother was disappointed because she loved school. When she told her teacher that she would be quitting, her teacher was shocked. "What?" she said. "With your grades?"

Even before Grandmother Au had completed the eighth grade, Miss Huntley, the supervising principal, asked her to serve as a substitute teacher at Lihue School. My grandmother would go to class for a while, but then when a teacher was absent, she would have to act as a substitute until the teacher returned. She felt honored and cheated at the same time.

Grandmother Au worked as a substitute teacher off and on until she was married. Her duties as a substitute teacher varied. One year, she had to enroll 102 first-year students. She pinned notes to their backs asking their parents to supply birthdates and other necessary information, and she completed the paperwork so that everything was in order by the time the regular teacher arrived. Her sister-in-law, Dora Peiler Ahana, became the teacher at Huleia School, and when Dora's parents died, Grandmother Au had to take over. She learned of her new responsibilities through instructions shouted to her from the road. With no warning, no books or other materials, she assumed Dora's duties. She worried about not knowing what to do, but she managed until Dora's return.

Following the customs of the day, my paternal great-grandparents stressed the education of the boys but not the girls. My grandmother's two older brothers were sent to private schools in Honolulu; Koon Chong graduated from Iolani and Koon Ming from St. Louis. My grandmother's two younger brothers graduated from Kauai High School. Of her six sisters, only the youngest, Harriet, graduated from high school.

Until she was in her early nineties and her eyesight became poor, Grandmother Au was an avid letter writer. She corresponded with dozens of people and for years mailed out more than 300 cards at Christmas. A member of the Lihue Baptist Church since 1937, she was active in church activities especially after her sons were grown. Because of her strong religious beliefs, she read the Bible nearly every day. She read many books and pamphlets with religious themes, and I do not recall seeing her read any secular material apart from popular women's magazines, such as *Ladies' Home Journal.*

My family, like other Chinese American families in Hawaii, experienced dramatic increases in levels of education, both within and between generations. The education of men and women did not follow the same pattern, in part because of beliefs brought from China about the education of women. One of my grandmothers did not have a chance to go to school at all, and the other did not go as far in school as she wished. Both treasured literacy, one because she could not read and write, the other because she found it to be of great social and religious value. As a child I did not know of my grandmothers' specific experiences with schooling, only of the value they placed on education. Later, when I knew to ask, I found that their feelings of disappointment about their own schooling had not been dimmed by the years or by the successes of their children.

In my parents' generation, education for women became the norm. Interestingly, in my mother's family it was an aunt, not an uncle, who received a graduate degree. This, I believe, was due to Grandmother Hew's influence. Because my mother and aunts were well educated, I grew up with high expectations for my own schooling. But access to higher levels of schooling, particularly for women, was new enough in the history of my family that I did not take education for granted.

CULTURE AND LANGUAGE

My interest in research on culturally responsive forms of instruction derives in part from my own experiences as a Chinese American. I do not hyphenate the term *Chinese American*, because I agree with the argument that a hyphen between *Chinese* and *American* suggests that the two can be broken apart. Rather, I prefer the view that Chinese defines a kind of American.[3] Every American is some kind of American, and I feel that issues of cultural identity should be explored by all students, not just by students of diverse backgrounds. However, for students of diverse backgrounds, it may be more difficult to find a balance between assimilating to mainstream culture and maintaining a commitment to their own cultural heritage.

My parents, like other Asian Americans of their generation in Hawaii, were deeply influenced by the events of World War II. A photograph of my mother, Mun Kyau Hew Au, receiving her high school diploma, shows her with a gas mask draped across one shoulder; Pearl Harbor had been bombed the previous December. Nevertheless, my mother moved to Honolulu from Maui to attend the University of Hawaii, where she received her training in laboratory science and medical technology. She spent her senior year working in the lab at Queen's Hospital in Honolulu and graduated with a bachelor of science degree in chemistry and biology.

My father, Harold Kwock Ung Au, moved to Honolulu from Kauai to live with relatives so he could attend the university. On the morning of December 7, 1941, he and his cousin saw planes pass overhead as they were on their way to play tennis. Assuming the planes to be American, they continued on to the courts. When they returned home, they learned of the bombing of Pearl Harbor. My father was already a member of the Varsity Volunteers, a unit of university students. Along with other Asian students determined to prove their loyalty to the United States, he quit school to serve full time in the Territorial Guard.

The war and its aftermath probably accelerated the process of assimilation of Chinese American families in Hawaii, although this process was already well under way. When I was growing up, we observed Chinese customs, such as the ceremonies of the new year and the memorial season, and we acquired a sense of family values. However, we lost the use of Chinese as the language of everyday communication. My parents both grew up speaking Chinese, but my father's family spoke Cantonese, whereas my mother's family spoke Hakka, a northern language similar to Mandarin. These varieties of Chinese are not mutually intelligible, so my parents' common language was English. But in my friends' families, even when both parents spoke the same dialect, the same situation prevailed: The language spoken in the home was English, not Chinese.

The summer I was ten, my brother, sister, and I attended a Chinese school in downtown Honolulu. The school primarily served families that had recently immigrated, and its program assumed that students could already speak Cantonese but needed to learn to read and write. We felt out of place and quit after three weeks. In high school, along with a number of my Chinese American classmates, I studied Mandarin for two years. Most of us were there because our parents thought it a good idea, and we did not take our teacher seriously.

As an adult I realized that, because I could not speak, read, or understand Chinese, I was cut off from part of my past. I was fortunate that all my grandparents could speak English. But I cannot read for myself the records in the Shinn temple in Man Kung Uk that list the names of my ancestors going back twenty-five generations. And there are nuances of meaning that I will never understand. After the death of my uncle Richard, I was seated downstairs in the Paia house next to my aunt, Ah Lun, when one of my grandmother's old friends came by to extend her condolences. The woman spoke to my grandmother in Chinese. On hearing her words, my aunt and the others nodded in appreciation. I asked my aunt what the woman had said. My aunt thought for a moment, then told me, "I can't explain it in English. But she said just the right thing."

The process of language loss is swift, can take place in just one generation, and in many cases is irreversible. The case of the Hawaiian language is particularly striking. The Native Hawaiian population at the time of Cook's arrival in 1778 numbered perhaps 400,000. But by the mid-1980s, there were perhaps as few as thirty Hawaiian children being raised to speak their native language. Before the advent of the Hawaiian-language immersion program, initiated in two of Hawaii's public schools in 1987, the language was in danger of being lost as a means of everyday communication.[4]

Certainly, culture is more than language, but my own experience illustrates a fact verified by recent research with students who come to school speaking a native language other than English. The language of power in the United States is English, a fact well known to these students and their parents, and these students are all learning English. At the same time, they are in danger of losing their native languages.[5] Clearly, we need to provide much more support for bilingual education, in order to maintain and improve students' command not just of English but of other languages, especially those already spoken in their families. American students, like their counterparts around the world, can and should be literate in at least two languages. Being literate, in this case, would extend to oral as well as written expression, along with knowledge of the cultural concepts and values important to speakers of the language.

LITERACY

In my research I have been interested in the question of how students of diverse backgrounds can become literate through means that do not require them to give up their cultural identities. Literacy can be taught in a manner that either empowers or disempowers. The dictionary defines *empower* as "to invest with power, especially legal power or official authority." I think of empowerment somewhat differently, as the confidence to act on one's own behalf. We work toward empowering students through literacy when we help them both to gain competence in written and oral expression and to understand themselves and their world better through reading, writing, listening, speaking, and observing.

My early experiences with literacy gave me confidence in myself as a learner and a sense of the excitement and power of words. They did not, however, enable me to understand or appreciate my own world and cultural identity.

In the living room of our home on Pacific Heights in Honolulu, my parents assembled a large bookcase from planks and glass blocks, and we children kept our books on the bottom shelf. Most of our books were Little Golden Books, including many of the titles being reissued today, such as *The Pokey Little Puppy*. We had a huge collection because my parents bought us one or two of these books whenever they went out for the evening or took us shopping.

Apparently, my affinity for books developed early. One of my mother's cousins, who came to Hawaii from Nam Wai as a teenager, remembers her first sight of me. I must have been three or four at the time, and I was sitting on the floor with a pile of books stacked higher than my head. She watched in fascination as I picked up one book after another, going through all of the pages and seemingly reading all the words. At the time she knew no English and so could not understand what I was saying, but this scene was fresh in her mind when she described it to me thirty years later.

My favorite of the Little Golden Books was entitled *Little Pond in the Woods*. As I recall, it did not have much of a story line, just one animal after another, including a bear, a deer, and a rabbit, coming to the pond to drink.

I had heard the story so often that I had memorized it and could recite the text word for word, page by page. Some members of the family were impressed by this feat, but I know that I did not yet understand how to deal with print. When I was in the first grade, my aunt Ah Lun, a teacher, gave me copies of the preprimers and primer from the Scott, Foresman series. I remember the weekend I suddenly discovered that I could read all the words. I read through all four books. It was an exhilarating experience but it took hours, and at the end I was exhausted.

My parents, aunts, and uncles all read aloud to us. My mother read us nursery rhymes and popular poetry, such as "The Owl and the Pussycat" and Joyce Kilmer's "Trees." We had two books by Dr. Seuss, *The Oobleck* and *The 500 Hats of Bartholomew Cubbins*. As we got older, adults read us chapters from *The Wizard of Oz*. In addition, we read comic books of all sorts, featuring Donald Duck and Uncle Scrooge, Casper the Friendly Ghost, Archie and his friends, Superman, Batman, and a whole array of other superheroes.

After I had learned to read, my mother bought copies of the books she had enjoyed as a child, so I made the acquaintance of the Bobbsey Twins and the Five Little Peppers. I remember having a book about King Arthur and the knights of the round table. My mother took us to the main branch of the Library of Hawaii, with its high-ceilinged rooms opening to grassy courtyards. The library was cool, quiet, and orderly, and all the books set neatly on the shelves seemed to be part of their own timeless world. I liked borrowing books from the public library and the library at school. I was overjoyed when I found a new series of books. I read all the Dr. Doolittle books but never discovered Nancy Drew. I liked the books of fairy tales by Andrew Lang and the novels by Louisa May Alcott, Walter Farley, and Laura Ingalls Wilder.

I did not connect reading in school with the rest of the reading I was doing, because the two were entirely different. Reading in school, through the sixth grade, meant reading aloud and working one's way through the basal readers, such as *On Cherry Street*. I liked some of the stories in the readers but, beginning in third grade, I had often read them all (surreptitiously) by the second or third week of school. I didn't mind doing workbook exercises, although I know that I didn't learn phonics, including the so-called long and short vowels, until after I could already read. Since I had the same classmates year after year, we developed games, such as racing to see who could finish first and still get all the answers right. Mrs. Awai, my fifth-grade teacher, let us go to the library often, and that was the year I read much more than I ever had in school.

The books in the library, as well as our basal readers, presented us with a world quite different from our own. I recall only two books with Asian settings: *The Five Chinese Brothers* and *The Story of Ping*. Illustrations of the brothers showed them to be horrible caricatures of Asians. Ping, while nicely drawn, was still only a duck. We read books of Hawaiian legends, but none with contemporary Hawaiian characters. As a student I do not remember thinking it odd never to come across a book written by an Asian American or with Asian American characters or, for that matter, with any but European American characters. I assumed that books were supposed to represent another world, not anything close to my own experience, since that was the case with all the books I had ever read.

In a sense, this disconnectedness between the world depicted in books and my own world paralleled the disconnectedness between school and life outside. I was fortunate to come from a family that valued schooling so much that I never thought to question why schooling should be so divorced from everyday reality. I believe my elementary school teachers, like my parents, leaned toward an assimilationist rather than pluralist ideology and were primarily concerned with teaching us what children all over the United States were being taught. In the years following World War II, in fact until the late 1980s, students in Hawaii's schools did not learn about crucial events in Hawaiian history, particularly the illegal overthrow of the Hawaiian monarchy plotted by American sugar planters.

I am overjoyed that so many wonderful children's books written by authors of diverse backgrounds are now available, and that social studies textbooks are beginning to move away from a Eurocentric bias. Yet I know that many teachers feel uncomfortable teaching literature and social studies from a pluralist versus assimilationist perspective. Many teachers and publishers seem to believe that the reason for introducing children to multicultural literature is to "teach them that people are more alike than different." They do not seem to understand that celebrating and maintaining differences may be equally, if not more, important to students of diverse backgrounds, such as Native Hawaiian students, who sense their cultural identity and heritage being threatened by the larger society.

BECOMING A TEACHER AND RESEARCHER

For my entire career I have worked at the Kamehameha Elementary Education Program (KEEP). KEEP is an educational change effort that has the goal of improving the literacy achievement of Native Hawaiian students enrolled in schools in low-income communities. The premise of KEEP is that Hawaiian students can achieve at parity with national norms. KEEP is the nation's longest running research and development project devoted to improving the education of students of a particular ethnic group.

I imagine that my choice of research topics might have been quite different had I been based in a university instead of a school. I have always tried to focus my research on the key issues facing KEEP. Sometimes the research has matched my personal preferences, and sometimes it has not. I like to conduct small-scale studies, such as those of videotaped small-group reading lessons, in which I have the opportunity to understand features of instruction in depth. I do not particularly like to conduct large-scale studies involving dozens of classrooms and hundreds of students, as in my recent work on whole literacy and portfolio assessment.[6] While my job has given me ample research opportunities and resources, it has forced me to become a generalist, exploring a wider range of topics than I feel would be ideal for a researcher. Usually I do not have the opportunity to tie up the loose ends before I must start work on a new issue.

My employment at KEEP came about quite by chance. After a year of courses at the University of Hawaii, I did my student teaching in a fifth-grade classroom at Wilson School, located in one of Honolulu's middle-class neighborhoods. When I received my professional diploma in June, I felt ready to have a classroom of my own. However, my prospects of finding a job were slim; Hawaii had far more teachers than it could use. One by one, the women who had completed their student teaching with me went on to other jobs: as a sales clerk in a department store, as a secretary in an insurance firm. I wondered whether my decision to teach had been a good one.

One day my mother noticed a newspaper ad placed by the Kamehameha Schools, a large private school for Native Hawaiian students. They were looking for two teachers to work for a new project. Desirable qualifications included teaching experience, especially with Hawaiian children, and previous work in curriculum development or research. I lacked these qualifications but applied anyway, because I had nothing to lose. I had a brief interview with the director of personnel, then a lengthy interview with the men who would lead the new project, including Ronald Gallimore, a professor in the psychology department at the University of Hawaii, and Stephen Boggs, an anthropology professor at the same institution. Later I went to the university for an interview with Roland Tharp, who with Ron was one of the project's principal investigators.[7]

I do not remember the specific content of these interviews, except for learning that research would be a part of the project. I decided it would be best to acknowledge right up front that I did not have the desired experience but that I was willing to learn and to work hard. KEEP's leaders took a chance on me. Their other choice was Arlene Granger, a teacher with many years of experience working with Hawaiian children, and they thought that we would be a good combination.

Arlene and I spent a year learning about curriculum trends in reading throughout the state and visiting public schools enrolling a high percentage of Native Hawaiian students. We observed a wide range of practices and discovered little consensus among educators about the best approach for teaching Hawaiian children to read.

By the fall of 1972, two more teachers, Sherlyn Franklin Goo and Sarah Sueoka, had been hired, and KEEP enrolled its first class of kindergarten students, most of them Native Hawaiians and from families receiving welfare. Our first classroom was the lounge of one of the dormitories on the Kamehameha Schools campus. My fellow teachers had all done much more teaching than I, so they took charge. I started by doing just a few lessons, reading stories to the students and teaching math to a small group using Cuisenaire rods. These children were unlike those I had taught at Wilson, in age as well as socioeconomic and cultural background. I found I had to learn classroom management strategies–quickly.

The enrollment policy at KEEP's laboratory school had been designed to give us the same population of students found in the neighboring public schools. In fact, we ended up with a population including more low-income students than any other school. Even at the age of five or six, the children had developed the skills needed to survive in the public housing projects of Kalihi. They could fight, swear, answer back, band together. They did not respect me just because I was supposed to be their teacher. I had to earn their respect by showing that I could take charge of the class, respond to challenges, make lessons interesting, be both kind and tough.[8] In turn, the students showed that they were bright, creative, thoughtful, and loving. I struggled during my first years in the classroom, and I was fortunate in having Arlene, Sarah, and Sherl to serve as models and to advise me. I know that many teachers learn to teach on their own. But for new teachers in inner-city classrooms like those at the KEEP lab school, I feel this must often be an unfair and overwhelming task.

The incident in my first years of teaching that stands out in my mind has nothing to do with the teaching of reading. It occurred during my second year of teaching, when I had the kindergarten class. In November, members of the State Board of Education were to visit the KEEP lab school. At the center of the school was an observation deck with one-way mirrors allowing easy viewing of events in the three classrooms. Video cameras and microphones mounted in the ceiling of each classroom could be controlled from a panel in the observation deck as well. All the teachers at KEEP learned to observe and be observed, through the glass and on videotape. Every year we took our classes to the observation deck so the children would know that their teachers, parents, and other visitors might be watching them at any time.

As planned, members of the board were in the observation deck as I brought my class in from recess. The children had cooperated well, especially given the schedule changes made to accommodate the board's visit. Before they entered the room, I reminded the class one more time about the important visitors. The children took their seats at once, and I told them that they could now go to a learning center of their choice.

Just as the children were making their way to the various centers around the room, I heard a loud crash of keys from the piano. The children froze. I turned to see what had happened. A new student, whom I will call Tommy, stood at the piano. Tommy had just come to us from preschool with a folder two inches thick, detailing his aggressive behavior and family problems. I knew I had to do something, but I had no idea how Tommy would react. "Tommy is new to our class and he doesn't know what to do yet," I said, trying to speak in the slowest, calmest manner possible. I told the children that Tommy would be choosing a center too, and that they should just go back to what they were doing. My words seemed to hang in the air for a moment. Then the spell was broken and the children began to move about and talk. I turned my back to Tommy and busied myself with some other children. Out of the corner of my eye, I saw Tommy go to his seat. He had a brown corduroy jacket he never removed, and he pulled the jacket up over his head and hid his face. He remained in this turtlelike position for a few minutes. Finally, he went off to one of the centers. The rest of the period passed peacefully.

After this incident, I knew that I would be able to survive as a teacher. But I learned that teaching students like those at KEEP would always be both challenging and humbling. There would be good days and bad days, and things might fall apart at any moment. I taught at the KEEP lab school in grades K through 3 for six years, then reached the point of burnout. Nothing in my professional life has ever proved quite as demanding in either mental or emotional energy. I have great respect and admiration for the successful teachers I have come to know over the years, first in the KEEP lab school and later in Hawaii's public schools and the Kamehameha Elementary School, who approach their teaching as a continual process of learning and self-renewal.

In my third year of teaching, I decided I needed to gain a better understanding of research on children's learning to read.

At the time, almost all reading research was psychological research, so I entered the master's program in psychology at the University of Hawaii. The first semester I enrolled in a required course on animal learning; it was so difficult that half the students dropped out. The professor, M. E. (Jeff) Bitterman, an internationally known comparative psychologist, gave brilliant lectures, always without notes. I admired Jeff's manner of thinking and command of the subject and asked him to be my adviser. At the time, Jeff was conducting experiments on the learning of bees, and he pointed out that he would not be able to help me with my interest in children's learning to read.

He did teach me the principles of experimental psychology, through a master's degree and all requirements for the Ph.D. except the dissertation.

I continued to teach but participated increasingly in curriculum development and research at KEEP. Perhaps because I was a classroom teacher, I sensed the limitations in the experimental research on reading available in the 1970s; this research did not take into account the complexities of classroom life. From the beginnings of my work as a researcher, I preferred to study classroom life, particularly the work of expert teachers.

My first publication described a study of oral reading errors I had conducted with my first-grade students.[9] I found that the students could use visual-phonic (letter-sound) information but showed little skill in using context or the meaning of the sentence or passage. The results of this study, along with others conducted at KEEP, contributed to the hypothesis that the emphasis in the beginning reading instruction of Hawaiian children should be comprehension, or understanding of the text, rather than decoding. At the time, the conventional wisdom dictated that children in kindergarten through third grade should "learn to read"–that is, decode–before they "read to learn" or read for understanding.

In 1976, as a first-grade teacher in the lab school, I taught comprehension-oriented small-group lessons for the first time. That year, my students' standardized test results looked promising in comparison with those of previous classes. As a result, the next year other teachers in the lab school began to teach similar lessons. We worked from our own instincts about how to emphasize comprehension instead of decoding, by teaching the children to comprehend the stories in their basal readers. Discussions of the type we tried to hold with kindergarten, first-, and second-grade students typically did not occur in conventional reading programs until the third or fourth grade.

I began studying videotapes of small-group comprehension lessons in the fall of 1977, hoping to detect a pattern that we could turn into a systematic instructional strategy. Ron Gallimore described this as a process of moving from the unconscious to the conscious. I learned to transcribe lessons with pointers from Steve Boggs, who with Karen Watson-Gegeo was completing research on a speech event called talk story, which they had observed among Hawaiian children outside of school.[10]

My fellow teachers knew that I was studying comprehension instruction, and I asked them to let me know when they thought they would be teaching an interesting lesson. The teachers had a clear sense of when such lessons would occur: when they were teaching a "meaty" story, one with ideas worth discussing.

In some of the videotaped lessons, I saw that the teacher showed great skill in drawing out and developing the children's understanding of the text. In my initial analyses, I transcribed the teachers' questions. One of the most promising tapes was of a lesson taught by first-grade teacher Karen Bogert, based on the story "JasPer Makes Music." I asked Karen to take a look at the list of questions she had asked during the "JasPer" lesson. A few days later, after looking over the list, Karen told me she had had an insight. She realized that she started with a broad discussion, narrowed the focus, then opened it up again. She gave me a drawing showing her strategy; it looked like an hourglass.

In studying other lessons, I verified the pattern Karen had seen. These results became the basis for the experience-text-relationship (ETR) method.[11] When opening a lesson, teachers ask questions that bring out the children's background experiences relevant to the topic or theme of the story. Then the lessons turn to discussion of the text itself. Finally, the teacher helps the children draw relationships between the text and their own experiences. ETR lessons became an enduring feature of the KEEP curriculum.

In the 1970s the social dimensions of instruction were little understood. In my first analyses of videotapes, I became frustrated at having to distill the key points in the discussion from the welter of voices. I found it easy to transcribe the teacher's questions but extremely difficult to sort out the children's responses, because the lessons contained a tremendous amount of overlapping speech. The children were quick either to dispute or to build on one another's answers. At times their speech overlapped that of the teacher, who might have momentary difficulty getting a word in edgewise. I became preoccupied with the problem of filtering out what I thought of as the social noise from the cognitive substance of the lessons. Finally I realized that what I had regarded as noise was actually the medium by which the children's comprehension developed. Through those rapid-fire exchanges, the students and teacher formed, questioned, and extended their shared interpretation of the story.

About this time I began to collaborate with Cathie Jordan, an anthropologist at KEEP. Cathie was interested in cultural compatibility, the idea that classroom practices should be compatible with the children's culture. While I was videotaping small-group reading lessons, Cathie was videotaping the children while they worked independently at learning centers. Her hypothesis was that the students would do well teaching and learning from one another. Because many were cared for by older sisters and brothers, they were likely to be more accustomed to learning from other children than from adults.[12] Drawing on the general notion of cultural compatibility, my hypothesis was that comprehension-oriented reading lessons would be more effective if conducted in a talk-story-like fashion.[13]

In the meantime, I continued to collect videotapes. In November 1977 I arranged to videotape Claire Asam, a second-grade teacher. Claire had chosen a day when she would be teaching a lesson based on a story entitled

"Freddy Finds a Frog." When I viewed the tape a few days later, I was struck by the liveliness of the discussion and knew I needed to study it further. I felt sure that this tape provided a clear example of the talk-story style.

After I had been analyzing the tape for a while, I went to speak to Claire. I said I was interested in how she got the students to do so much talking. Although she did not have a label for her approach or know exactly how she did it, Claire was aware that she could turn up or limit the amount of student talk at will. She turned up the talk when she wanted to bring the ideas out of the students. She said she did not turn up the talk with all groups, because some groups were talkative anyway and did not require this approach.

I realized that what I was learning in graduate school at the University of Hawaii was not helping me to pursue the research questions I thought important. Jeff and Roland both suggested that I needed the experience of working in an active research lab where people were doing research closer to my interests. I arranged to spend the spring semester of 1978 at Rockefeller University, where Michael Cole had established the Laboratory for Comparative Human Cognition, applying in American classrooms ideas shaped by comparative research in Africa.[14]

By now I had met Frederick Erickson, a noted educational anthropologist. Fred taught me the theory and method of studying participation structures, that is, the rules for speaking, listening, and turn taking as they varied within and between speech events. By applying these methods to the "Freddy" tape, I was able to confirm the talk-story hypothesis. One could not study these lessons and come away unimpressed by the speakers' intellectual and social skills. The teachers and students needed to be remarkably in tune with the rhythms of the discussion to coordinate their utterances in the rapidly shifting participation structures of the lessons.

At Rockefeller I became acquainted with Ray McDermott, who introduced me to ethnomethodology and showed me how to look at the nonverbal aspects of interaction on videotape. I also met Bill Hall, a developmental psychologist with contacts at the Center for the Study of Reading at the University of Illinois, Urbana-Champaign. Bill made it possible for me to work as a research assistant at the center, and I decided to transfer my degree work to Illinois.[15] After a year there, I returned to Hawaii to conduct my dissertation research on talk-story-like reading lessons. While collecting and analyzing the data, I spent my last semester as a classroom teacher.

REFLECTIONS

My attitudes toward schooling and literacy were shaped by the experiences of family members. I saw my grandmothers' longing for educational opportunities, and I have been particularly intrigued and affected by the stories of their lives. As a Chinese American with an interest in my own cultural heritage, I have explored avenues of bringing students to high levels of literacy through forms of classroom instruction respectful of their cultures.

One conclusion to be drawn from my research on talk-story-like reading lessons is that effective instruction may take more than one form. Definitions of effective teaching need to be broad enough to take into account a range of practices beyond those typically seen in mainstream settings. Another conclusion growing from my research is that students of diverse backgrounds can become excellent readers and writers when they receive well-conceived, culturally responsive instruction. Conversely, the reason many students do not succeed is because they are denied high-quality instruction. The slow acceptance of these ideas is due, I believe, to the continued dominance of assimilationist ideology,[16] which leads to a narrow view of what it means to be a good student or a good teacher, deriving from a narrow view of what it means to be a good American. This narrowness also affects views of what counts as literacy, in terms of written and oral expression, mainstream and diverse cultural knowledge, standard English and other codes.

A pluralist view of instruction takes into consideration the content of the curriculum as well as the process of instruction. I think the curriculum must be expanded to include time for students to explore their own cultural identities. I did not receive this opportunity in my own schooling and wish that I had. Students of diverse backgrounds will still be taught to read and write in standard English at high levels of proficiency. But they will be encouraged to use their literacy skills not just to learn mainstream content, as I did in school, but to deepen their understanding of their own worlds. We must balance the need to find common ground with the need to recognize and support the differences in culture and language that allow students of diverse backgrounds to maintain a connection to their family histories.

NOTES

1. Au, 1980.
2. Au and Mason, 1981.
3. Lum, 1990.
4. Wilson, 1991.
5. Pease-Alvarez and Hakuta, 1992.
6. Au, Scheu, Kawakami, and Herman, 1990; Au, 1994.
7. Over the years Ron proved to be the model of a thoughtful scholar, generous with ideas and credit. Roland gave KEEP a grand and ambitious vision.
8. For a discussion of classroom management issues with Native Hawaiian students, refer to D'Amato, 1988.

9. Au, 1976.
10. Watson-Gegeo and Boggs, 1988.
11. Au, 1979.
12. Gallimore, Boggs, and Jordan, 1974.
13. Au and Jordan, 1981.
14. Cole and Scribner, 1974; Scribner and Cole, 1981.
15. At Illinois I met colleagues with whom I have continued to work over the years: Jana M. Mason, who was my adviser; Richard C. Anderson; P. David Pearson; and my fellow graduate student, Taffy Raphael.
16. For a discussion of assimilationist and pluralist ideology, see Gollnick and Chinn, 1990.

BIBLIOGRAPHY

Au, Kathryn H. 1976. "Analyzing Oral Reading Errors to Improve Instruction." *The Reading Teacher* 31 (October):46–49.

Au, Kathryn H. 1979. "Using the Experience-Text-Relationship *Method* With Minority Children." *The Reading Teacher* 32 (March):677–679.

Au, Kathryn H. 1980. "Participation Structures in a Reading Lesson With Hawaiian Children: Analysis of a Culturally Appropriate Instructional Event." *Anthropology and Education Quarterly* 11 (Winter):91–115.

Au, Kathryn H. 1994. "Portfolio Assessment: Experiences at the Kamehameha Elementary Education Program." In *Authentic Reading Assessment: Practices and Possibilities*, Sheila W. Valencia, Elfrieda H. Hiebert, and Peter P. Afflerbach, eds. Newark, DE: International Reading Association, 103–126.

Au, Kathryn H., and Cathie Jordan. 1981. "Teaching Reading to Hawaiian Children: Finding a Culturally Appropriate Solution." In *Culture and the Bilingual Classroom: Studies in Classroom Ethnography*, Henry T. Trueba, Grace P. Guthrie, and Kathryn H. Au, eds. Rowley, MA: Newbury House, 139–152.

Au, Kathryn H., and Jana M. Mason. 1981. "Social Organizational Factors in Learning to Read: The Balance of Rights Hypothesis." *Reading Research Quarterly* 17 (Fall):115–152.

Au, Kathryn H., Judith A. Scheu, Alice J. Kawakami, and Patricia A. Herman. 1990. "Assessment and Accountability in a Whole Literacy Curriculum." *The Reading Teacher* 43 (April):574–578.

Cole, Michael, and Sylvia Scribner. 1974. *Culture and Thought: A Psychological Introduction*. New York: Wiley.

D'Amato, John. 1988. "'Acting': Hawaiian Children's Resistance to Teachers." *Elementary School Journal* 88 (May):529–544.

Gallimore, Ronald, Joan W. Boggs, and Cathie Jordan. 1974. *Culture, Behavior and Education: A Study of Hawaiian-Americans*. Beverly Hills, CA: Sage.

Gollnick, Donna M., and Philip C. Chinn, P.C. 1990. *Multicultural Education in a Pluralistic Society*, 3rd ed. Columbus, OH: Merrill, 32–34.

Lum, Wing Tek. 1990. "Matrices, Paradoxes, and Personal Passions." *Bamboo Ridge* 47 (Winter):5–16.

Pease-Alvarez, Lucinda, and Kenji Hakuta. 1992. "Enriching Our Views of Bilingualism and Bilingual Education." *Educational Researcher* 21 (March):4–6.

Scribner, Sylvia, and Michael Cole. 1981. *The Psychology of Literacy*. Cambridge, MA: Harvard University Press.

Watson-Gegeo, Karen Ann, and Stephen T. Boggs. 1988. "From Verbal Play to Talk Story: The Role of Routine in Speech Events Among Hawaiian Children." In *Child Discourse*, Susan Ervin-Tripp and Claudia Mitchell-Kernan, eds. New York: Academic, 67–90.

Wilson, William H. 1991. "Hawaiian Language in DOE Unique." *Ke Kuamo'o* 1 (May):4–6.

CHILDREN'S LITERATURE CITED

Baum, L. Frank. 1903. *The Wizard of Oz*. Indianapolis: Bobbs-Merrill.

Bishop, Claire H., and Kurt Wiese. 1938. *The Five Chinese Brothers*. New York: Coward-McCann.

Flack, Marjorie, and Kurt Wiese. 1933. *The Story About Ping*. New York: Penguin.

Lowrey, Janette Sebring. 1942. *The Pokey Little Puppy*. Racine, WI: Western.

Ousley, Odille. 1961. *On Cherry Street*. Boston: Ginn.

Seuss, Theodore G. 1938. *The 500 Hats of Bartholomew Cubbins*. New York: Random House.

Seuss, Theodore G. 1949. *Bartholomew and the Oobleck*. New York: Random House.

Ward, Muriel. 1948. *Little Pond in the Woods*. New York: Simon and Schuster.

* *CHAPTER 6* *

Ways Without Words: Learning from Silence and Story in Post-Holocaust Lives

Anna Neumann

ABOUT A YEAR AGO, I began to look closely at the relationship between my work as a researcher-interviewer–as a scholar who seeks to view the space that exists within and between my subject and my self–and my own existence as a post-Holocaust Jew who has learned how little I can truly know of another person's experience. I wrote a paper that described what it meant for me to listen to my father as he spoke, first to his brother and much later directly to me, about his captivity in Auschwitz. I described how my father, speaking to us in post-Holocaust times, tried to tell what could only be told in the words–the utterances–of the camp itself; no other words and sounds, emerging beyond the camp, could begin to contain or convey what he knew. What he wanted to tell was, of necessity, incomplete in its telling. What he said and what we heard consisted of text we could scarcely comprehend and silence we simply could not fathom.[1]

What I learned from that writing, for my self and for my work, is that how I now relate to others, even in the conduct of my professional work, notably my research–how I listen for the knowing of persons whom I interview, how I imagine their lives, how I sense the limits of their words to convey what they feel and know, how I sense my own inability to comprehend what they know and learn even as they speak–reflects what I learned through my father's efforts to tell his stories years back. While at one level the paper described how I learned of another's life by listening and by trying to understand, at another level it pointed at what I could never hope to learn of a life apart from my own, no matter how hard I tried. It spoke of the silences that emerge inevitably in every text, that grow in every effort to imagine

Learning from Our Lives: Women, Research, and Autobiography in Education. ISBN 0-8077-3593-0 (pbk), ISBN 0-8077-3594-9 (cloth).

another's life, that accompany every gesture of empathic imagination. It taught me that the stories I hear of others' lives are composed only partly of text; they are also composed of silence for which no text can exist.

As I finished the paper, I was surprised to see how very incomplete even my own writing of my experience with my father had been–how in attending to the silence and text that comprised his story, I had neglected to describe how my mother's life, existing in wordless form, enabled my father to tell his story. I was surprised at how absent the story of her survival, in the Holocaust and beyond it, was in what I had written–how little I even knew about it, how little she'd ever revealed to me. While my father's silence emerged from the text of a story he actually told to those of us who listened, even as thoughts he could never fully articulate or ever completely share, my mother's silence seemed to emerge from the dissolution of story itself, from the absence of virtually any recognized text, however flawed, and from the lack of people who would listen. While my father had a story that I and others acknowledged as real, though few–if any–could grasp it, my mother's story, as real as it was for her, has remained largely unknown, even to me.

In this chapter I speak once more about the interplay of text and silence in stories of human lives, but this time I draw on my mother's life and stories, in various versions of their telling, more so than on my father's, though his stories (and mine) intertwine with hers in ways I can hardly take apart. I learned from writing my father's story that with every text that's told comes a silence that cannot be converted into words or understanding that is fully shared. I learned from my mother's life that even in the silence of a story that lives without words, there exists a text to know and to tell, though its telling may occur in unexpected ways.[2]

In this chapter I draw on my understanding of my mother's experience in the Holocaust, including how I constructed it within myself (and how I continue to do so even now), to describe the place and meaning of untold stories in the lives of those who could tell them, and in the lives of those who could learn from their telling. I also try to describe how stories (like my father's and my own) may emerge, in articulated form, from within other stories that (like hers) exist untold, or that are told in unconventional ways, that is, without words. I conclude by exploring what it might mean to bring words to stories that have existed without them for much of the space of a life.

In the pages that follow I present and discuss three versions of what I have come to call my mother's story of her experience of the Holocaust. The various "tellings" or revelations that the three versions imply occurred at different times in my life, and over diverse lengths of time, and thus the three differ from each other in important ways. The last two tellings, which reflect my mother's talks with me just over the past few years, occurred more closely in time to each other than the first, which occurred initially during my childhood, although it continued throughout my adolescence as well.

The three versions of story also represent different forms of telling (for example, oral, written, enacted, or a combination) constructed for different audiences. For example, the first version largely reflects the "voice in my head" recounting the story I constructed out of fragments of story that she told me out loud and that I gathered by existing in her presence over many years, for example, by watching her alone or in interaction with others around her. In other words, the first version represents, in part, a "protected" story told to a child in bits and pieces; it also represents multiple, mostly unintended tellings that the child "read" into her mother's presence. The second version represents my mother's tape-recorded voice, presented here as a fine-grained transcription, as she recounted her story to me, this time as an adult, and with my husband present as well. The third version presents her voice again, but this time in the form of a written testimonial that she recently composed for the German government in application for long-overdue reparations payments.

The questions that lie behind my retelling of three versions of her story and with which I struggle in this chapter, and in my work more generally, are: How can we think of untold stories? What are they? How do untold stories manifest themselves, especially in the lives of those who would tell them, and what is their significance? How might we gain awareness of the existence of untold stories, even if we cannot know their contents specifically, and how important is it for us to do so? To what extent should we, as researchers, pursue untold stories? What good or harm might come from such pursuits?

I

I begin with the earliest version of my mother's story that I can remember—one I have constructed, in my own words, from my earliest memories of what she said of her life, and my memories also of how I saw her live in the present, though in terms of what I believed to be her past.

My mother says that when I was young, I hated to eat. One of her ways of convincing me to have a meal was by promising to tell me a story as I ate. She would pick me up and put me on the large cement block near the gate of our veranda so that I was just at eye level with her. Then, while she spooned soup or eggs or sour cream into my mouth, she'd point at the picture she'd just taken down from our living room wall, and she'd begin the story it brought to her mind—about a girl who lived in the house by the lake and with mountains nearby that I could see right there in the picture I held in my hands. The stories she told were largely make-believe, emerging from pictures or from images and problems that she thought up–about girls who were lost, or who went in search of flowers or friends. But every once in a while, and I think mostly at my urging, she told me a piece of a story in which the girl at its center was herself. I learned, in this way, small bits of her life that, over the years of my childhood, I strung into text until, in my childhood mind, a semblance of story emerged:

> My mother's real name is Yehudit Fuhrer Neumann, and she was born in the early 1920s in a land far away–far from Tiberias, Israel, where I was born and where we lived when she first mentioned her past–in a town called Suceava in a country called Romania, a place to which she told me, time and again, she would never return.
>
> As a girl, she lived in Suceava with her two younger brothers, her mother, and her father. Her father was a merchant who descended from a family of mystics and scholars who studied *Zohar*, the Jewish Book of Splendor, but whose own father or grandfather had left the family during hard economic times to become a traveling merchant. As this great-grandfather guided, with one hand, the horse that pulled his wagon, he used the other hand to hold the book that he read and studied even as he rode. This is how his family gained the name of Fuhrer, meaning "one who travels."
>
> My mother was an excellent student, especially good in arithmetic, but she learned languages quickly and easily as well. She loved to read, and her studies were the center of her life. All this changed, however, when, in her fifth-grade year [*],[3] the Romanian government banned Jewish children from Romanian schools, and she had to drop out. This was right before the outbreak of World War II. An aunt [*] taught her privately, but soon those lessons ended as well because, in those days and in that place, "what did it matter if a girl had school?"
>
> Shortly after this, my mother and her family were deported, with the other Jews in Suceava, to a Russian labor camp far away in "U-kraina," as my mother called it, where they were forced to work in terrible cold and had little to eat.
>
> Her life in Ukraina was hard, but even as she said this, she would remind me, with a sidelong look at my father, that "there [in Ukraina] they did not kill us." And she would tell me that she and her family, unlike my father and his, were able to stay together throughout the war, except for the time that her youngest brother was abducted by Russians [*] searching for workers. He disappeared for several months, and they

> thought he had died—my grandmother cried every day—until one day he miraculously reappeared, thin and very, very sick.
>
> After the war, my mother and her family returned to Romania, and shortly thereafter, to avoid Communist rule, they left for Israel.

This is the text that grew in my head over the years of my childhood and adolescence as I collected bits of information that she shared with me, or with my sister and me, initially in the Yiddish that, for much of my life, we spoke at home. But I never heard her say these words, in any language, to anyone else. Usually she listened to others tell of their lives rather than revealing her own to them, or she spoke of her life in the present as though a past did not exist for her, or as though the past did not matter.

But I did not construct my mother's story only from selected fragments of text such as these. I constructed it as well out of thoughts I had in watching her, and in watching also those around her as they talked or stood with her, sometimes as they forgot her, sometimes as they fought against her, even as they struggled to surpass the growing intensity of her voice and her thought. I constructed it, not through listening to her talk directly about her story but through watching her absorb the stories that others would tell, watching her play with thoughts about the places of those stories in the extraordinarily varied lives from which they emerged and which they reflected. I constructed it through attending to her silences, when she sat and thought, gazing into spaces ahead. And I constructed it through watching her confront her own stories silently, as she seemingly battled the present moment of remembrance, as she forced her attention onto what simply had to be done by the end of this afternoon and within the next hour. I constructed it through observing her close attention to the lives of others—doing for them, wondering about them, planning what she'd say to them next. And I constructed it through thinking back on what she had once said—or what others had once said to her or about her—combining one small thought from conversation and watching today with thoughts even more slender, more fragile, more compressed, that I'd recall from conversation and watching years back.

These fragments and splinters of story—and of story about story, story emerging from the shell of a story I'd heard long ago—grew and joined, interweaving thought-from-right-now with thought-recalled-from-a-long-time-ago into thought-I-constructed-for-myself, perhaps not in pure fact, but in mind and in love and in wanting to know who she was, who I imagined she was, wanting to believe I knew her, wanting her image in my life right now.

I chased after the ghosts, and shells, and splinters of her stories, as I heard them—coming out of my memories of past conversations, or uttered in the moment–trying to hold and understand, trying just to have an image of what she might be. I wrote in a paper not too long ago how even in the void of not-knowing, we nonetheless come to know, how even when we have no interpretation, we nonetheless construct one, gathering wisps of sight and sound that surround us into images that, through the weaving of interpretation, become real for us.[4] I know that while my mother never told me, never told anyone (as my father tried to), about the harshness of her life in the war, about the resentment and anger out of which her life grew, I absorbed a story nonetheless, constructed it through weavings of bits of talk, and touch, and looks, and sighs, through moments of closeness and distance, through remembrances of conversation that flowed and conversation that stopped and switched and turned even in mid-thought. What emerged as my story of my mother was less a story composed of the knowing that words can bring than a story constructed from the knowing that unworded feeling creates.[5]

I constructed, in this way, a story that, like her, I did not tell out loud–of how embattled she was with her past but how determined she was to live right now, of how bitter her losses had been yet how vigorous and filled with hope her efforts to restore and remake had become, of how much had been taken from her but how much will and strength she had to take so much of it back. I sensed this story long before the person-to-person talks, cast in real spoken words, that we finally had just two years ago, when, with tape recorder in hand and my husband close by as well, I asked her to talk of herself, and he then asked why, before this time, she had not.

II

From notes I made to myself:

> *September 26, 1992 [morning].* I now live in Lansing, Michigan. I am married, have a house, furniture, a schedule, a profession, an adult life. In all those years when I heard my father talk–mostly to others because he could not talk directly to me, though later in his life he could–my mother said little. She said little about herself to me or to my father or to friends in front of me. I knew she was from the northern part of Romania, a piece of land that, before the war, was contested territory, having once belonged to the Austro-Hungarian Empire. And when I had once looked at a map, I realized she was talking about Transylvania [*], what to me was only a fictional land, something I had read about in books. She used to talk about Suchava [*sic*], where she was born and lived, but in my mind it was a far-off place and she always minimized it. She never

said much. And I knew in general terms of her war experiences, what happened, some of the events, little more. She would always point to my father and say that his story was more horrible.

When my mother visited me at the end of September 1992, I was in the midst of writing my autobiographical account of what and how I learned, about myself and about learning itself, from listening to my father's accounts of his life throughout the course of mine. I was devoting immense energies to remembering the substance and form of past conversations with him–what he'd said about his life in the war and beyond it, what I'd felt as he spoke–in part because his advancing Alzheimer's made me fear that soon his memories would be lost and, with them, perhaps, the person I'd become in living among them. But as I struggled to remember what it had been like for me to learn of his life, I couldn't help but ask, as well, what I knew of my mother's life in that war. I couldn't help but wonder why I was not writing about her in the same way that I was writing about him. Why wasn't she more in my story? My paper, after all, was supposed to be about me–about my life and my work. Why was my understanding of myself, as a scholar and as a post-Holocaust Jew, not framed in terms of my relationship with her inasmuch as it was framed so clearly in terms of my relationship with him? Why hadn't her experiences permeated my life in the same way? Why did I know so little about her life? Why wasn't her story more present in mine?

I started one of our morning conversations that week by asking her questions about her life in Romania. I learned enough, from that brief talk over breakfast, to appreciate that there existed, in her head, mountains of details about her experience of the war that I simply knew nothing about. I came to understand, from that snippet of talk, that she had never spoken to me of her life in more than the vaguest of terms. Rather than searching for words, she would cut herself off, switch topics, or just say she did not remember. I wanted to ask her more, and to ask her why she'd always said so little, but I hesitated. If she hadn't spoken, perhaps it was for a good reason, that it might hurt too much, that she'd have to recall something horrible, that I would have to hear it and live with it and live also with knowing that for much of our life together, I just hadn't asked, or that I hadn't asked in ways that would help her talk. But I was also frustrated and angry in realizing how her life had simply not entered into mine in the same way my father's had. Back at my computer, I made notes of what she'd just said and my feelings about it: "I know, from all these years with her, that her memory for detail is outstanding, and frankly I find it hard to believe she does not remember."

Later that day I asked if she would mind repeating our breakfast conversation after dinner when Aaron, my husband, and I could both listen. I asked if I could tape-record what she said. She seemed surprised at my interest, but agreed immediately, and agreed again later that day when I asked her once more if it would be okay to talk.

September 26, evening

JUDITH: I was born in Suceava, Bukovina, Romania[6]. . . . My years //[7] til // fifteen years // I had a regular life // more or less. But as I was fifteen years I couldn't continue in my education any more. I had to take private lessons because Jews were not allowed in school any more. [Soon after this] we were // we were deported at // deported from our town. That means all // all Jews had // were deported from Suceava to Transnistria [a portion of the Ukraine].[8] We went // with // by train in very bad condition to // to Bessarabia // to Bessarabia // which is at the *grenetze* [border] // which is // there we had to take the boat and go // went over to Transnistria which is Ukraina. We were // when we came to Mogilev which is the town after we // which is the other part of Romania that's in the Ukraina // we had to walk for a few days til // til another town // town that was Shargarod. We were together, my // my mother, my father, my aunt, my cousin, and my two brothers. When we arrived // when we arrived in Shargarod we // the situation was real bad. We found // we found a very small room for our // for the whole family and . . . after // uh // after // after a year, they took all the young men // all // uh // the young men to work // to the other part of Ukraina // which was occupied by the Germans. We were occupied by the Romanian. And // but we // right away as Bubi [the older of her two brothers] was already sixteen years old and very tall, we // sent him to a village so he won't be caught. And Ianu [the younger brother] was home // he was thirteen years old and // a child at that time and we were thinking he wouldn't be taken, but they took him instead of Bubi.

ANNA: Who did the taking?

JUDITH: Uh // they were policemen, Jewish policemen, and they had a list of // young boys to be taken. Ianu was not on the list, but as they did not find Bubi, they took Ianu. And we never thought that Ianu was going to come back. Because he was very thin and he was sick. But he was a few months there. We haven't heard of him anything // and on one [day] he just appeared, he just came back. . . . He was in the hospital for a long time. At that time we were very bad [things were very difficult for us]. . . . Bubi used to work as // as a mechanic. He used to be a schmidt // schmidt. And we had a little bit money and so we could // we could live. But we were extremely sad until Ianu came back. We were thinking we won't have him any more.

ANNA: You were living in a little room?

JUDITH: In a little room // this was all [that there was] [describes dimensions of the room, in terms of my dining room, as about eight-by-eight feet]. . . . And it had an oven and there I used to sleep on the oven. And down [used to] sleep my father, my mother, and the two boys. And that's the way we lived. . . . A piece had an oven and on the oven you know // was // was empty // I could sleep there. I slept by myself. And they slept all down you know. . . . We were there for three year. After the three years // when the war // I mean // the Germans retreat, they retreated, and Romania got normal, more or less normalized. They said all the Jews to come back. So my brother made a *vaigaleh* // a carriage.

ANNA: Why did they move everybody over there?

JUDITH: They just wanted // because Jews were very rich // we [her family] were not . . . rich people, but we had three houses. They [Jews] had everything you know. Everybody had a business. They [Romanians collaborating with Nazis] wanted everything. They just had a // the Germans asked them to move // to // to move. They were thinking. After a while we would have been taken to Auschwitz too. They wouldn't have kept it, kept us over there. But the war it was very bad, and they had too many people from // from the other countries. If they would have finished them [in Auschwitz] we would have, they would have taken us. This was the plan. The plan was to take us too. After a while we would have gone to Auschwitz too. But thanks God, the war got to an end. And so // uh // we had to go back. Bubi made a carr– // a *vaigaleh*, yah? // and not a horse . . . with a donkey. We put all our things and we started // we started walking til Mogilev. Then from Mogilev we went with a boat // not with a boat, I think it was already a bridge // it was a bridge there. So they went with this carriage on the bridge, you know, with everything. And when we came to Bessarabia, it was very many days to walk home. I could[n't] walk, and my father couldn't walk either, and the aunt. I mean they were already sixty years old there, fifty-five or sixty // so we three went to catch a train and // and my mother // the babbeh [my grandmother] // my mother with my two brothers // they, they walked with this carriage and with the things and with the donkey. We [my mother, her father, her aunt] went by train, and on the way I had lots of difficulties, I was a young girl and they took me // they were some drunk // drunk soldiers. They took me there to a room. I had very much luck because some officer came in and I // I went out and // I found the fa– // the aunt. Because my father went by train // somebody took him // he couldn't walk at all. And // the aunt waited for me. She didn't // didn't want to go away without me. . . . My aunt and myself, we started walking to our town. It was a few days we had to walk. It was very far // from north Bukovina to south. . . . And myself I told I don't want to stay there [in Romania] for a minute [more]. I didn't even have a dress to wear. I had this dress // nothing. . . .

AARON: So you've talked about your experiences to // [Anna before]?

JUDITH: No, I never talked. That's right? [*Turns to Anna*] I never //

ANNA: Why not?

JUDITH: First of all //, it was //, you know, I always worked. . . . I was very little with you and with Lily [my younger sister]. [*To Aaron*:] You can't imagine how hard I worked. You can ask this. [She turns to Anna.] Anna can tell you. . . . So I didn't have time, and I wasn't interested for them to hear many *tsurris*, you know, all these problems.

ANNA: Why not?

JUDITH: Because I wanted you to think about good things when you were young. If I didn't have a good life, I wanted you to have a better one.

ANNA: But Daddy talked about them–

JUDITH: Daddy used to talk maybe more. I don't know why. Because, like you say, with Uncle Nandor [his brother]–[*to Aaron*] his brothers used to come [to our house]–and there he used to tell them the story of the whole family [his family]. But whom should I have // ? I didn't have whom to tell it.

ANNA: No, you didn't have anybody to talk to.

JUDITH: I didn't have any family. I didn't have // And my children had other things to do. You know, I wanted them to have friends. I wanted them to be happy [*indrawn breath on tape*].

For all of the years of my life with her, my mother did not put words to her own life. There was no one, no other adult, who could ask her to talk, who would really listen to what she said, who would respond if she called. She had left her own mother and father and brothers in Israel, where they had immigrated after returning to Romania from the Shargarod ghetto at the war's end. After marrying my father, and after eleven years in Israel, she moved with him and with my sister and me to a South Texas town with a small Jewish population. Few of the people she encountered in her life there cared for a survivor's tale, and fewer still cared to hear stories of deportation that, in the still-emerging discourse of the Holocaust, had not yet been legitimated as a survivor's tale.

But while my mother said little, about her life, through the course of both of ours, she was never still, and even today she is not. She worked, she continues to work, extremely hard. Through the years of her life with my father, she engaged in a labor that displaced her telling, but that displaced, as well, the silence of what she did not tell. It was work that–despite the silence it invoked for her–created, for my father, a place and time in his life within which he did struggle to tell, with words and with silence, what I now believe he had to tell to survive the fact of his own survival.

My mother's work, driven in part by her silence, became the human context of his telling. She left him alone with his brothers to talk, often expressly removing herself from conversation, withholding her own story in a way that positioned his at the center of our lives and at the center of our understanding of ourselves as a family. She spoke for him when he failed to express himself clearly to others, and she helped him understand why others thought and spoke and acted as they did. She carried out, even invented, the detailed work of the clothing store that he managed, making it exist as a store day by day. Through her labors, she crafted the place and time, the activity and thought, that became their daily work and that became the means for earning the living that let us live, and think, and speak, and exist as most middle-class American families in Brownsville, Texas, did, that gave us the livelihood that in every way supported our lives.

My mother immigrated to America with my sister and me, aged three and six, in 1958, following my father who had made the trip by himself several months before. My sharpest early memories of our lives in the new America–in Laredo and then Del Rio, Texas, in Waco, then for many years in Brownsville, Texas–portray her behind a waist-high counter, leaning forward over an upper counter, lifting parcel after parcel of women's and young girls' clothing well above her head, asking after the customer's daughter and husband and neighbor, exclaiming how happy she was to see her again and how long it had been since she'd last come in, counting pesos and dollars interchangeably, stashing hangers, storing customers' bags, calculating rows and rows of figures in her head (still in the Romanian I would never comprehend) as she ran her pencil down the page. Turning from customer to customer, helping two at a time, three in the busiest seasons, marking tickets, tearing stubs, taking money, making change, catching up on the lives before her and urging each to come back–switching from the Spanish of her talk with them, to the Spanish-with-English of her talk with the clerks, to the

English of her talk with Lily and me as we scrambled behind her, to the Yiddish of her talk with my father, to the Romanian of her talk, I think, with herself as she thought through the motion and sound all around her.

Franklin's Store in downtown Brownsville was, for me, something of a magical place with my mother behind the counter always at its center, always surrounded by women's voices almost all in Spanish, laughing, counting, inquiring into each other's lives, pointing to other dresses, other coats that other friends just had to see, the radio blaring polkas and Spanish love songs, the salesclerks inquiring after prices, retrieving layaway merchandise that months back she'd boxed in pink-and-black-striped containers. She was the store's main bookkeeper, cashier, chief of credit, head salesclerk, and assistant manager, but to most of her customers and to many of the women with whom she worked closely, she was also a friend. She listened to the stories they told of their lives and tried to understand the families and friends for whom they shopped and cared. She worked this way twelve hours a day, sometimes more, six or seven days a week, maintaining the store as a store, for herself and for us, turning its insides into spaces on which we constructed our American lives.

I learned, from watching my mother those many years, that there are lives, like hers, upon which others' lives are written and lived and told, and without which these other lives simply would not be. My mother's successes in that small downtown store on East Elizabeth Street that she and my father managed together became the context within which the members of my family configured our lives in America–my father continuing throughout his life to try to make sense of his own ravaged past in a postwar world to which he could scarcely relate, my sister and I struggling for some semblances of meaning amidst American ways, even amidst intellectual pursuits, that seemed oceans apart from the simpler, clearer, everyday knowing of our parents' lives.

Even as I write this I labor over words that will bring what my mother wrought for us to the front of my story, placing the text of my father's life and my own farther back. Through her work in that store, virtually every day of her life, she crafted a netting of time and place and being, within which we could come to be what, in fact, we all became. My language falls short–I stumble over the intricate shadings and interlacings of distance and relation, silence and sentence, feeling and word that might begin to capture the untold details of how her life spread out as a place and time for ours to become. The silence of her life–its submergence in the lives of others, its displacement in work–created the space on which my father, my sister, and I could write and tell and make our own.

III

The last retelling of my mother's story came about a year after her visit to my home in Lansing and as a quick, straightforward, and painfully honest response, on her part, to one of those unexpected turns of history, when unknown faces suddenly become known, when nonevents are named, when those who have stood silently in the background of history come forward to reclaim their parts in its making.

This last iteration of her story began when my husband, Aaron, in reading *The New York Times*, ran across an announcement that the German government was just revising its long-standing reparations policy so as to recognize (that is, to treat as real and legitimate) the claims of those who existed during World War II in ghettos and in labor camps, though not in the torturous death camps that have, for years, been associated with images of the Holocaust survivor. After days of hesitating, I broached the topic with my mother over the phone, knowing that the pension resulting from a successful application could mean a great deal to her, instrumentally and expressively, but fearing also the substance I knew she would have to unearth to make her case.

She literally jumped at the chance. "I'm a survivor too," she said, with an edge and quickness that made me feel that she actually knew and regretted how little I, like so many of those with whom she'd lived, understood of what her life had been. I sent her the clipping that Aaron had found, but before I could really ask what she wanted to do about it, she informed me that she'd already phoned New York, that she'd given the basic facts to the woman who took her case over the phone, that she'd called her brother in Israel to find two old friends who would testify to the veracity of her claim, and that she'd started already the essay of testimony that she would have to make.

She called me two nights later to have me listen to her account . . . was this right? was the English good? I told her, after I'd listened and after I learned what that New York office wanted, that she would have to be much more specific, that the language was fine, but that she would have to tell more than she'd told, and maybe more than she wanted to tell. "What? I don't understand. You mean my English is no good?" she said. "Maybe you can write it for me." "No, Mama," I replied, "your English is very good. And I can't write it for you because I'm the one who doesn't understand." And I gave her an example, from specific bits of what I remembered she'd said to me just the year before, about how one turns a story about "terrible things," about "suffering very much," or about a "situation that was very bad," into a detailed account of living through hunger and dirt in a space so small that she had to sleep on an oven. She said she understood and that she would write again. I asked if this was what she really wanted. She insisted it was.

She called me a few nights later to read to me the most explicit account I've ever heard her make of her life:

> The anti-Semitism in Suceava-Bucovina started in 1940. Jews had to wear a yellow Star of David on their chest. I always wore a yellow Star of David to identify me as a Jew. Jews were not allowed to be seen in groups, it was punishable by incarceration. In winter of 1940 I went to visit a friend. As I entered his house there were 5 friends visiting her [*sic*]. After me came the police, we were all arrested and taken to the police station. I was severely beaten there, because they said I had to confess that I am a Jewish communist. As I did not confess to anything, I was sent to Jasi-Moldova to the terrible penitentiary. There I was kept for a few months. I suffered very much there. I was beaten by the guards and humiliated.
>
> In September 1941 every Jew from Suceava had to be at the train station. We were put in a train in cattle wagons without water or food or air. After days of traveling in this situation, we arrived in Basarabia [*sic*], weak hungry and thirsty. We stayed there for a few days, we did not have food and lost all our belongings. We were transferred in little boats over the Niester [*sic*] to Transnistria-Mogilev. From Mogilev we were marched to Shargorod. On both sides of the marching transport were soldiers with bayonets. People who could not walk were hit on the head. I was one of them hit badly. We marched for a few days and ate only a piece of bread we were given. We arrived in Shargorod hungry, dirty and sick. With much difficulty we found a little room in Ghetto Shargorod 3 feet by 3 feet [*]. We were 5 people, my parents, my 2 brothers and myself. All this time I slept on the stove, ate once daily, bread was not available.
>
> In Shargorod I was taken by soldiers to work in the fields. I was beaten with sticks by them. My hands were all swollen.
>
> In winter was very very cold, I had no shoes, my feet were full of frostbeits [*sic*], open wounds.
>
> In 1943 I had typhoid fever [* typhus]. I was in a hospital–around 80 people to a room lying on the floor, with no medical help, left to die, but survived by miracle.
>
> In May 1944 we had to walk home for weeks from Shargorod to Suceava, Bucovina. On our way back, as we were in Basarabia, I could not walk anymore and waited for a train. A train arrived with Russian soldiers. The soldiers took me to a room at the train station, they wanted to rape me, some officer knocked on the door and I was able to escape. I

> was very scared and someway after many days I found my way home to Suceava. I arrived home only with the dress I wore and torn shoes. After a few months I decided to leave Suceava. I saw no possibility to continue my education. I left for Bucharest . . . and then left for Israel.

Even in this retelling I knew there was much she'd left out and much more that, even if she'd tried, she could never retell in a way that I and others would understand. She told me that her efforts to write had made her cry, that she hadn't slept, that in writing she'd found thoughts she'd long tried to forget. I called her every night for some time after that, and when, six months later, she called to tell me that her application had been approved, I asked if I could have a copy of the text I've reproduced above and that she read to me that night.

While I've cast my mother's story as three versions of text and silence, as though each version were discrete and singular, this was not the case at all. Each version consisted of multiple versions and multiple tellings stretched over time. For example, the first version stretched over the years of my childhood and adolescence, and even in my adulthood, it existed as my primary interpretation of my mother's life in the war.

The second version, situated within my adult life, represents a response to the silences I discerned in the paper I wrote about myself with my father; it continued through the course of an initial conversation I had with my mother over breakfast one morning, which I did not tape-record though I wrote about it privately and later reread and rethought what I wrote; it even continued later that day as I tape-recorded our talk of her life, as I reflected on it later in conversation with my husband and in my own thought alone, and as I listened again to the tape I made, though much later on; it continued also in my own transcribing of parts of the tape into a fine-grained script that, in addition to hearing, I could actually see with my eyes. The transcript helped me discern the density of breaks in her voice – the hardship of finding words to fill silence, to replace what has always stood in silence. Ironically, while this version started as speech, it ended as writing.

The third version was, in some ways, the converse of the second. For this telling, my mother prepared a narrative that she read to me over the phone; she sent me the narrative and I read it again and again, silently to myself; I also read it out loud, trying to absorb what it might have meant for her to live this life, and then to write it down in English, a language she'd never before used to express it. This version, while starting as writing, ended as speech.

With each rereading and retelling I've come closer in myself to the story I know of my mother's life, and she too has come closer to me. Learning her story became a project for me that I think will continue in my life for years; it has involved (and continues to involve) much more than a one-time telling, for example, as she elaborates, in telling that builds on telling, on what she said some time before, and as I repeatedly retell and rethink to myself what I hear her say. The retelling of her story continues in my mind. I think it will for a long time to come.

I have also learned about my mother's personal experience of the war through sources beyond herself–by exploring the tragic historical events, officially recorded, in which her personal experience was cast, but to which the post-war world has, until recently, given little heed, thereby overlooking the lives of those (like her) who endured those events, and who endured also their aftermaths.

In 1930 approximately 145,000 Jews lived in the Romanian region of Bukovina where Suceava is located. It is estimated that 125,000 Bukovinian Jews perished in 1941 alone on the death marches to the ghettos and labor camps in Transnistria,[9] the Ukrainian territory that Romanian and German forces conquered and that Hitler awarded to General Antonescu and his son, the Romanian heads of state. Aron Hirt-Manheimer describes the plan of the Romanian government in conducting the deportations to the ghettos and camps of Transnistria, including Shargarod where my mother and her family were interned:

> Here [in Transnistria] the exiled Jews were expected to perish of "natural causes," nameless victims of a world at war; accordingly, the Romanian administration denied the deportees food, water, soap, clothes, fuel, shelter, and medicine. Forced on death marches to remote localities throughout the approximately 16,000-square mile territory, thousands died of exhaustion, disease, and exposure. Those who fell behind were beaten or shot. Naked, decomposing corpses on the roadside became the leitmotif of the Romanian Government's crusade to exploit a "historical opportunity" to rid the nation of its unwanted Jewish minority. (p. xxvi)

In November 1941, after three months of deportations, Franklin Mott Gunther, the U.S. representative in Bucharest, sent the following message to Washington: "'[The Bukovinian Jews] are being evacuated eastward into the war-devastated territory of the Ukraine under conditions so appalling that they would seem to afford a substantial share of the evacuees little chance to survive. . . . This modern Captivity would seem deliberately calculated to serve a program of virtual extermination . . . '" (p. xxix). According to Hirt-Manheimer, the younger Antonescu's justification for the deportations was straightforward: "'We are now at the moment in time most favorable for ethnic liberation, national revision and the purification of our nation from all those elements alien to her soul, which have grown like weeds, darkening her future. In order that this unique moment not be lost, we must be implacable . . . '" (p. xxv). The elder Antonescu clarified this point:

> I am for the forced migration of the entire Jewish element from Bessarabia and Bukovina, which must be thrown over the [Russian] border. . . . You must be merciless . . . I do not know when . . . the Romanian nation will again enjoy this total freedom of action, with the possibility for ethnic purification and national revision. This is the hour when we are masters on our territory. Let it be used! I do not mind if history judges us barbarians. . . . If need be, shoot with machine guns, and I say that there is no law . . . (p. xxv)

Yet even with documentation such as this, the experience of Romanian Jews in Transnistria during World War II is hardly known and hardly remembered, existing, for the most part, as "the forgotten Holocaust" and "the forgotten cemetery."[10] In many ways, I think of Transnistria as one of many untold stories encased in history itself.

It is, however, so hard for me to comprehend how horror can actually compete with horror in the chronicling of history, whether in terms of generalized, large-scale events or, more particularly, in the lives of individuals. In many ways, the particular and personal silence of my mother's experience in the war parallels the more general silence of the Jewish-Bukovinian exile to Transnistria defined as historical event.[11] In the eyes of recorded history, Transnistria, compared with Auschwitz, exists as horror in the shadow of greater horror. But *how* does the world even begin to compare two such events? And how do we dare to classify the horror of one's experience, encased in event, as greater or lesser than another's, encased in the same or another event? There are times when comparison makes absolutely no sense, when neither likeness *nor* difference matters at all, when all we can do is try to attend, with all that we have in our selves, to stories of life and stories of death–told and untold, then and now and later–one by one by one.

ON STORIES TOLD AND STORIES LEARNED IN SILENCE

As I look back at my mother's story–and at my story of how I discerned her past–I realize what I learned from her about the existence of wordless stories in people's lives, and how the telling of such stories proceeds nonetheless.

People live their stories as much as they tell them in words. They live them in what they do not say. They live them in attending to the words of others rather than their own. They live them in the gaze that comes with inward thought and inward talk while others all around are conversing. They live them in the feelings that come to surround them, that they give off in sighs and looks and gestures, or simply in the feeling that their presence evokes in others. All of these are forms of telling, though without words, and they are forms of telling that we can begin to read and hear, though also without words.

I am coming to believe that the telling of a story, however it occurs, is part of the living of a life and that to shut a story down is to shut down, as well, the life of which it tells and from which it flows. An untold story, or one that is told unconventionally without words, relates the teller's continuing struggle to live. For a survivor, it relates the teller's continuing struggle to survive.

The texts that some people speak out loud, or that they commit to writing, emerge within the time and space that surrounds them and within which they are told. Conversation as text is embedded in the silence that surrounds it, that breaks it up into words and spoken thoughts, letting those words and thoughts exist as distinctive sounds; written text exists on a page that is otherwise blank and whose blankness lets black print emerge, word by word, as part of distinctive statement. While oral and written texts, emerging as conversation and as writing from silence and blankness, have clear and identifiable authors, so, too, do the silence and blankness that exist *with these articulated texts*, holding and supporting them, serving as wordless backgrounds against which the spoken or written words of authors may appear and become real. What I have learned from my mother's story is that though story and author existing *in text* are readily identifiable, a story and an author exist, as well, but in far less visible form, in the silence and blankness that exist *with text*, around it, as context. Even context can hold a story of life and one who would tell it. In the case of my family, my father's partially articulated story, and certainly my own, came to exist as text that grew in the context of my mother's unarticulated story.

But how can we find such stories? How can we even know they exist in lives around us? How can we hear or see, sense or absorb their very existence, even without glimpsing their content? Discerning untold stories is bound to take an unconventional ear and eye, and mind and heart, for the evidence we collect—even that these stories exist—will be drawn less from text than from the silence and diffuseness of context. It requires attending more to what is absent than to what is present, more to what remains unsaid than to what is said, more to what is unacknowledged than to what is acknowledged, more to what remains unknown than to what is known. In Henry Greenspan's terms, this discerning requires attending more to the "not story" inscribed between the words of text than to text itself.

Stories, to me, are the sense and meaning we derive from our selves and our lives, for ourselves and for others. They appear less in the clear, hard, textually rendered lines of setting and event, action and plot, movement and sequence, plan and accomplishment, than in the often fragmented, even wordless expressions of experience and emotion.[12] Stories are what we feel and tell ourselves, about how we know our pasts, even in the contexts of our present-day lives. We also tell these stories–of our selves and our pasts, with words and without–to others in our lives.

But there is another dimension to story that exists in the present, and that is the story of the story's telling. It is also the story of others' coming to know of the story that is told, both with and without words. It is the story of how the story of the past, and/or the story of the self, lives in the present. Even with my mother's untold story, there are multiple stories: the story of her life in Transnistria, the story of how she lived with that story (and without expressing it in words) through much of her life after the war, the story of how she came to express it years later in words. And there is the story as well of how I and others in my family came to know her story, how we lived in the past with what we knew, however vaguely, how we lived with its wordlessness, how we live now with the telling she has begun, how we live with our telling of what she tells. Though I've come to believe that few, if any, untold stories exist in pure untold form (they tell themselves in other ways), I believe that the story of their telling, and the present-day "reading" by others of that which is the subject of their telling, can itself exist in untold form. We can sense another's life without acknowledging or appreciating the meaning and value and feeling of what we are learning.

I think there are many untold stories we already know, or whose existence we sense in the present moments of our lives, though we do not speak of them. Nor do we speak about our not-speaking, or about the personal pain and distortion that silence engenders when, in Henry Greenspan's words, the would-be tellers "live rather than . . . speak their retelling," in this way constructing a "mode of recounting that severely reduces the lives of recounters" (p. 163).

Even an untold story, existing for years in the silence of a life, can come to be told, in words, to someone who enters a life and who may come to be trusted to listen and to care in ways that make its telling, with words, possible. But such telling is never easy. It can, in fact, be incredibly hard, as I learned through my mother's efforts to tell, and especially through her last account. I think that her telling has, on balance, been a good thing–for me as I've come to understand how closely her story of silence is braided with mine of articulated text; for others who, as the bureaucratic descendants of the government that oppressed her, have been forced to come to terms with the experienced reality of her life; and for herself as she, too, comes to terms with who she is now and how she exists, not just as one who survived but as one who vigorously lives.

ON EFFORTS TO RESEARCH SILENCE AND STORY IN ACADEMIC LIVES

What have I learned (what do I continue to learn) from my mother's life, and her story, for my own research, and through it, for my own life?

I have learned, first of all, how closely life and story are intertwined–how life is lived through story and how story lives in life itself. I have also learned that story often lives unworded in people's lives though it is often rendered in other ways, without words. And I have learned that the rendering of story, with words or without, itself becomes a story, though I believe that *this* second story (the meta-story) can, in fact, exist untold and in unrealized or partially realized form in the present day of its enactment. The issue for me, then, is as much the question of "what is this person's story?" as it is "what are we doing with this person's story and with the person herself as we come to know what she 'tells' us, whether conventionally, in words, or without?"

I am trying to make a career of studying lives–and the making and rendering of articulated story–in college and university settings. Initially I did this by joining with senior colleagues who were studying how people with formal leadership responsibilities related to others who did not exist as leaders in the same way.[13] More recently, I have been studying how professors construct themselves as scholars, alone, but also as they relate to others under the rubric of professorial colleagueship and other forms of intellectual relationship. Within this study, I am hypothesizing (that is, "finding" through my own thoughts and, until recently, without data) that professors tell stories of themselves and their lives through the medium of their work, notably through their scholarship, and that their scholarship often stands (at least, in part) as a statement of personal identity.[14] Viewed this way, scholarship–a topic that, by virtue of its "professional" nature, is often separated from life itself–becomes, ironically, an expression of one's personal self in one's work.[15] Though it is hard to imagine scholarship literally as untold story, it might nonetheless be construed as a series of stories of self told unconventionally, that is, through the words and substance and rituals of scholarly practice.

Given this perspective on scholarship, it becomes possible to ask how the story-of-self emerging in a professor's scholarship exists as part of a second story (a meta-story) of how the professor tells her story-of-self-in-her-work to others, and also how others "read" and come to know and feel about her story. As I noted above, this meta-story may itself be largely untold and hard to grasp by those who live within it. It may be more discernable to an outsider (or to a wise insider) who can listen to the holder-of-story while listening as well to others who exist with her, attending to what they all say, but also to what they neglect to say, of themselves and each other.

My aim, in pursuing this line of work, is to salvage the stories-of-self that I believe exist, at least in some professors' scholarly work, in institutional settings that, I fear, often suppress or distort them. I want to know how the organizational worlds, and the worlds of colleagueship in which professors exist day by day, may diminish (or otherwise shape) their stories, for example, through pressures to conform. I particularly want to know how professors may resist and persist in the creation of their stories-of-self through their work, perhaps through alternative inventions of colleagueship and self. And I want to know how we might re-create the settings in which we, as professors, live and work, so as make these settings more conducive to the construction of scholarly work that more authentically reflects our selves, even as we ourselves continue to be shaped by others around us.[16]

Through my mother's story, I have also extended my understanding of how silence may intertwine with articulated story, supporting its very existence as story, but also how silence may itself bear story. I have learned that often both story and, for that matter, data exist as/in that which, in standard terms, is not-story or not-data at all, but which mingles and mixes with the articulated story and data that become the texts of research. The study of unworded story requires the study of that which exists, as con/text–literally, with text–in the spaces between words, in the momentary stops between speakers in conversation with each other. And it requires a research approach that is antithetical to standard research practice that attends mostly to text–to articulation–ignoring the silence that exists with text, behind it, around it.

In particular, I have come to appreciate how research that seeks to find, and possibly to articulate, untold stories raises significant moral issues–for example, the question of what might happen if the subject of a research study should find herself at the center of a clearly articulated meta-story that she herself may never have told–that is, directly, in words–but that the researcher derived by examining the words and actions of this subject in relation to those of other persons existing with and around her. To what extent can untold stories, derived through research that draws from the texts of multiple people existing in a single shared social space (what I have called the meta-story), be shared with the people whom they are about and who might someday tell them, and at what risks? But what risks are involved in neglecting these stories altogether?

I wish to address these questions by discussing an example that emerged in my own work. In 1991 I wrote a paper entitled "Interpreting Silence: Constructing the Role of the Lone Woman in a Male-Dominated Leadership Group." The paper told the story of Elizabeth Collins, Academic Vice President of Meridian College, one of thirty-two sites in the Institutional Leadership Project.[17] Elizabeth Collins was the lone woman on Meridian College's presidential leadership team. Through interviews with the president, other senior administrators, and faculty leaders, I developed a picture of what life was like for Elizabeth Collins as the only woman in the president's "cabinet." I learned that she defined the college and its leadership needs quite differently than did her male colleagues. This recognition drew me to the question of how to pursue the experiences of individuals whose ways of understanding the world place them in the minority. In this case, I found that Collins was uncomfortable with the poor fit between her natural sense of self and the demands of her professional leadership role, but that (as best I could determine) she had not reflected on the source of her discomfort and its origins in the differences between her own conceptions of organization and leadership and those of her male colleagues. Rather, because no one in that site had articulated those differences, they were interpreted by most others as flaws in her leadership abilities, thereby undermining her ability to carry out her job.

I learned also that the president and other male administrators used several strategies in the course of their work that had the consequence, whether intentional or not, of "silencing" Elizabeth Collins. Their actions perpetuated misunderstandings about who she was and what she believed by failing to take advantage of opportunities to interpret her ideas, role, and behaviors to each other and to the college community. Moreover, in their own interactions with Elizabeth Collins, they urged her to temper her natural voice, encouraging her to act and think more like her male colleagues. While Meridian College was widely deemed a successful institution, Elizabeth Collins's contribution to that success was scarcely acknowledged, even though my analysis pointed to the important role that she had played.

The paper was difficult to write. I found myself revisiting and reinterpreting data that I and my colleagues had used primarily to characterize the president and his campus leadership. As I reimmersed myself in the data, the silences–what was not said by and about Elizabeth Collins–became more apparent. The stories we had crafted about Meridian College had left Elizabeth Collins's story untold. Her story was not a comfortable one to tell, in its descriptions of the systematic silencing of a capable individual–doubly so in the way her gender contributed to this silencing–but perhaps even more in its portrayal of the seeming lack of (articulated) insight Elizabeth Collins had about her situation and the forces that shaped it. Collins was uneasy with the demands of her job, her relations with faculty, and her need to submerge her natural self in performing her job. But she did not articulate an understanding of how her role as the lone woman on a male-dominated leadership team could have contributed to her discomfort.

When I presented this paper at a professional meeting, a member of the audience asked if Elizabeth Collins had seen the case report I had written. I replied that she had not. This was largely because of the promises of confidentiality that we had made to our respondents. Because the story of Elizabeth Collins drew on the voices of nine different actors at Meridian College, showing the manuscript to her (or to any of the others) would have immediately divulged the identities and responses of all of these respondents.

While this was a compelling ethical rationale, another moral issue emerged shortly thereafter. A reader of the paper, unaware of the promises of confidentiality my colleagues and I had made to our respondents, questioned the decision not to share this paper with Elizabeth Collins. The reader cast the issue as an ethical one, arguing that Elizabeth Collins had the right to see what I had written about her, and the right to withdraw data about herself that portrayed her as weak or incompetent. This reader invoked Yvonna Lincoln and Egon Guba's principle of member checking in qualitative research, described in *Naturalistic Inquiry*, which involves sharing case reports with respondents who provided the data on which the reports are based. According to Lincoln and Guba, failure to member check abridges the rights of research participants and thus violates the primary ethical imperative in social science research to minimize the potential harm to these participants.[18]

This perspective, however, fails to acknowledge another source of harm to participants that may outweigh the potential harm to respondents stemming from a decision not to member check. In some cases, a research report may tell a story that may be harmful to an informant, perhaps revealing uncomfortable truths or critiquing the status quo or the informant's fundamental assumptions. The risk to a research participant may be especially great when the research is reporting an untold story (in this case, an untold metastory). As I have suggested earlier, some stories may remain untold for good reasons.

I believe that returning "Interpreting Silence" to Elizabeth Collins may well have been harmful to her. Her life at Meridian College was difficult. From my point of view, she had constructed a personal narrative that was clearly at odds with the narrative I constructed through my interviews with her and others but that nonetheless enabled her to live and work in a hostile environment. The story of Elizabeth Collins that I told in "Interpreting Silence" could have burst this delicate bubble. I do not mean to be melodramatic, but the risks are real. My mother's reaction to telling her long-untold story is ample evidence of this.

This moral issue – the potential harmful consequences of telling an untold story–poses some interesting dilemmas for naturalistic inquiry. Lincoln and Guba contend that naturalistic inquiry involves a blurring of the line between researcher and researched, with both parties collaborating equally in collecting and interpreting data.[19] Naturalistic inquiry also involves intense negotiation between researchers and respondents over the collection, analysis, and interpretation of data. How can this be done when stories are untold? Will respondents be willing to participate in research projects that may lead to results and interpretations that make them sad, angry, or uncomfortable?

The process of naturalistic inquiry proposed by Lincoln and Guba leads to the disconcerting conclusion that it may not be ethical to study–or to report–untold stories. This runs counter to the critical tradition of much qualitative interpretive research. Although there are no clear-cut solutions to a dilemma such as this, it seems to me that it should be possible simultaneously to pursue the telling of untold stories and to protect research participants from the harm that might come from exposing them to these untold stories. It is possible that, in some aspects of naturalistic research (for example, in the pursuit of untold stories), there can be no general methodological rules that apply uniformly to a class of research settings but rather that decisions to tell or not to tell all or part of a subject's story are part of the complicated, particularistic, ungeneralizable, and very human stuff that comprises this research endeavor. In this case, the potential harm of returning an untold story to a respondent, who may have a very hard time living with what s/he learns from it, may overshadow the potential harm of withholding the interpretation from the respondent.[20]

If untold stories come to exist in our research, inasmuch as I believe they already exist in our everyday lives, then we will need to think through, with extraordinary care, what it means to relate to the people who exist in our studies in much the same way we think through what it means to relate to those who exist in our lives every day.

CODA

My mother often tells me how awkward she feels that she never finished her education, that she doesn't have a high school or college degree, that her English is not smooth or refined, when so many around her–especially her children–have, in her eyes, accomplished so much. I wonder if, when she reads this paper, she'll realize how this daughter, who's "finished with school" so many times over, who's credentialed to the hilt, and who writes and speaks in this American world with relative ease, still struggles to learn–from what her mother seems always to have known–what it means to create and preserve a story of self in a life (yes, even a scholarly life) so thickly inscribed with others who struggle to do the same.

POSTSCRIPTS, 1994–1995

On my mother. I wrote this chapter in 1993 with my mother's knowledge and encouragement. But when she read my draft, she wanted to know why I had revealed her lack of a formal education. This was not something she was proud of; rather, it was something she wanted to hide. I talked to her—as did Aaron—about the difference between really learning and mere schooling (though not in these words), and that to us, the former (which reflected so much of her life) meant so much more than the latter (to which she had so little access). So to make up for any possible mischaracterization of what this woman has done with her life, as a learner and maker of her own and others' stories, I add the following:

My mother compensated for her loss of schooling by reading Hebrew translations of Tolstoy and Shakespeare, among others, an unusual endeavor in the Israel of the 1950s. In her lifetime she has been both fluent and literate in seven languages: Romanian, French, Yiddish, German, Hebrew, Spanish, and English. She maintained, in Franklin's Store, an incredible bookkeeping system, personally tracking, with paper and pencil, thousands of accounts over the years, and with them the lives and faces and words of the people whose names they bore. Although she had access to an adding machine, she was actually faster in the computations she carried out in her head, and no one but no one ever caught her in error. She handled all her own and, in his late years, my father's affairs, and she seemed to have no trouble at all bringing the bureaucracies of schools, hospitals, department stores, nursing homes, and Medicare itself to their knees. She's far better versed in world affairs and community affairs, and the personal affairs of those around her, than I will ever be. And to this day, neither my sister nor I nor her friends can keep her in books.

I can only begin to imagine how rich and full and clear, how accomplished and refined, her story might have been had it just been cast somewhere else and in some other time.

On others who have written this with me. In writing this chapter, I learned that in composing autobiography, I do not (and cannot) write only about myself; I write also about others in whose presence I become my self. But I also learned that I do not (and cannot) write only *by* myself. I am indebted to those who have read and talked and listened and, literally, written with me, in particular . . . to Aaron Pallas with whom I talked (and continue to talk) incessantly about lives and about research, and who, in many substantive ways, shares in the authoring of all my autobiographical endeavors; to Penelope Peterson whose careful questions helped me realize that what I search for in others' lives, even as untold story, has sources in my own, untold as that may be; to Chris Clark who responded to me in ways that helped me discern what I was just beginning to sense. My thanks also to Maxine Greene, Steve Weiland, Estela Bensimon, Diane Holt-Reynolds, and Sheryl Welte for encouragement and helpful comments. My deepest thanks, of course, are to Judith Fuhrer Neumann for letting me tell a piece of my story in the terms of a story that is hers.

NOTES

1. This paper was entitled "On Experience, Memory, and Knowing: A Post-Holocaust (Auto)Biography." For thoughtful commentary on differences between the language of the camps and the language of post-Holocaust existence, see Lawrence L. Langer's *Holocaust Testimonies: The Ruins of Memory* and Sander Gilman's *Inscribing the Other*, especially Chapter 13, "To Quote Primo Levi: 'If You Don't Speak Yiddish, You're Not a Jew,'" pp. 293–316.

2. "Lives as Texts," Henry Greenspan's examination of how Holocaust survivors recount their lives, contributed in important ways to my understanding of untold stories and to unconventional modes of "telling."

3. When quoting or referring to myself at earlier times in my life, and occasionally when quoting others, I use a bracketed asterisk [*] to indicate a belief or statement, articulated by the speaker, and which was later corrected; the correction is noted elsewhere in this chapter. For example, the bracketed asterisks in this narrative indicate that at one time in my life I believed that my mother had been forced to stop school when she was in fifth grade, that an aunt taught her privately for a brief time after this, and that her youngest brother was taken away by Russian soldiers. As I indicate in later text, I learned, through conversations years later, that she actually left school when she was in eighth grade, that a cousin taught her, and that her brother was abducted by "Jewish policemen" collaborating with Nazis in Transnistria. When no correction appears later in the chapter, I note the correction after the asterisk.

4. See Neumann, 1992a.

5. I have found interview-based accounts of how other sons and daughters of survivors learned their parents' stories to resonate closely with mine. An example is Helen Epstein's *Children of the Holocaust*. One respondent in this book says, "The fact that it wasn't talked about made me know it more. . . . [My parent] would lapse into thoughtfulness and for me the lapse was an answer. . . . I don't know how or where or when I heard stories from the war. It's as if they came through thin air to my ear" (p. 179). Epstein, herself the daughter of survivors, adds, "Like most survivors neither [of my parents] imagined how, over the years, I had stored their remarks, their glances, their silences inside me, how I had deposited them in my iron box like

pennies in a piggy bank. They were unconscious of how much a child gleans from the absence of explanation as much as from words" (p. 335). In *In the Shadow of the Holocaust: The Second Generation*, Aaron Haas quotes the adult children of Holocaust survivors describing how they learned of their parents' lives, for example, by attending to "snippet[s]" and "tidbits" (p. 74), "bits and pieces" (p. 82), and to "undercurrent[s] . . . often nonverbal" in family talk (p. 71), which they then constructed into stories themselves. "'The story,'" said one interviewee, "seeped into my consciousness in an accidental manner since the age of six'" (p. 69). Other works that consider the intergenerational transmission of survivor stories include Randolph L. Braham's *The Psychological Perspectives of the Holocaust and of Its Aftermath*, Art Spiegelman's *Maus: A Survivor's Tale* and *Maus II: A Survivor's Tale: And Here My Troubles Began*, and Dina Wardi's *Memorial Candles: Children of the Holocaust*.

6. According to Martin Gilbert, in *Atlas of the Holocaust*, on the eve of World War II, the city of Suceava had the third largest Jewish population in Bukovina, a region in northern Romania.

7. In the text that follows, I use a double slash (//) to indicate a stop or break in the speaker's flow of words as recorded on tape. I use three dots (. . .) to indicate deletion of one or more words on tape.

8. In the introduction to *Jagendorf's Foundry*, Aron Hirt-Manheimer describes Transnistria as "an artificial geographic entity that existed from 1941 to 1944" (p. xxvi). Located in the western Ukraine east of the Dneister River, it was about twice the size of New Jersey. In fall of 1941 the Romanian government deported between 140,000 and 150,000 Jews from Bukovina, Bessarabia, and Dorohoi (all regions of Romania at that time) to ghettos, labor camps, and concentration camps in Transnistria. As best I can determine, the area which was Transnistria is over 150 miles north and east of Suceava.

9. Gilbert, p. 73.

10. In his edited volume of Siegfried Jagendorf's memoirs, Aron Hirt-Manheimer references a small literature on Romanian Jews' incarceration in Transnistria, including *The Forgotten Holocaust, Holocaustul Uitat*, by Ion C. Butnaru, and *Transnistria: The Forgotten Cemetery*, by Julius S. Fischer.

11. I worry that the juxtaposition of Auschwitz and Transnistria, viewed in terms of my parents' experiences in the war, will be interpreted, by some readers, as a gender issue in which the man's story dominates (that is, silences) that of the woman. While my father held fairly traditional views of men's and women's roles in society and in the family, the dominance of his story and the relative silence of my mother's appears related to far larger and more complicated issues concerned with the social construction of historical text. Stories derived from other survivor families bear out this proposition, as in this interview with a woman whose mother was interned at Auschwitz and whose father was deported to Transnistria (the exact opposite of my family's experience): "'My father doesn't talk about it much . . . it doesn't become a very melodramatic issue at all. From what I understand, the Germans arrived in Rumania relatively late. My father was in what they call a work camp for three years. I have no idea where, I really am ashamed to say. Somehow, we always minimized my father's experiences. In work camps, where he was, people did not get killed. They

just worked, like prisoners of war in so-called normal circumstances. . . . My mother and her family were taken to Auschwitz the last years of the war . . . '" (Epstein, 1979, pp. 119–120).

12. Mary Gergen also refers to this view of story in "Life Stories: Pieces of a Dream" in the volume *Storied Lives*.

13. Some examples of my research on college and university leadership include Neumann, 1991, 1992a, 1992b, 1995a, 1995b, and Bensimon and Neumann, 1993. These studies focus on the cognitive and symbolic aspects of academic leadership viewed as interactions among administrators and faculty, and among administrative peers, particularly during financially stressed times. Several of these articles have emphasized how people who are not in leadership positions make sense of their leaders' words and actions, and how leaders themselves make sense of their own roles and others' responses to them.

14. My initial explorations of this topic are recorded in a working paper entitled "The Ties that Bind: Notes on Professorial Colleagueship as Academic Context," a literature review constructed in autobiographical perspective. I have also initiated a three-year longitudinal, interview-based study of professors' learning, scholarly identity, and colleagueship after tenure in order to study professors' engagement in scholarship in the early stages of mid-career. Though this study focuses on others, it is strongly self-reflexive in that I am, by virtue of the date of my tenure, a member of the generation of faculty I am studying. Early results of this study are reported in a working paper, "'What Do I Do Next?': Constructions of Self as Scholar in the First Post-Tenure Year." Though I began this line of work in reflection between several literatures and my own life story, I have recently brought the stories of others to bear on my learning as well. I consider my writing in and editing of this volume as further extension of this work.

15. Susan Krieger's *Social Science and the Self: Personal Essays on an Art Form* helped me to shape this view.

16. For an elaboration of this perspective, see Dorinne K. Kondo's *Crafting Selves: Power, Gender, and Discourses of Identity in a Japanese Workplace*.

17. I worked as assistant director of the Institutional Leadership Project, a five-year national study of college and university leadership supported by the National Center for Postsecondary Governance and Finance, from 1986 to 1990; the project is described in my publications on this topic. "Meridian College" was one of the study institutions; all names and titles, of persons and places, are pseudonymous.

18. See Lincoln and Guba, 1989.

19. See Lincoln and Guba, 1989, and Lincoln, 1993.

20. There are times when the masking of identity in research reports, and the withholding of other information about a research site, has greater import for what persons at the site might learn from reading the report than what readers existing outside the site might learn from reading it. In such cases a researcher will need to think through how much of the report should be withheld, and in what ways, both in terms of what the general public will see and what individuals on site may learn about themselves and each other.

BIBLIOGRAPHY

Bensimon, Estela M., and Anna Neumann. 1993. *Redesigning Collegiate Leadership: Teams and Teamwork in Higher Education*. Baltimore: Johns Hopkins University Press.

Braham, Randolph L., ed. 1988. *The Psychological Perspectives of the Holocaust and of Its Aftermath*. Boulder, CO: Social Science Monographs.

Butnaru, Ion C. 1985. *The Forgotten Holocaust, Holocaustul Uitat*. Tel Aviv. Cited by Aron Hirt-Manheimer, ed., *Jagendorf's Foundry: A Memoir of the Romanian Holocaust, 1941–1944*, by Siegfried Jagendorf. New York: HarperCollins, 1991.

Epstein, Helen. 1979. *Children of the Holocaust: Conversations with Sons and Daughters of Survivors*. New York: Penguin.

Fischer, Julius S. 1969. *Transnistria: The Forgotten Cemetery*. New York. Cited by Aron Hirt-Manheimer, ed., *Jagendorf's Foundry: A Memoir of the Romanian Holocaust, 1941–1944*, by Siegfried Jagendorf. New York: HarperCollins, 1991.

Gergen, Mary. 1992. "Life Stories: Pieces of a Dream." In *Storied Lives: The Cultural Politics of Self-Understanding*, George C. Rosenwald and Richard L. Ochberg, eds. New Haven, CT: Yale University Press, 127–144.

Gilbert, Martin. 1993. *Atlas of the Holocaust*, rev. ed. New York: William Morrow.

Gilman, Sander. 1991. *Inscribing the Other*. Lincoln: University of Nebraska Press.

Greenspan, Henry. 1992. "Lives as Texts: Symptoms as Modes of Recounting in the Life Histories of Holocaust Survivors." In *Storied Lives: The Cultural Politics of Self-Understanding*, George C. Rosenwald and Richard L. Ochberg, eds. New Haven, CT: Yale University Press, 145–164.

Haas, Aaron. 1990. *In the Shadow of the Holocaust: The Second Generation*. Ithaca, NY: Cornell University Press.

Hirt-Manheimer, Aron, ed. 1991. Introduction to *Jagendorf's Foundry: A Memoir of the Romanian Holocaust, 1941–1944*, by Siegfried Jagendorf. New York: HarperCollins, xi–xxix.

Kondo, Dorinne K. 1990. *Crafting Selves: Power, Gender, and Discourses of Identity in a Japanese Workplace*. Chicago: University of Chicago Press.

Krieger, Susan. 1991. *Social Science and the Self: Personal Essays on an Art Form*. New Brunswick, NJ: Rutgers University Press.

Langer, Lawrence L. 1991. *Holocaust Testimonies: The Ruins of Memory*. New Haven: Yale University Press.

Lincoln, Yvonna S. 1993. "I and Thou: Method, Voice, and Roles in Research With the Silenced." In *Naming Silenced Lives: Personal Narratives and the Process of Educational Change*, Daniel McLaughlin and William G. Tierney, eds. New York: Routledge, 29–50.

Lincoln, Yvonna S., and Egon G. Guba. 1985. *Naturalistic Inquiry*. Beverly Hills, CA: Sage.

Lincoln, Yvonna S., and Egon G. Guba. 1989. "Ethics: The Failure of Positivist Science." *The Review of Higher Education* 12(3):221–240.

Neumann, Anna. 1991. "The Thinking Team: Toward a Cognitive Model of Administrative Teamwork in Higher Education." *The Journal of Higher Education* 62(5): 485–513.

Neumann, Anna. 1992a. "Colleges Under Pressure: Budgeting, Presidential Competence, and Faculty Uncertainty." *Leadership Quarterly* 3(3):191–215.

Neumann, Anna. 1992b. "Double Vision: The Experience of Institutional Stability." *The Review of Higher Education* 15(4):341–371.

Neumann, Anna. 1992c. "On Experience, Memory, and Knowing: A Post-Holocaust (Auto)Biography." Paper presented at the annual meeting of the Association for the Study of Higher Education, Minneapolis.

Neumann, Anna. 1993. "The Ties that Bind: Notes on Professorial Colleagueship as Academic Context." Paper presented at the annual meeting of the American Educational Research Association, Atlanta.

Neumann, Anna. 1995a. "Context, Cognition and Culture: A Case Analysis of Collegiate Leadership and Cultural Change." *American Educational Research Journal* 32(2):251–279.

Neumann, Anna. 1995b. "On the Making of Hard Times and Good Times: The Social Construction of Resource Stress." *The Journal of Higher Education* 66(1):3–31.

Neumann, Anna. 1995c. "'What Do I Do Next?': Constructions of Self as Scholar in the First Post-Tenure Year." Paper presented at the annual meeting of the American Educational Research Association, San Francisco.

Spiegelman, Art. 1986. *Maus, a Survivor's Tale*. New York: Pantheon.

Spiegelman, Art. 1991. *Maus II: A Survivor's Tale: And Here My Troubles Began*. New York: Pantheon.

Wardi, Dina. 1992. *Memorial Candles: Children of the Holocaust*. London: Tavistock/Routledge.

Clockwise from top:
Kathryn H. Au
Anna Neumann & Judith F. Neumann
Maxine Greene
Martha Montero-Sieburth

Photo by Sandy Middlebrooks

Photo by Jane Hoffer

Clockwise from top:
Nel Noddings
Concha Delgado-Gaitan
Penelope L. Peterson
Gloria Ladson-Billings

Photo by Leidner Studios

Photo by Don Fraser

Photo by Bruce A. Fox

From top:
Patricia J. Gumport
Ellen Condliffe Lagemann

Photo by Visual Art Services/Steve Gladfelter

Photo © Jeff Dodge

* *CHAPTER 7* *

The Weaving of Personal Origins and Research: *Reencuentro y Reflexión en la Investigación*

Martha Montero-Sieburth

LIKE THE THREADS IN A Mexican Indian weaving, representing visible color lines that can be followed until they become knots in life's cloth, my research expresses cultural, language, and social differences that make me who I am. Unlike some other weavings, mine is threaded from the mixture of soft-washed European wool mixed with raw, naturally colored Latin American burly wool. Close-up, the knots in my weaving reveal an intricate combination of multicolored woolen threads–uneven in size, rough with burrs and thorns, and exquisitely variable in deep earth tones–in their complexity much like each research project I have worked on. Yet, just as each research experience becomes woven into a continuum of many and is strengthened by what comes before and after, so each knot on its own exudes the strength and durability that comes only from being braided together as a whole. Viewed from a distance, the individual knots disappear against the dominant backdrop of stamped bright colors. The conglomerate design of the weaving mirrors the form and meaning of my life's learning and research experiences.

At the risk of overextending the weaving metaphor, I will use it to identify different moments in which my life has been inexorably intertwined with re-search (the search for knowledge), reflection (the paused mirroring of my own and others' experiences), and investigation (the deep inquiry of issues and why things are the way they appear to be).

FIRST KNOT: CHILDHOOD REFLECTIONS

As a baby boomer of Costa Rican and Mexican parentage, I discovered that even though these two countries share a language, the differences in meanings

Learning from Our Lives: Women, Research, and Autobiography in Education. ISBN 0-8077-3593-0 (pbk), ISBN 0-8077-3594-9 (cloth).

between the Spanish of one and the other may, at times, be embarrassingly great. One single word could have opposite meanings from one country to another and without your knowing could end up shaming you as well as others. Innocent words such as *güila*, which meant "child" in Costa Rica, referred to a lady of the night in Mexico; *pisar*, which throughout Latin America literally means "to step on something or someone," connoted copulation in Costa Rica; *chingar*, which as a verb in Mexico literally means "to fornicate or to send someone to hell," in Costa Rican usage means "being totally naked" as an adjective, or as a noun refers to the butt of a cigarette. Distinguishing between colloquial uses of Spanish depended upon my acquiring the sensitivities of "appropriateness" within each culture and hence maintaining the decorum that was expected.

Keeping such distinctive language usages straight was difficult as I was growing up, but learning English proved to be an even greater challenge; it was a language that was neither written the way it sounded nor spoken the way it was written. When I was brought to the United States at age three, I had heard French spoken as a first language by my Belgian grandmother in Costa Rica and Spanish as the colloquial language of the home. English was clearly the language learned outside the home as well as the expected norm of the school. Yet because I had already developed an ear for the phonetic structure of Spanish, I found it hard to learn English through rote memorization and drills.

Instead I turned to *Little Lulu* comic books, where I identified with Lulu, her dark curls and wit. Little Lulu was a comic strip character of the 1950s who was portrayed as having brains and as outsmarting Tubby, another character in the strip. I used language cues and accents in ways that let me outsmart others who thought I would have difficulty with English. Lulu outwitted people like a trickster, and, borrowing from her, I learned not just to read but to read between the lines and with the appropriate accent. In other words, I came to see the learning of a language as like learning to take a standardized test. I mastered the process so that I became quite proficient in many types of English usage and displays and could readily fit. Later on in life, the chameleonlike adaptability that I learned from Lulu and other sources allowed me to perfect a southern or Texas drawl, a midwestern twang, and even an eastern effect in the presence of people from each of these areas.

This sense of making choices and searching for appropriate cues–regarding when to speak, in what language, with what accent and inflection, and with what voice projection–probably affected my own sensibility in designing and conducting research. I have learned to hear and respect the voices of others and to not speak for "them." In doing research, I have chosen to become an instrument to channel the unstated ideas, or words, or meanings people share when using their own voices. In this respect, I have become suspicious of research that sets out to empower communities, because I know that no one can empower another. Rather, I have come to appreciate that one may serve as a catalyst to create the space within which others may discover their power. Thus having the knowledge about what communities are really like in their everyday life requires more than spending time in the field. It means actually understanding the negotiations that take place, the contradictions that exist, and the interpretations people have of the rhythms of their lives. Few researchers live in the communities they study; they are "outsiders" despite their constancy within a community. Gaining access to the "inside" histories of people's lives and becoming part of the fabric that binds people together can only be approximated. Thus, I often wonder, who is speaking for whom in such studies?

SECOND KNOT: TRICULTURAL EXISTENCE

Aside from language, there have been other obstacles to overcome in my life of research and reflection. Moving in and out of different contexts during my childhood and teenage years, between the 1940s and 1960s, provided me with a dual and, in some cases, triple existence–living and studying in Mexico, visiting with family in Costa Rica, and living and studying in different parts of the United States. I developed a veritable catalogue of different schools, approximately ten in all, over a wide geographical range, from elementary schools in Mexico, South Dakota, Kansas, Nebraska, and Connecticut to high schools in Texas and Mexico. The last high school I attended forbade the use of Spanish because the policy of the school was that the only way to perfect one's English was by speaking English all the time. The price I paid for indulging in my mother tongue is ever present in the collection of demerit slips that I still conserve as a reminder of my language transgressions. I did not think then how the foundation of one's language can be so readily and symbolically violated.

I grew used to accepting such differences and attempting to balance the demands of the U.S. mainstream culture with my own. As the strangeness of the newfound culture wore off, I began to adjust by recognizing that I was being defined not by my country of origin but by the categories of race, color, and minority status that prevailed. If I did not think of myself as a minority, I simply became one by being Hispanic. My *mestizo* (mixed Indian, Spanish, and European backgrounds) became categorically a single race, derived solely from my Spanish-speaking roots. I became cast in the rubric of the "other" when I entered the United States and ended up being classified under the categories designated for whites, Hispanics, Asians, or blacks in my later years.

Closer to home, the class-based differences in my Mexican and Costa Rican backgrounds represent more accurate approximations of who I am. The saying "Dime con quién andas, y te diré quién eres" (Tell me who you are with, and I will tell you who you are) rings home, as I attempt to identify myself in Mexican and Costa Rican class-conscious societies. I came to appreciate the soulfulness of my Mexican relatives, their closeness to the earth, religious and mystical fervor, and respect for wisdom, mostly carried on by my grandmother and the women in the family. Such wisdom often made me think of my mother's family as being matriarchal, where women made hard choices, sometimes of life and death. Their pragmatism and realism about life and death stand out in my mind as symbols of their resilience. These women lived through the Mexican Revolution, experienced single-parenting, were married and then divorced, lived out the gender differences of a traditional Mexico, and lost family members to death. Their way of life contrasts sharply with the more formal, highly educated, continental European lifestyle of my Costa Rican family, where males became the professionals and decision makers of the family. I found it ironic that even though both families shared a common language and general culture, the differences between contexts, class, and behaviors were dramatic.

Both families believed that females had no need to study beyond secondary school. Going on to a university was a privilege only expected by and granted to males. In fact, my role as a future wife and mother was already defined, despite my own desire for further education. However, because all of the males in my father's family had access to study and obtained professional degrees, a tradition of educational advancement was established by my great-grandfather, who was a historian and educator, my grandfather, who became a psychiatrist, and my father, who also became a doctor. In my case, such patriarchal capital created the space for me to follow in their footsteps and to become the first female in both families to complete a doctorate. This does not mean that the women in my family, particularly on my mother's side, were not influential in helping me set goals. On the contrary, even though my grandmother and aunts could not break out of their traditional roles, and my female cousins resisted such roles—for example, by leaving the family, marrying young, or simply rebelling—the defiance of these women taught me to be persistent and resilient. My cousins defied the status quo set by the patriarchy by being feminists while also being feminine. They could be outspoken and direct while being captivating in their dresses and latest hairstyles. Although my cousins were not educated beyond high school, they taught me to have access to the power males had achieved. They believed in having an education, a privilege denied them. That privilege I have passed on to my children.

As great as the differences between these two families were, they seemed minor compared with the acute differences, particularly around issues of identity, encountered by my immediate family within the U.S. context. Questions about *who you are* and *how you are defined* assume inordinate importance when you are defined immediately as the "other." Learning about your own heritage and background become even more pressing issues, not just as survival mechanisms but, more importantly, as a means to define yourself, before you are defined.

Undoubtedly, my own vision of research and the biases I have are colored by the types of multicultural differences I have experienced. I often felt as if I were, in the words of a popular Latino song, "neither from here nor there" but most likely "everywhere."

THIRD KNOT: EARLY RESEARCH EXPERIENCE

Re-search probably began with my earliest childhood experiences when I uncovered the lens of reality with which researchers frame their inquiry questions. I lived, for close to thirteen years, on the grounds of several state-run mental institutions in the United States where my Costa Rican father was a psychiatrist in residence. The world of the mental hospital appeared from the outside to be secluded and private, in contrast to the life of hustle and bustle beyond. Yet within the grounds of the hospital, life went on with daily routines, public displays by patients, and events such as dances, which I attended. The hospital and its environs became the site of my first field experiences. I had at my disposal a unique culture where I could venture forth and avidly explore peculiarities to which many were not privy.

I understood that the purpose of mental hospitals was to take care of people who were mentally disturbed, the *loquitos* (the crazy ones), as my mother would often say. Yet through my father's work, I discovered that many of the patients who were interned were not actually ill but were wards of the state who had been committed by families unwilling to send them to nursing homes, because of the costs involved. Thus, within these settings, I was exposed to many patients who were mentally healthy yet could not be part of the outside world and in their loneliness sought friendships. Over time, I acquired many pseudo-grandmothers, who shared their stories of woe and resilience as they looked after me. These adopted grandmothers spent hours mentoring me, as they would have their own grandchildren. Missing my own paternal and maternal grandmothers from Costa Rica and Mexico, I found their care rewarding. I learned to listen to their oral histories, heard their pain, took mental notes about who they were, and observed their demeanor. They became the basis of my later interest in collecting oral histories of different women.[1]

I also observed another side of mental illness through experiences ranging from hearing cries in the night from unknown sources to witnessing patients who sat staring fixedly within their cagelike cells–knowing they had lives to speak of but were mute. I simply came to accept the culture of the state hospital as it was. It was orderly, ritualistic, and organized around the patients and doctors. Yet because there were not many children to play with, I found myself learning to play "imaginary golf" with Ms. Ellis, one of the adult female patients. I knew, even then, there was no real golf ball, but Ms. Ellis's elation at "teeing off" and sending me to retrieve the golf ball from the bushes presented such a euphoric demand that I could not disappoint her. Ms. Ellis's admonitions taught me a great deal about playing golf "by the rules." I learned to follow her directions carefully, a lesson that has served me well in fieldwork. I have learned to rely on being guided by others as I attempt to learn about their cultures. As a stranger, the more I allow myself to know the context through their eyes, words, and wisdom, the greater is the perspective I gain.

That status of stranger influenced the way I learned to do ethnographic research. In my anthropology classes in the 1960s, I learned to study a given culture or cultural group through the use of informants. However, by the 1970s that typology had given way to the concept of learning through co-researchers, or co-members of a team, people within a cultural context who actively constructed reality from different perspectives, including their own. During the 1980s and 1990s, I learned to acknowledge that even co-membership in research was not enough. "Giving voice and legitimacy" to those with whom you work and participate seems to make perfect sense. In such relationships the notion of subject-object (the researcher studying the "other") becomes one of subject-subject (the researcher becoming the "other," and the "other" becoming the researcher). Today, the notion of teacher as researcher or community member as researcher is commonplace in my research repertoire.[2]

What I gained from these reality-testing experiences between the imaginary and the real helped me develop several perspectives that I have used in framing and designing research. I have come to respect the insider's and outsider's perspective (the emic and etic) as sacred, having learned that communities do forge their own cultures. I have also understood that the framing of questions is as important as gaining the participants' meaning and formulating a working hypothesis. I have learned to listen intently as I probe with open-ended questions. I know that the wealth of experience gained will depend on the comfort, confidentiality, and trust shared, so that participants are able to share their stories safely. I have also learned to be heard, making sure that I anticipate needing to negotiate, negotiate, and renegotiate my entry each time into the community. Research is not about uncovering a reality but rather the multiple realities of any given situation. Thus my past experience of being a newcomer and "learning by the rules," of raising my own consciousness of the imagined and the real, the fictional and nonfictional, the mentally healthy and mentally ill, has influenced my research. I have often wondered whether Ms. Ellis knew she was mentally ill or whether, like me, she was also willing to forgo reality, intent on playing and willing to pretend in order to have a playmate. Our individual realities were bridged through play, and our engagement allowed us to "see" the golf ball as a means to interact with each other. In retrospect, I wonder if this is not the sort of negotiation that constitutes the basis for conducting "good" research.

As an adolescent, I learned to take notes while my father interviewed his patients about their life histories. Groomed as his secretary, I learned to use shorthand as another vehicle for communicating ideas, much like learning another language. As my father dictated his scribbled notes to me, in order to develop his case histories, terms such as *schizophrenia*, *paranoia*, and *manic depression* became secondhand vocabulary for me. With awe, I watched as my father interviewed patients, masterfully incising their minds through the types of words and questions he raised. The precision with which he drew out their childhood memories and stories in order to assess their present illnesses gave full credence and meaning to his "having a clinical eye." In witnessing such sessions, I discovered the power of description in the notes I took, finding myself captivated by the patients' innermost secrets and explanations of their sexual histories and behaviors, as well as the descriptions of their current illnesses. Little did I know that I was already doing fieldwork and had begun to search and reflect about people's hidden meanings.

I rarely looked at the patients directly during those sessions, since I was intent on not missing a word and focused carefully on the note taking. Yet as I reread these notes, I found refuge in their use of simple words and actions. Their language, once removed from their mouths, became another symbolic structure in the hands of the specialist. The rawness evinced by sadness, fear, shame, guilt, and rage became subdued and artificially transformed into convoluted and complex notions of "paranoia," "schizophrenia," or "manic depression." Their individual idiosyncrasies gave way to generic and all-encompassing labels. With single words, their essence became transformed, and in some cases, the power of the new labels seemed to obliterate their spirits.

As a grown person, I experienced the same sense of powerlessness when confronted with terms such as *at-risk students*, *disadvantaged or deprived populations*, or *culture of poverty*—terms directed at Latinos/as, African Americans, and anyone who was not from the mainstream, dominant Anglo culture. I could see how glibly these terms were applied by researchers during the 1960s, even into the 1990s, to explain the "culture of failure" of certain ethnic groups. I wonder whether the converse would be true in studying and describing mainstream Americans? Would the labels be so portentous or foreboding, or would they simply speak of privilege and status as a given?

These initial experiences of uncovering the patients' illnesses through the use of monolithic terms that defined their lot and explained away their differences represented some of my primary insights into re-search, the search for knowledge. This includes unraveling packed ideas and notions back to their essential reality, their unique meaning. Thus growing into adulthood in the mid-1960s, I once again experienced the explaining of differences, but this time in the American heartland.

FOURTH KNOT: COMING OF AGE

The notion of home as a place, or a location where a person lived, became in my life a state of being. The push and pull of families between Mexico, Costa Rica, and the United States created a constant adaptation and readaptation of experiences. Thus the *frontera*, or United States–Mexican border, became a revolving door for our entry and reentry. Crossing the border became a commonplace expectation. It seemed as though we grew restless and needed to refuel back in Mexico but at the same time needed to return to the United States to follow my father's residencies in different states and to sustain our education. Thus we went back and forth between Mexico and different parts of the United States to attend schools, visit with relatives, and deal with family illnesses and deaths. In total, we crossed the border more than a hundred times. Returning to the United States often meant moving from one state to another, but it also meant learning new things and having the latest fashions. Such catapulting between homes, languages, and friends meant roots were not set down anywhere. It also meant that except for the emotional ups and downs of living in two countries, the notion of a border was always blurred. I came to expect rejection from both my Mexican friends and American colleagues. My Mexican counterparts often called me a *pocha* (an Anglicized Mexican) whenever I spoke Spanish with a slight Anglo accent or used Anglo words. My American counterparts would spout off a litany of words associated with Mexicans—*bean eater*, *frito bandido*, *taco bender*—or other derogatory stereotypes when I announced I was Mexican. Had I not been secure about my identity during that time, I would probably have suffered from low self-esteem and a feeling I did not belong. Yet this derision of Mexicans, and Latinos in general, served only to make me even prouder of my Mexican and Costa Rican heritages. What mattered was the way I saw and knew myself. I knew the richness inherent in Latino cultures and I saw my cultural background as a source of strength, not weakness. I was not willing to allow the bad-mouthing to reflect upon the 5,000-year-old traditions of my Spanish and Indian cultures.

I realized in time that my unique differences, of which I was proud, were perceived by others as negative and contrary to the assimilation and accommodation expected of immigrants to the United States. I learned to adopt a chameleonlike response to such difficult situations and resolved to take the best of American culture along with my own. Being a chameleon, I *chose* the situations in which I would blend–for example, matching the words and actions of my acquaintances of the moment–and those in which I would assert my differences. The latter required teaching others about Mexicans and Costa Ricans, a process that could become tiresome if the learners had no *real* interest. Hence it was through judging situations that I decided to roll with the punches or to defy ignorance with knowledge.

During my last two years of college, I studied at a mid-western women's Methodist college, where I was the only Latina. Given my background, I found sock hops, engagement-ring parties, panty raids, and "mooning" of people to be strange social rituals but accepted these as part of the rites of passage of American college life. Where I could be myself was in some of my classes, like the "Sociology of Deviance" and "Urban Sociology," where the professor in charge initiated us into mini-research projects on issues that interested us.

Some of my first insights about applied research in different contexts emerged here, where I became observant of my milieu and midwestern culture. Attempting to investigate what prejudices existed in this college town, where "town and gown" differences were marked, I began to interview townspeople and students about their own sense of well-being. This allowed me to conduct forays into the countryside and into people's homes. The results indicated that not only were the college students not welcomed by the townspeople, but black students in particular were denied access to the local barbershops and dance places. Issues of injustice began to surface for me. I questioned the purpose of social science research in its outcomes and felt that it should be used to document the processes of inequality that persisted. Not finding actual reasons for the townspeople to negate black students' access to services, I led a boycott against the only local barbershop and stood with a crowd of students while Kiri, my friend from Kenya, had his hair cut. I also frequented the dance places where Kiri and other friends enjoyed dancing to southern and African tunes and I to Latin American rhythms. We learned to avoid the crowds of white males with chains who awaited us at the front door by leaving through the back door.

Such experiences shattered my naiveté and led me to consider reflective action, that is, to use research to identify, name, and document the processes of discriminatory actions. I spent my senior year in the community, documenting the factors that seemed to sustain the "separate but equal" mentality of the town.

FIFTH KNOT: ACADEMIC SOCIALIZATION

Once in graduate school in the late 1960s, during the heyday of the Vietnam War, I took courses in anthropology and met Jules Henry. As an anthropologist, sociologist, philosopher, and educator who was concerned with the relations among culture, personality, education, and socialization, he was known on the Washington University campus for his criticism of social scientists who did not oppose the Vietnam War. His daily impassioned messages on his door reminded me that social scientists could not avoid ethical and moral concerns.

In class, Henry challenged our conformity by pointing out the fallacies of our naiveté. To him, the role of anthropology in education was a quest for philosophical understanding. Many of the readings for his classes were from classical literature. He showed us how social science research originated with the ideas of the Greek and Roman writers. By grounding our learning in history and tracing the origins of ethnographic research to the enlightened principles embodied in Greek and Roman thought as well as the grand theories of the British school of anthropology and the American development of the field through Franz Boas, Ruth Benedict, and Margaret Mead, he helped us comprehend global, cross-cultural understanding before the field was popularized. His own research in urban schools influenced much of today's discourse in urban education.

Henry was not content with describing a culture. He unyieldingly challenged the mores and norms of that culture by making the connections between theory and practice explicit. *Culture Against Man* is perhaps one of the most incisive books to challenge the state of American culture during the 1960s. Henry is especially well known for his analysis of how the technological drivenness of American society (where even fun must be orchestrated) defines humans after age forty as obsolescent. His classic description of high school life and its psychological boundaries for students presents a set of issues as compelling today as they were during the 1960s. His chapter on nursing homes and the dehumanization of patients by staff in such homes became painfully poignant when he himself was placed in a nursing home after suffering an embolism. Notable among the qualities that Henry asked of researchers was a commitment to examine closely the implicit messages of our everyday life, which are so often sustained solely through our unwillingness to be critical.

For me, his influence lies in the power of his critique, particularly evident in the arena of American education, which he considered to be "education for stupidity" or "aimlessness." His critique in defining social policy for educational purposes had an impact upon my own research. Henry believed that social science, rather than simply describing change, needed to be instrumental in creating it. He was influential in helping the government of Mexico develop its socialist educational plan under President Cardenas in the 1940s. In the 1960s, Henry created a unique typology in his *Current Anthropology* article, "A Cross-Cultural Outline of Education," which addresses the universal factors affecting learning–the very processes of learning, establishing values, communicating information, who educates, in what ways, and with what attitudes. When I had the opportunity to present the educational program of Mexico to our education class, I found myself not simply portraying or describing the type of education Mexico had but also questioning and critiquing its values and orientations as well, based on his typology.

In many ways, Jules Henry was a precursor, during the 1950s and 1960s, of the tradition of the "new sociologists of education in America." He espoused ideas about critical theory that today have become interwoven with the discourse of educational theorists. Through his teaching, I became aware of the difference between anthropological description and cultural critique, the latter requiring deeper and more thorough analysis of any given social situation in relation to its social, economic, and political influences. I also became aware of the importance of cultural systems analysis and the ways in which different aspects of a culture contribute to a person's socialization into that culture. Henry's description of the hidden curriculum, even before it was known as such, is another influence that has lasted. His analysis of the fears of the cold war between the United States and the U.S.S.R. were creatively set forth in a series of articles and handouts he shared with our class. He reminded us that in the final analysis, it was our own fears that immobilized us. In my own professional work today on issues of diversity and multiculturalism, as well as in my analyses of racism/discriminatory practices, his influence is evident–for example, in my need to configure ethnographic research within historical, social, cultural, and educational frameworks, and in my efforts to understand the convergence or divergence of meaning for different stakeholders in a culture.

At the same time I was learning about critique, my work in graduate school also thrust me into a series of skill-building apprenticeships that led me to transcribe audiotapes of Latin American oral stories and folklore; develop interviews, code, and prepare them for programming; and connect these with a comparative educational research study that was being conducted in Brazil, Chile, and the United States. Learning how to interview African American teachers and their families about the opportunities they experienced in "busting out of the ghetto" as they acquired middle-class status through education became the main focus of my research. *Because I was in the community*, I began to acquire and learn how to use the language of the streets through "playing the dozens." The oral dueling characteristic of the dozens was similar to the oral retorts (*piropos*) Mexican males engaged in with women passing by. Knowing when and how to escalate or deflect the retorts became an art form. Such social learning made a great deal of sense to me as the "real" gathering of data, in contrast to the more formal, structured interviews that were coded and prepared for computer programs.

I came to realize that even though much of the data gathered in social science research as it developed was in the form of interviews–people's sharing of their lives and histories as my father's patients had–the words and ideas shared by participants became reduced to categories and codes, later represented by some numerical value and meaning. In the hands of researchers, such analyzed data became translated into interpretations and findings and eventually materialized as publications placed on the library shelf of a university–but without having reached the people who initially contributed their ideas, thoughts, and time. Such a process raises important questions: For whom is the research? For what purposes is it being designed? What are the expected outcomes?

Even more perplexing are the differences between the questions and interpretations of university-based researchers studying communities outside the academic domain and those of the people who actually live in these communities. The community might even have a different set of words to identify its issues, but academic research appropriates the community's meaning into its own discourse and rationale. Because in some instances the community's input may not be regarded as legitimate social science research, the very questions raised by community members become modified versions of the academic discourse. Only the university and its faculty appear to have the true essence of the community's thinking. Yet there is now a need for a connection between the folk theories of the community and the more scholarly theories of the academy; there is a need for a common discourse. Only then can the content and power of meaning found in the community and the knowledge base of academicians come to approximate each other and, in this way, be validated by both. It has been my experience that the researchers and scholars of the universities have much more to gain in such an exchange than do the individuals in the communities they have undertaken to study. Renato Rosaldo's confrontation of the academic establishment, in *Culture and Truth*, poignantly expresses this sentiment:

> The agenda for social analysis has shifted to include not only eternal verities and lawlike generalizations but also political processes, social changes, and human differences. . . . Social analysis must now grapple with the realization that its

> objects of analysis are also analyzing subjects who critically interrogate ethnographers–their writings, their ethics and their politics. (p. 21)

SIXTH KNOT: RESEARCH FOR ACTION

During the 1970s, I returned to Mexico to work as a professional at a major university located in an Indian village. The town has served as a ceremonial center for thousands of years and has the world's largest pyramid. The university seems out of place in such an environment, yet it represents the connection of academia and community that I have found lacking in the research field. Here the usefulness of research in influencing change, particularly at the community level, was revived for me in the work that I undertook.

Returning as an adult to one of my homelands began to close the circle for me. I regained much of what my Mexican grandmother had taught me through her story telling about the Mexican Revolution–the connections to my historical past. I knew my European and Spanish backgrounds but had no idea about my Indian heritage. I came from the Huasteca region in Mexico and surely had Bribri Indian blood from Costa Rica. As a way to find my Indian roots, I learned to speak Nahuatl, the native language of Mexico's highland Indians. I discovered, in using Nahuatl, a sense of meaning not inherent in Spanish. Instead of using the pronoun *me*, I learned to refer to *us*; instead of using *mine*, I learned to refer to *ours*. I also began to understand that the complex layering of this language enabled me to identify the self to the group, to connect the concept of culture to power, and to recognize the oppression brought on by colonialism. Transcending the limitations of language allowed me to expand my ability to become a good researcher. Thus I gained respect for the educator-anthropologist who spends time living and studying in a setting where she becomes part of the landscape and begins to acquire the skills and knowledge of the very people from whom she is learning.

Yet Mexico exposed me to more than my roots; it also exposed me to *Pedagogy of the Oppressed*, by Paulo Freire, the world-renowned Brazilian educator. Through my reading of this volume, I gained a new understanding of the relationship of power to knowledge, particularly between those who are privileged (and oppress) and those who are powerless (and oppressed). Freire's literacy campaigns with illiterate peasants in northern Brazil uncovered reasons why the peasants did not read. He advanced both a theory and a method for literacy attainment based on the process of *conscientization* (knowing with purpose, reflection, and action). Through conscientization, in order to know, one needs to confront one's own concrete reality. That means being able to identify and give expression to the experiences of one's daily life.

When such experiences are named and codified as generative themes, their vocalization becomes the basis for reading. In learning to read relevant information, the reader moves through four different stages, starting from an *unknowing* and ending with a *knowing with purpose* stage. Through this process, illiterate people "break out of their silence" as they gain access to the power of the "alphabet." Such a process contrasts sharply with traditional "banking education" in which teachers deposit knowledge inside students' heads without ever asking the students to question. "Liberatory education" enables students to experience the power of their own dialogue by questioning reality and thus gaining understanding.

Freire's thinking allowed me to realize the urgency for helping peasants to read in the context of Mexican villages where reading is inaccessible. Armed with Freire's theory of conscientization, I began to look at Mexico with critical eyes. I experienced the educational inequalities between rural peasants and middle-class urban dwellers from Mexico City. I witnessed the discrimination toward Indians[3] and the continual silencing of women by men. Such reflections drove home the point that research needs to be oriented to social action and the creation of public policy. Clearly, research that sits on the shelf in a library or a school is ineffectual if it cannot be used, especially by those who most need to understand its power.

I left Mexico in the mid-1970s to complete my doctorate in the United States and decided to focus on administration and public policy. Instead I gravitated to curriculum theory with a concentration in bilingual education, because these fields combined most of my interests. Henry Giroux introduced me to the critical pedagogy of the "new" sociologists of education, the curriculum making of the reconceptualists, and the theories of resistance that he and Paul Willis espoused. I again encountered Paulo Freire and liberation theology and became enthralled by postmodernism and poststructuralism—areas that complemented my past experiences. Giroux's weaving of theory and history with education in *Ideology, Culture, and the Process of Schooling* not only appealed to me but offered a grounding I had found generally lacking in American education. His influence reaffirmed the need to problematize issues—that is, not simply to describe educational issues in a vacuum but, more importantly, to relate these to social, economic, political, and cultural influences and to critique their internal dynamics.

I wrote a qualitative thesis at a time when quantitative research was the *norm* and critical pedagogy had not yet gained a foothold in academia. I also selected a highly controversial topic—bilingual education, combined with qualitative, ethnographic research and critical pedagogy. Faced with writing a thesis for academia versus writing one that could be used by the teachers in my field site (a more time-consuming and field-demanding task), I opted for the former. It was the only way that, as a researcher and a woman, I could complete my dissertation while raising a combined family from two households, working full-time, and taking care of an elderly parent.

Once my thesis was completed, the postdissertation stage was anticlimactic. Tenure-track positions in my areas of interest were not readily available, and the competition for the limited openings was such that I turned to teacher training for several years. The near impossibility of being able to conduct one's own research without institutional backing further hampered my academic advancement. As I look back at the process of becoming a professor and researcher, questions about how gains are made in the world of academia have certainly challenged me. I question whether the realm of academe offers space for one individual to be a mother, wife, caretaker, mentor, researcher, and teacher. Or do some of these roles need to be negated in the name of professional advancement? And in two-career families in which the choices for moving are constrained by a companion's position, whose career must suffer?

SEVENTH KNOT: WAYS OF KNOWING AMONG THE MAINSTREAM

The preceding questions concern how one can fit one's personal life in with academic demands. But there is another question: How does one fit within the academic culture? This raises vital moral and ethical questions about research itself and one's own paradigm in research: Whose knowledge is represented? What values are evident? How are these understood? Whose research is it, after all?

These reflective questions about power and value relationships as well as status differences are rarely asked in academic circles because the focus on research tends to be driven largely by white, Anglo, middle-class cultural norms. The status of mainstream researchers affects the relationships that underrepresented (Latino/a, Native American, Asian, or African American) researchers have in the field. In this regard, much of the academic struggle that I have experienced as a researcher is related to the way mainstream researchers are regarded and upheld vis-à-vis underrepresented researchers.

Since the 1920s, mainstream researchers have dominated the field of anthropology and education. They have focused on under-served communities using paradigms emanating from Europe and reflecting mostly white, male, middle-class perspectives. These paradigms have been used extensively to characterize underserved communities. They were used first in national culture studies, like those done by Margaret Mead and others, and then in the popular analysis of "cultures of poverty," like Oscar Lewis's studies of Mexican and Puerto Rican families. Then with the War on Poverty and the need for compensatory education, a rationale for helping "disadvantaged students and families" was created. Most recently, the focus of research has been on "at-risk" students and families.

Of concern is that many of these studies were written primarily from the perspective of white Anglo researchers who knew little about the communities they researched, and what little they knew came from informants who themselves may not have been from the community. Local people's lore was not considered, nor were the people within those communities regarded as knowledgeable. Moreover, without having lived the experiences of people within the community, these researchers were providing causal explanations for their educational "failures," explanations to be used ultimately in defining public policy. Many of these researchers remained outsiders to the communities they studied, but their recorded accounts and analyses became bases for major community interventions. For underrepresented researchers to study the same issues, but from their own perspectives, was simply not accepted as objective or scientific. Having firsthand information about your own ethnic group worked against your entry into the mainstream. So, like that of many of my colleagues, the research I conducted did not focus on Latinos/as but was mainstream in nature. Only recently has that shibboleth been broken, mainly because the need for other explanations–beyond those provided by the mainstream–has emerged through the work of Renato Rosaldo, Henry Trueba, Pedro Pedraza, Concha Delgado-Gaitan, Ursula Casanova, Carmen Mercado, and Luis Moll. With the overturning of such barriers, different paradigms are appearing and gaining acceptance for explaining and problematizing the culture of dropouts, community knowledge, and cultural continuities.

Another salient issue is what I call the "silencing" of nonmainstream researchers. This is a subtle process not manifested in overt actions but generated by omission, disregard, or condescension. Examples abound: being left out of the school catalogue even though the necessary materials were submitted, or having your degree omitted beside your name when everyone else has been listed with the appropriate degrees; being told with surprise that you are "quite articulate" for someone not an English-speaker; and being referred to by a different name because the pronunciation of your own may be difficult or hard to remember. I cannot enumerate the times I have been referred to as María instead of Martha, even when I have introduced myself and have shared papers with my correct name; the invitational letter for a recent conference presentation, where I was to share personal and professional experiences that have influenced my choices as a teacher, mentor, and educational researcher, came addressed to María.

It should be noted that this silencing does not occur simply between mainstream and nonmainstream researchers but is also evident among underrepresented researchers. Issues such as gender bias and cultural mores and expectations may hinder your role as a researcher. The concerns in this case are not only who endorses, promotes, or mentors you but, more importantly, under what conditions you can count on their support. It has been my experience that even when an established relationship exists and support is expected, especially from a colleague within your own ethnic group, such an assumption may be wrong, especially if both of you are competing for the same position or grant. It is clear that in the current academic climate of competitive research, the degree to which collaboration is engendered by diverse groups may help reduce such differences. However, the magnitude of intragroup differences has only recently become a focus of research, as interested researchers seek to discover how their work methods serve either to create conflict or to consolidate the group.

Another silencing effect relates to whose voices are heard. At academic conferences, when some of my mainstream counterparts describe Latino/a communities and make assertions about what they deem to be the central issues or problems Latinos/as face, their assertions are taken at face value. But if I or other Latinos/as articulate our understanding of what is happening from our own perspective, our assessment may not be regarded similarly; it may be viewed as anecdotal or unimportant. A case in point is the all too common usage of the term *macho* only in reference to Mexican males. This is usually a pejorative statement about excessive "male-ness." Yet as a Mexican, I know that there are women also who are regarded as *muy machas*–in other words, very *macho* in a female sense, because they take matters into their hands, make decisions, and are highly respected leaders. Thus a *mujer muy macha* is a compliment for a good leader! The validity of this dual interpretation, one of the complexities inherent in Mexican culture, is rarely acknowledged within mainstream research not only because it is not known but also because such connotations are seldom studied or uncovered.

The same lack of understanding of perspective between mainstream and underrepresented researchers is evident in the "publish or perish" dilemma that most academicians face. The very act of publishing is a matter of knowing how to access mainstream thinking and audiences. It requires presenting research findings and discussions in expected, specific ways. Thus writing directly about your community and the issues that most concern you may not be what is in "vogue" in academia and hence not of interest to funding agencies. You are left with the task of finding publishing markets that are specifically interested in your work or are willing to take the risk of supporting your ideas. During the 1960s, research about African American teachers was of interest, fueled by civil rights and studies of black culture, but attempts to document similar processes within the Latino/a community were not supported to the same degree. My own initial publications met with rejection at that time because doors were not open to collaborative, field-oriented research within teacher education, particularly with linguistically different teachers, nor were explanations emanating from Latino/a researchers salable. Today, I have learned to walk the fine line between publishing articles on general-consumption issues, such as classroom management, multicultural education, and teacher training, and at the same time writing about specific topics that also interest me. I publish in Spanish to keep my connections to Latin America alive, and I publish research about bilingual education, ethnohistorical accounts, and Latino/a high school students in journals that are committed to "being educated as well as educating others."[4] Thus the marginalization that comes with the territory of being a Latina researcher is somewhat mitigated by my efforts to ensure that my research finds an open-minded audience. I often test my writing at conferences and symposia to see how other researchers respond and to gather useful and needed feedback. I even try to find colleagues who are willing to present their findings as a united front, so as to begin to influence mainstream research itself.

One of my greatest learning experiences in academe was when I taught and conducted research as a non-tenure-track faculty member. Hired as "a qualitative researcher and teacher who works in poor communities either in the U.S. or abroad," I was the only outsider among the finalists considered for the position. In joining the faculty, I became the first Latina full-time assistant professor at this prestigious graduate school. In my fourth year of teaching, one of the administrators asked me whether I didn't find it difficult to be at this school, because, after all, I was with such distinguished faculty.

I dismissed such comments readily and focused on the quality of the classroom experiences, which have stayed with me despite the rupture I experienced between my personal life and academic demands. My personal life was crushed under the weight of academic competition, writing, conducting research, and publishing. Though I realized that research would be the mainstay of my visibility as an academic, teaching–in particular, being a good teacher–was a challenge I welcomed. My students came from different parts of the world and had a wealth of backgrounds to share. I attempted to create communities within my classes by having students do a great deal of group work, fieldwork, or practicums and requiring them to integrate their readings and class discussion with concrete situations. All of my classes required students to be involved in different communities–schools, agencies, community-based organizations, peer teaching programs, and after-school programs. Students completing their theses in community settings were required to share their findings with the community people and to deposit their theses at their local libraries. Many of these students have continued this policy in their own teaching and research. Likewise, community members participated in our classes through presentations and problem posing. Such collective experiences made our classes open dialogical forums.

The research projects I engaged in – university and school collaboratives, teachers' theory building, and community-based learning – were generally viewed by my colleagues as pilot projects or course initiatives and not as actual community outreach.[5] My involvement with such projects gained me a reputation as a clinical faculty member and as a generalist, a role considered inferior to that of a specialist, who works on single-focus and specifically targeted research. I did not question these issues openly at the time, but in retrospect I find it ironic that the very inquiry-based research I developed with teachers, and which constituted much of the content of the teacher-education program at the school, was not seen as contributing to the "traditional" core of knowledge.[6]

My research during those years was a solitary experience, expanded by the circle of graduate students who were working on their theses or teachers involved in collaborative research. While I mentored my students, I did not have other faculty mentoring me, even though the topic of mentoring was regarded as being on the "cutting edge" at every faculty meeting. During the time I was at the school, I received most of my advice for career advancement and mentoring from outside faculty.

Although teamwork was heavily emphasized through course work in teaching and curriculum development, it was rarely practiced by the faculty. Faculty got together at faculty meetings and for specific course-work tasks, but they worked independently in their own areas. Only when I became the research coordinator of a multimillion-dollar research study did I work closely with a few colleagues. This was one of the rare opportunities I had to learn about how some of my colleagues thought or acted.

Even the notion of time had its own meaning. I quickly learned that the implicit message in concerns about time use was that time is to be valued for personal production, publishing, and research, not necessarily for advising students. To the degree that I clocked my time, I could squeeze more time for such production. I began to reduce the one-hour appointments with students to only twenty minutes, realizing what the ante was. Hence I expended less and less time interacting with students and faculty and more and more time working alone. It was clear that the lines between private and public space were tightly drawn.

The culture of this institution made it abundantly clear that no matter how hard you worked, taught, or extended yourself in conducting research, teaching, or participating in the community, securing a tenured academic slot was simply not possible. The stakes you confronted were of tremendous magnitude, beyond the merits of your work. One administrator's remark, that there were "simply no world-class minorities out there to be tenured at this school," poignantly brought the message home.

During my last year of teaching, I also took care of my father, who suffered from diabetes-related problems. I brought him for treatment from Costa Rica where, otherwise, he would have had his leg amputated. For six months, I juggled daily visits to the hospital, witnessed his growing fear during five operations, and took care of his home-recuperation while teaching, writing, and completing a school-based research project. When he left for Costa Rica, walking on his own, I felt satisfied with my decision. In the midst of his stay, one of my colleagues remarked, "You are hurting yourself academically by not putting your personal issues aside and completing the book for promotion to associate professor." Little did I realize how vacuous such comments were until my father suddenly died six months later. Today, the memories of washing his hair with his favorite soap, shaving his face, grooming his clothes, and cooking his very special dishes linger as loving father and daughter conversations that sharply contrast with the demands of publishing. When I offered a mass in his memory a few months later, the teachers from the field sites, friends, and graduate students were those who accompanied me.

I was not prepared to face my father's death, even though, as a Mexican, I had grown accustomed to accepting death as a continuous ritual and cycle that began at the moment of birth. Death had been my companion since childhood. I had experienced the death of more than twelve relatives, participated in the wakes and crying, and observed my grandmother wear only black dresses for mourning. I had even fed the spirits of the departed souls with their favorite foods during the celebration of the Day of the Dead each year. Yet the sudden loss of my father, when I was most enjoying him, shattered the link to the cultural connections of my being, to family and friends in Costa Rica, Mexico, and Europe. It also ruptured the linkages my father had begun to share with his grandchildren–the traditions and history of the family, its lore, the influence of different generations, and, most importantly, his teachings. His departure left an incomprehensible void.

Not finding solace alone in my academic work, and in need of filling the void, I have consciously decided to focus my energies on my remaining family, friends, and colleagues, and to conduct research aimed at uncovering those issues that have the most impact on the lives of Latinos/as–education, parents, and community. Whereas over the past twenty-five years I tended to work at the periphery of my interests, feeling intimidated by the demands of mainstream academia and the lack of interest in Latinos/as, today I find myself returning to where I started, with the oral histories and folk stories of my grandmother and others' lives. I am recording the life history of my mother, her thoughts about being a traditional woman in Mexico, living through the Mexican Revolution, coming to America at mid-life, learning how to raise children and grandchildren in this milieu. The first part of the oral history of her life is in the repository of the Latinas' oral history project at the Schlesinger Library of Harvard University. Moreover, I have begun to immerse myself in a series of community-based research and advocacy projects as a means to generate collaborative research grants that will address the needs of Latino/a youth and parents.[7]

I have also committed myself to using research to document the processes and practices of unequal education in its manifestations. Naming practices of discrimination and racism and how they are institutionalized in both mainstream and underserved communities have become major thrusts of my current research. Clearly, identifying the manifestations of racism is not enough. Equally important is to name how such manifestations are perpetuated and how their intended outcomes can be deconstructed. It is my intent to develop re-search that overpowers the systemic conditioning of racism and discrimination by identifying its persistence.

EIGHTH KNOT: CURRENT RESEARCH, STRUGGLES, AND CHALLENGES

After leaving Mexico over twenty years ago, I did not expect to stay in one place. However, having made the choice to study and work as well as raise my family in the Northeast, I have tried to combine the learning from social science and educational research with community advocacy. My research interests are in ethnohistorical accounts of communities, both in the United States and abroad, the effects of schooling on secondary school students (particularly Latinos), professional development of teachers and academicians, and individual and collective oral histories.[8]

I began what is now a seventeen-year analysis of a community undergoing tremendous demographic and economic change.[9] Informed by Louis Smith and William Geoffrey's seminal ethnohistorical account of a school district in St. Louis, I have observed schools, classrooms, and bilingual classes. I have interviewed teachers, parents, and administrators and have joined a community-based advocacy organization for the interests of Latinos/as. I have also trained Latinos about cross-cultural understanding. I have come to respect the dimensions of ethnohistorical accounts for their usefulness in "grounding" research and in providing a context for developing "new" research.

It is only now, after all these years, that I can speak less as an "outsider" and more as an "insider" about issues in the community I have been studying for so long. Yet I am constantly aware of my own limitations in not living within this community. I am aware of my own perspective in relation to the perspectives of other community members and participate in the initiatives that grow out of the folk theories fed by the community's activism. I recognize that such an awareness is hard to describe to researchers who spend anywhere from two to six weeks in a school or community, come up with an analysis, and call their research "ethnographic." Ray Rist's description of blitzkrieg ethnography reverberates in my mind as I encounter reports that short-term research is in vogue. What is being called "ethnography" in some cases lacks the rigor and systematic analysis that I have come to expect from traditional and more current "good ethnography."

I also believe the researcher has an ethical and moral commitment to use time adequately in uncovering those issues that are being studied purposefully. I do not condemn ethnographic researchers who are limited by funding contracts to short time frames for their work, but I do feel that the design of such research and the methodologies proposed to pursue it should result in findings that can be used, mostly within the communities of study and those in need.

I have made it a personal choice not to parlay ethnographic research into quick-fix studies of time-limited duration. In fact, I will not initiate studies that do not allow for the negotiation of entry and building of trust and relationships, the cornerstone of ethnographic research. Like Shirley Brice Heath, who spent over ten years researching her study *Ways with Words*, I believe it takes a great deal of time to sort through what is actually going on within a community setting. Understanding the context, the stakeholders and gatekeepers of the system, their interactions, negotiations, and the consequences of these, requires time and reflection. Ethnographic research is an organic process intertwining fieldwork, critical thinking, reflection, revisiting of contexts, reflecting about oneself, and redefining the research time and again. At times, one must leave the field in order to regain one's perspective before reentering. Qualitative research is also research for action. In that regard I have found that participatory action research is often easier to conduct in Latin America than in some U.S. contexts. I attribute these differences to the fact that in Latin America, qualitative or participatory action research requires *compromiso* (commitment to advocacy), an issue not taken lightly, but in the United States, descriptive analysis with recommendations from the field is often all that is necessary.

Thus conducting qualitative research entails learning about communities–including learners, teachers, community members, parents, and families–and it involves negotiation and reaffirmation of the researcher's values as well as those of research subjects and community members. Creating such temporal space in which one's personal life intersects with research is not typically expected in the academic world.

The other issue in current ethnographic research is its lack of theoretical and practical grounding. Instead of schools of theory informing or guiding the process, methodology often becomes the grounding of research. The facileness with which the theory and method of qualitative and ethnographic research become separated out into discrete descriptions of theory versus practice, or the way theory becomes diluted through poorly designed studies, or the way methodological explanations that are grounded in theory are sometimes side-stepped in favor of attention to the sorting capacity of computer programs—all these point to some of the weak links that have been constructed in the name of efficiency of research. Instances like these lead me to ask: When am I truly hearing the data speak to me? When am I construing meaning without having heard the participants' own voices or interpretations? When do I know that I have captured enough of an understanding of the universe of the participants to fully describe and interpret their realities? And when do I know that I know?

The output of my research is also affected by the push and pull between research and teaching. While teaching is second nature to me, it is viewed as secondary to research in many institutions. Yet the research I engage in, uncovering the theory in teachers' minds or defining knowledge as it is constituted in classrooms by students and teachers, becomes the content of my teaching. Why should such content not be what schools of education are about: the interactions of classroom and community contexts and the issues that practitioners and parents confront daily? At the academic level, this tension between research and teaching becomes resolved by identifying faculty along clinical and/or theoretical lines. Yet being a clinical faculty member carries with it specific disadvantages to academic advancement, because one is not viewed as contributing to the building of new knowledge in the field. At the community level, being a researcher demands that knowledge of academe be fairly exchanged with community people for their use. In fact, in my own work I am moving away from the idea of the researcher as one who uses his or her skills to identify "issues" within the community; rather, the researcher's role is to encourage collaborative inquiry within the community, working with community members to train them in the skills of conducting outreach, gathering data, creating data bases, elaborating observational guides for working in the schools of their children, and training the second cadre of community researchers.

It is my belief that if we continue to sustain the dichotomy between research and teaching, we will continue to fragment the self. I do not believe one can be a good teacher without being a good researcher, or a good researcher without being a good teacher. I also believe that research devoid of self becomes immobilizing.

TIED KNOTS: CONCLUSION

As I have attempted to make some sense of research across my lifespan of childhood, coming of age, adulthood, and maturity, it has become evident to me that the differences and border crossings of my life have added value to my research. Language and cultural differences, as well as symbols, have been the metaphors that have given content to my teaching and research. My mobility within and without different contexts has also allowed me to fit into many diverse environments–whether playing with Ms. Ellis or participating in community advocacy. The status of stranger has also given me access to domains unknown to others. I have been privileged in learning about these contexts. In recognition of the entry given to my research, much of my work has been with the teachers, students, and communities collaborating with me. Through such encounters, I have come to regard research with reverential respect, knowing that its power in the hands of those most in need results from the knowledge they gain, which they can reflect upon and ultimately convert to action on their own behalf. I contemplate conducting collaborative research projects in the future as the most challenging and rewarding area of my teaching and learning. In collaborating, I have learned about myself as well as about what is entailed in working with others, but I have also learned to take the disenchantments in the field as opportunities for growth. My mission is clear, like the Mexican weaving, where each rough knot gives the emerging cloth depth and character. The research I expect to do will undoubtedly continue to intersect with my personal life and will braid threads of diverse texture, passion, and feeling to make its form come alive.

NOTES

This chapter is dedicated to my husband, Charles, whose support of my professional commitment has been unconditional.

1. Extensions of this interest have included my collection of Latinas' oral histories in relation to the work of the Ad Hoc Committee on Latinas' Oral Histories at the Schlesinger Library, Radcliffe College, and my article "Beyond Affirmative Action: An Inquiry into the Experiences of Latinas in Academia" (Montero-Sieburth, 1996a).

2. See, for example, Montero-Sieburth and Peŕez, 1987, and Montero-Sieburth and Gray, 1992.

3. An example of such discrimination is the common use of the term *naco* for "Indian"; the term connotes "country bumpkin," or one who is backward and stupid. Drivers in Mexico City are often heard to shout "Stay out of the way, you *naco*," a reference to the offending party's incompetence.

4. Some of the articles I have published in Spanish have to do with explaining to Latin American audiences ethnographic research as used in the United States and in particular in education. At the same time, I have been interested in documenting how Latin Americans define qualitative research. Gary Anderson and I have a forthcoming publication on *Educational Qualitative Research in Latin America: The Struggle for a New Paradigm*, which will orient U.S. researchers to what is happening in the field within Latin America.

5. Some of this work is described in Montero-Sieburth and Gray, 1992.

6. I developed a four-year collaborative with urban high school teachers in which they were paired with graduate students who were also teachers but who wanted to observe and experience teaching from the vantage point of being "outsiders." The urban high school teachers identified the areas of research they wanted to explore, and the graduate students collaborated in conducting the research, which was primarily directed by the teachers. The outcomes of the first year led to an AERA conference presentation on the absenteeism of their students by program, ethnic background, and motivational levels. The second year, specific projects were initiated by the teachers with another set of graduate students, and the third and fourth years, teachers asked for individual attention to their teaching and to their classroom management.

7. In my former role as the director of educational research at the Mauricio Gastoń Institute for Latino Community Development and Public Policy, University of Massachusetts-Boston, I was involved in projects such as "Al Nuevo Mundo," which attempts to tie the five campuses of the University of Massachusetts to community-based organizations and their constituents through cultural and artistic events. I continue to be involved in an ad hoc school-reform networking group delineating basic reform issues for the Boston Public Schools. In addition, the Educational Research Group, which I continue to direct, is working on several collaborative grants directed at analyzing school reform from within schools and developing public policies for Latino students and parents; this group is also examining the role of counselors in advising Latino students and the actual participation of parents in policy and classroom initiatives. Latino leadership, particularly of undergraduate Latinas, is another initiative that I have undertaken at the university. In the community, I will be collecting the oral histories of seasoned and emergent Latino leaders in one of the fastest growing Latino communities in Massachusetts.

8. Examples of my work in these areas include Montero-Sieburth, 1989, 1993, 1996a, 1996b, in press, and Montero-Sieburth and LaCelle Peterson, 1992a.

9. See Montero-Sieburth and LaCelle Peterson, 1992a, 1992b.

BIBLIOGRAPHY

Anderson, Gary, and Martha Montero-Sieburth. In press. *Educational Qualitative Research in Latin America: The Struggle for a New Paradigm*. New York: Garland.

Freire, Paulo. 1973. *Pedagogy of the Oppressed*. New York: Seabury.

Giroux, Henry A. 1981. *Ideology, Culture and the Process of Schooling*. Philadelphia: Temple University Press.

Heath, Shirley Brice. 1983. *Way With Words: Language, Life and Work in Communities and Classrooms*. London: Cambridge University Press.

Henry, Jules. 1960. "A Cross-Cultural Outline of Education." *Current Anthropology* 1(4):267–306.

Henry, Jules. 1963. *Culture Against Man*. New York: Vintage.

Montero-Sieburth, Martha. 1989. "Restructuring Teachers' Knowledge for Urban School Settings." *The Journal of Negro Education* 58(3):332–344 (Summer).

Montero-Sieburth, Martha. 1993. "The Effects of Schooling Processes and Practices on Potential 'At Risk' Latino High School Students." In *The Education of Latino Students in Massachusetts: Issues, Research, and Policy*, Ralph Rivera and Sonia Nieto, eds. Amherst: University of Massachusetts Press, 217–239.

Montero-Sieburth, Martha. 1996a. "Beyond Affirmative Action: An Inquiry into the Experiences of Latinas in Academia." *New England Journal of Public Policy* 2(2): 65–98.

Montero-Sieburth, Martha. 1996b. "Teachers, Administrators, and Staff's Implicit Thinking About 'At Risk' Urban High School Latino Students." In *Teacher Thinking in Multicultural Contexts*, Francisco Rios ed. Albany: State University of New York Press, 55–84.

Montero-Sieburth, Martha. In press. "Reclaiming Indigenous Cultures: Students' Oral Histories in Talamanca, Costa Rica." In *Students as Researchers of Language and Culture in their Own Communities*, Ann Egan-Robertson and David Bloome, eds. New York: Hampton.

Montero-Sieburth, Martha, and Cynthia Gray. 1992. "Riding the Wave: Collaborative Inquiry Linking Teachers at the University and the Urban High School." In *Research and Multicultural Education: From the Margins to the Mainstream*, Carl A. Grant, ed. Philadelphia: Falmer, 122–140.

Montero-Sieburth, Martha, and Marla Perez. 1987. "Echar Pa'lante–Moving Onward: The Dilemmas and Strategies of a Bilingual Teacher." *Anthropology and Education Quarterly* 18(3):180–189.

Montero-Sieburth, Martha, and Mark LaCelle Peterson. 1992a. "Immigration and Schooling: An Ethno-Historical Account of Policy and Family Perspectives in an Urban Community." *Anthropology and Education Quarterly* 22(4):301–325 (December).

Montero-Sieburth, Martha, and Mark LaCelle Peterson. 1992b. "Linking Critical Pedagogy to Bilingual Education: An Ethno-Historical Study Contextualizing School Policies in an Urban Community." In *Critical Perspectives on Bilingual Education*, R. Raymond Padilla and Alfredo Benavides, eds. Hispanic Research Center, Tempe, AZ: Bilingual Review, 125–161.

Rist, Ray. 1980. "Blitzkrieg Ethnography: On the Transformation of a Method to a Movement." *Educational Researcher* 9(2):8–10.

Rosaldo, Renato. 1989. *Culture and Truth*. Boston: Beacon.

Smith, Louis, and William Geoffrey. 1968. *Complexities of an Urban Classroom*. New York: Holt, 1968.

* *CHAPTER 8* *

A Subjective Necessity: Being and Becoming an Historian of Education

Ellen Condliffe Lagemann

I DON'T REMEMBER WHEN I first read *Twenty Years at Hull House* by Jane Addams. But the distinction Jane Addams drew there and in other of her writings between "objective" and "subjective" necessity has always provided a way for me to think about who I am and what I write. It was not easy for me, as a woman and as the particular creature I am, to admit and pursue scholarly ambitions, and I think this may have spurred my early realization that at least for me writing was both means and end, subjectively necessary and objectively worthwhile. Writing was a means to be things that I was not meant to be as a woman–seriously intellectual, publicly articulate, independent minded, interested in public affairs, and deeply committed to work; and it was a worthwhile end in itself because it enabled me to address important social questions in which I was keenly interested.

Although I had liked writing letters and had kept a diary as a child, I began to acknowledge that I wanted to be a scholar only during my last two years at Smith College. Of course, during the late 1960s when I was there, it was still generally presumed among Smith students that our purpose in life was marriage and motherhood. In consequence, we spent inordinate amounts of time escaping from Northampton to New Haven or Cambridge or Williamstown, often for what turned out to be truly gruesome blind dates. Although I now shudder at the memory, our behavior was not entirely unintelligent. Given the expectations held out to us, one might even describe it as a prudent form of goal-directed vocational education. Be that as it may, Smith had vast intellectual resources in its faculty, its library, and its student body, and when it came time to declare a major, I chose to enroll in the honors program in history, which was in a very real sense a declaration that I would be a serious student.

Learning from Our Lives: Women, Research, and Autobiography in Education. ISBN 0-8077-3593-0 (pbk), ISBN 0-8077-3594-9 (cloth).

Because I was in "honors," I had a carrel in the library, where I began to spend most of my time. I also began to haunt the local bookstores, where, one day during my junior year, I happened upon *The Transformation of the School* by Lawrence Cremin. I will never forget finding that book. I read it instantly, sitting on the floor of the Quill Bookstore. It captivated me. Much that I was curious about was there, in one book. I still have the copy I bought that day with three lines scribbled on the front page: "Robber barons, the settlement movement, and the Lincoln School." When I think that those were the things I wanted to study in 1965 and that those are the things that I have studied since, I come close to believing in foreordained destiny. But I am much too rooted in this world for that, and it still took quite a lot of time and struggle and luck before studying "Robber barons, the settlement movement, and the Lincoln School" became a central part of my life.

"VIDA DUTTON SCUDDER"

One could perhaps say that I took the first step in that direction when I decided to write a biography of Vida Dutton Scudder as my honors thesis. She was a Wellesley professor who was one of the founders of the College Settlement Association. But the truth is that I picked Scudder on the advice of my advisor, Peter d'A. Jones, who also suggested including the section I called "A Generation of Women," comparing Scudder to Jane Addams and Lillian Wald. Nevertheless, writing Scudder's biography did introduce me to some of the exciting aspects of doing history. I still recall reading Scudder's journals, and being keenly aware that they were the real ones, not copies, and talking with Josephine Starr (the niece of Ellen Gates Starr who founded Hull House with Jane Addams), who tried to convince me to join the Society of the Companions of the Holy Cross, a group of Christian socialist women to which Vida Scudder had belonged; and visiting Florence Converse in the house she had shared with Scudder for many years; and spending many a long night in the basement "smoker" of the house I lived in at Smith trying to figure out how Scudder could really have believed that prayer could foment a revolution. However much I enjoyed doing that thesis, though, it took seven more years before I was ready to begin a Ph.D.

This relatively long hiatus was a result of several things. In part, it was caused by the fact that I very much wanted to teach high school. It was the 1960s and I was idealistic enough to believe that I could help save the world by teaching kids to read and think, a belief I have stubbornly held on to, though, of course, I now realize how much more is also involved. In order to teach, I had to be certified, which led me to Teachers College, where I quickly enrolled in Lawrence Cremin's history of American education course.

Had I been less shy and more confident or Cremin less engaged in the beginnings of the first volume of *American Education*, I might have switched from the M.A. program in social studies in which I was enrolled to a doctorate in the history of education. But Cremin's announcement in the first class that we should see the teaching assistants about routine questions led me disdainfully to dismiss the course as an impersonal impediment that stood between me and a teaching license. Although I found Cremin's lectures fascinating, I sat in the back row, chewing gum and whispering with a Smith friend, and handed in a paper that was only a slightly revised version of a paper I had written at Smith. So much for a foreordained straight line between reading *The Transformation of the School* and becoming an historian of education.

But there was another, more important reason it took me seven years to return to the doing of history. To seek a Ph.D. required that I avow and pursue my intellectual interests even more openly than I had done at Smith. It meant that I had to take my capacity to think seriously and that was very difficult for me to do. In very subtle ways, intellect had been an important source of power in my family. Among my relatives, my father seemed to be most respectful of his father, who was an economist who wrote and read constantly, and my mother seemed especially to admire her brother, who was a publisher of serious, scholarly works. Although both my parents were bright and well educated, neither developed deep intellectual interests, even though one sensed they might have liked to. Our house was filled with serious books and magazines, most of which were not actually read.

This deference to intellect doubtless encouraged my own intellectual aspirations, although those were difficult to square with the fact that I was a woman. Through unspoken means, most of which I cannot now precisely recapture, it was very clearly conveyed to me as a child that women were not to be publicly powerful or assertive or intellectual. Although this happened later, I find it telling that at my (paternal) grandfather's memorial service, all the female grandchildren were asked to read and all the male grandchildren were asked to speak. That my grandfather had mused with surprise that his granddaughters seemed to be accomplishing more than his grandsons made the gender division not a little ironic. Regardless, the incident helped me appreciate how taken-for-granted it had been in my family that women might read the words of others, but neither write nor speak their own words in public.

Given the power of these expectations, I suspect I would never have dared to pursue a doctorate if many good things had not happened to me between graduating from Smith in 1967 and enrolling at Columbia in 1974. Central among these was marrying someone who held, as did I, lots of the restricting assumptions about gender that were common in our generation, but who believed in me as a person. Marriage and a few years thereafter motherhood, combined with the reemergence of the women's movement, made me aware of the unfair and constraining norms that governed my life. As it was for many others, reading feminist literature, including articles about "the politics of housework," was a truly radicalizing experience for me. All of a sudden, picking up my husband's socks was no longer my unalterable responsibility; now the question of the socks became a not-always-comfortable issue around which my husband and I and many of our friends debated and fought about our respective rights, roles, and responsibilities.

As part of this process of rethinking and renegotiating who I would be and how we would live our lives together, I decided to go to graduate school. My husband, who had been a law student when we married, had become a very busy and successful litigator; I had stopped working to stay home with our son, who was born in November of 1972; and we had bought a house in Riverdale, New York, which was lovely, but lonely and isolating. I needed a counterweight to the daily demands of being a wife and mother. In our house, I quite literally had "a room of my own," a study to which I could and did retreat, but I had no reason to go there except to pay bills or write letters. I was not strong enough to justify my own space merely on the basis of my inherent rights and needs as a person. I needed the reinforcement that can come from an occupational role. Being a graduate student offered that, without requiring that I leave home for long stretches. In fact, until our son began prekindergarten, I was only away two afternoons a week and on Saturdays, when my husband could cover things.

This schedule was made possible by the unusual arrangements under which I earned my Ph.D. Having fortunately decided to set aside the alienation I had felt in his history of education class, I had sought out Lawrence Cremin as a graduate advisor. He had very few students at the time and was soon to become president of Teachers College. Partly because of his own schedule, he seemed more than ready to allow me to spend virtually all of my time (and to accrue all the necessary graduate credit) in independent study. After one semester, he also asked me to become his teaching and research assistant. This meant that I spent four years helping Cremin write the second volume of *American Education*, assisting him in his large lecture courses (including the one I had disdained only a few years before), and reading and writing on my own, usually at home late at night or very early in the morning, in the room to which I now began to feel a little more entitled.

A GENERATION OF WOMEN

Even with this flexibility and freedom, becoming an historian was not an easy transition for me, although it was certainly eased by the dissertation I wrote. Building on the work I had done at Smith, I decided to expand the section of my thesis that had been entitled "A Generation of Women," this time studying the education of a number of progressive women. There were many compelling academic reasons to do this. In the middle 1970s, there was still very little writing about the history of women's education. Thomas Woody's *A History of Women's Education in the United States* remained the lonely classic in the field. Despite this, important methodological works were beginning to appear in women's history, generally, and these, it seemed to me, were highly suggestive for the study of women's education. I remember being particularly impressed by the argument that women's history needed to define criteria of historical significance that could bring into fuller view the activities and institutions important to women as women. Applied to education, I reasoned, this would require dropping all assumptions concerning which institutions and experience were educationally important and searching actual lives to find out where and how women had acquired the skills, sensibilities, and ideas important to them as individuals, wives and mothers, nonvoting citizens (until 1920), and workers.

Proceeding in this way had the advantage of fitting nicely with Larry Cremin's interests at the time. As part of his concern to broaden educational history, he was eager to have students define the genre of educational biography, although, at one point, he tried to convince me to switch my topic to the history of museums as educational institutions, his argument being that many others were beginning to write about women and no one was writing about museums, a history of museums therefore being more likely to result in a publishable book. However, once he became convinced of my determination to write *A Generation of Women*, Cremin invested abundant interest, energy, and encouragement in my work. Because I needed to learn a lot about education to write an *educational* biography, he spent countless hours talking with me as I read my way through his library of books on educational theory, everything from William James's *Psychology* to Joseph J. Schwab's writings on curriculum.

Thus armed with very good academic reasons for studying the educational life histories of a number of women, I was less aware than I am now of the reasons this project mattered so much to me. I was, of course, aware that personal curiosities had some influence on the selections I made of women to include. Lillian Wald had been a friend of my maternal grandmother, who had been active at the Henry Street Settlement; and Grace Dodge had lived near where I lived in Riverdale, New York. But it was only after I finished the dissertation and the book was published that I came fully to appreciate that in writing *A Generation of Women*, I was searching for and finding examples of women who had been able to do the things I, too, wanted to do.

This was important because in the affluent, insulated world in which I had come of age, most women did not work. They were wives and mothers.

They went to the supermarket and drove car pools and took their children to the doctor or dentist or orthodontist. They talked on the telephone, gave dinner parties, and met their friends for lunch. The exceptional ones read books or had "interests"–gardening, or children's books, or painting. The deviant ones, of whom I personally knew two, worked even though they did not have to and everyone felt sorry for their (doubtless neglected) children.

As Betty Friedan would soon report, many women in this world apparently felt something was lacking. Certainly, along with the unquestioned expectation that being a wife and mother would be the center of my life, this sentiment was communicated to me. My mother and aunt talked endlessly about the possibilities of work or further (graduate) education, and my great-aunt, who talked so often of her undergraduate years at Bryn Mawr that one got the sense that all had been downhill since, handed me *The Feminine Mystique* as soon as it was published.

Knowing of this discontent and having experienced it myself, albeit for a brief time, I wanted to be more than a wife and mother. But even at the time I began graduate school I still found it hard to admit this, especially since my interests led in directions that were within my experience taboo for women. Had I wanted to be a nurse or to have resumed high school teaching, I might have had an easier time. Then again, as I learned later from studying the history of nursing and other professions in which women have predominated, such traditional female occupations might not have satisfied my wish to be allowed to think and speak for myself. Not because it offered cookie-cutter models to follow but rather because it allowed me to learn and write about women who had self-consciously and painfully become effective, autonomous, public women, writing *A Generation of Women* helped me address a vital subjective necessity while also producing a book that had objective value for women's history and educational studies. Means and ends, process and product, *A Generation of Women* enabled me to become a scholar.

PRIVATE POWER AND *THE POLITICS OF KNOWLEDGE*

At the time I finished my Ph.D. there were few jobs for historians of education and none in the New York area, so I spent the first years of my professional life earning soft money and working as an adjunct assistant professor at Teachers College. This turned out to be extremely fortunate because it gave me much more time to write than a full-time assistant professor would have been likely to have. I wrote several articles and book chapters about the education of women and edited two books, one about nursing history and one about Jane Addams's educational thought, but I quickly moved away from women's history as a primary research focus.[1] I did this for two reasons.

First, I was dismayed by the orthodoxy that then seemed to prevail in that field. I was frequently chided in reviews and at professional meetings for not making lesbianism a central focus of my work. I had first encountered this at the 1976 Berkshire Conference where, as a very green graduate student giving her first professional paper, I was loudly and personally condemned for not discussing lesbianism in the life of Lillian Wald, which, it was charged, was tantamount to a vicious, homophobic denial. I had been totally unprepared for this attack and was vastly grateful when Patricia Graham, in her capacity as chair of the session, stepped in to save me. Nevertheless, I found pressure to define my work in ways that were "politically correct," unpleasant, and constraining, and I was also coming to believe that it was more important to try to understand gender as *a* force (one force among many) in history than to continue studying women as a distinct social group.

The second reason I moved away from women's history was because I became involved in writing about the history of philanthropic foundations. I wish I could say this was an entirely self-motivated and purposeful move from one to another of the interests I had noted on the first page of *The Transformation of the School*. But, if there is some truth to that, my shift from writing about the settlement movement to writing about the robber barons was more immediately the result of grants from the Carnegie Corporation. Having tried to recruit Merle Curti to write a seventy-fifth anniversary history of the Carnegie Foundation for the Advancement of Teaching, Alan Pifer, who was president of both the Carnegie Corporation and the Carnegie Foundation at the time, had called Larry Cremin in search of recommendations. Soon thereafter, I found myself in a mid-Manhattan office tower sorting through old pension applications and wondering whether there could possibly be a story to tell in what seemed initially to be extraordinarily boring records of grants and state school surveys. Where were Vida Scudder's journals now?

As things turned out, I was lucky and stumbled onto an interesting story quite quickly. That story began to take shape when I discovered that Andrew Carnegie and Henry Pritchett, the first president of the Carnegie Foundation, had not seen eye to eye at all. Carnegie had wanted the Carnegie Foundation to be nothing more than a pension agency, while Pritchett had wanted it to be "one of the Great Agencies . . . in standardizing American education."[2] This resulted in a good deal of cleverly effective maneuvering on Pritchett's part, which appalled me. So did the veiled alliances and behind-the-scenes negotiating that surrounded the famous 1910 Flexner report on medical education and other supposedly "objective" surveys. However naive it may sound, I had assumed that people like Pritchett were disinterested, maybe even selfless, public servants—the "good guys." It had not occurred to me that their aims and purposes might be controversial and that they would seek to accrue and use power to advance their priorities over and against people who disagreed with them. I had also assumed that an "objective" survey was an "objective" survey and not, as I came to describe it in *Private Power for the Public Good*, "a technology of influence."

My innocence now seems astounding, but I had not previously considered issues of power and politics except in their veiled, subtle, domesticated forms, as manifested in who could or could not speak for him- or herself and who would or would not pick up the socks. It quickly became clear, however, that to write the history of the Carnegie Foundation and then the history of the much larger and more complicated Carnegie Corporation, I would need to learn more about the ways in which people define and negotiate different, often conflicting interests.

Responding at the outset merely as the scholar I had now become, this realization prompted me to immerse myself in a variety of literatures that were entirely new to me. I began to read political philosophy and political theory, and especially liked Michael Walzer's *Radical Principles*, Sheldon Wolin's *Politics and Vision*, Peter Bachrach's *The Theory of Democratic Elitism*, Carole Pateman's *Participation and Democratic Theory*, and, most of all, John Dewey's *Liberalism and Social Action* and *The Public and Its Problems*. I read widely in the historical and sociological literature about professionalization, which, as luck would have it, was then taking a newly critical turn thanks to important studies by Mary Furner, Thomas Haskell, Magali Sarfatti Larson, Paul Starr, and Nancy Tomes and Joan Brumberg. And through works by Ellis Hawley, Martin Sklar, Grant McConnell, and Guy Alchon, among others, I began to wrestle with questions concerning regulation and state formation.[3] Eventually those books helped me frame, first, *Private Power for the Public Good*, and then, *The Politics of Knowledge*.

As had been true when I wrote *A Generation of Women*, I became totally caught up as I began to write. I was interested in what the two foundations had done and in the people who had worked for them, benefited from them, and, in some cases, resisted and fought with them. Most of all, though, I was deeply and personally engaged by the political issues that became inescapable as I was forced to confront my own reactions to the ideas, events, and people I was investigating. I seemed unable to let go of my dismay at Henry Pritchett and his "technologies of influence"; I kept feeling disillusioned when I encountered what seemed to me to be arrogant and elitist attitudes and actions. Clearly, therefore, in order to write anything that might resemble a balanced account, I needed to do more than act as a responsible scholar, reading up on her new topic; I needed also to come to a clearer understanding of my own views and values, my own politics.

As was the case for many people of my generation, I had been intermittently engaged in political causes as a student. At Smith, I became deeply interested in the civil rights movement and even flirted with the idea of going to Mississippi during the summer of 1964. As things turned out, I did not do that, but after Marion Wright (not yet Edelman) came to speak I did help raise money to buy shoes and clothes for kids in the Mississippi Delta and later registered voters in Springfield, Massachusetts. During my senior year, as the Vietnam War escalated, many of us also began to march and protest. More important, perhaps, we talked at length about the anger and confusion we felt as we watched our brothers and friends go into the armed forces (some never to come back) or leave for Canada or somehow get medical exemptions. We did not favor the war, but we also did not want to be ineligible for military service while our male peers fought, died, and dodged the draft.

Then I went to Teachers College, where, in the spring of 1968, everything exploded. This was real politics, I thought at the time. Smith protests had been ladylike, a far cry from those led by Mark Rudd, who postured as an unshaven, rowdy urban guerrilla. To my untutored eyes, he seemed tough, savvy, defiant, and maybe even brave. In those days, I was reading *Ramparts* and a short-lived journal called *Working Papers for a New Society*, I. F. Stone and Mao, and like so many others, I was quite awed by all the chanting and marching and climbing in and out of barricaded buildings. I remember being furious when police guarding the entrance to the campus tried to flirt and, much more, I remember feeling totally betrayed when police were called in to "clear" the campus.

Although participating in events like those did force one to declare one's position, as did the then common claim that "if you are not with us, you're against us," my positions were largely derivative. I was easily swayed by charisma and my friends and I tended to respond to issues framed by other people. I knew nothing about Columbia's plans to build a gym in Morningside Heights until Mark Rudd and others announced that the plans had to be resisted. I do not think I was unusually frivolous or mindless, but I was young and my politics were more activist than reflective and more centered on events than on ways to realize known, considered, and articulated convictions.

That had to change and did change, or so at least I think and hope, after I became a scholar. I could not write the kind of history I wanted to write unless I understood how fundamentally I believed (and still believe) in social and economic equality, racial integration, and participatory forms of governance. Put otherwise, I had to clarify what was socially and politically essential to me, if I were to formulate problems and issues, for myself, on my own. To use the relevant jargon, I had to know where I was coming from.

Of course, in writing the history of the Carnegie Foundation and then the Carnegie Corporation, I could have written fairly straightforward, institutional chronicles. There was enough human interest and self-evident significance in the activities of these foundations to have made that possible. But I did not want to do that. I wanted to write history that was broadly contextualized and built around powerful "so what" questions. I did not want merely to record the doings of others. That would have been analogous to reading, but not speaking, at my grandfather's memorial service. I wanted to *say* something, which to me seemed to require addressing the matter of who was doing what, to whom, for what purposes, and with what consequences. Most likely those questions seemed the "natural" ones to ask because they were rooted in my earlier experience of familial politics. There is no doubt, however, that, in conjunction with the reading I was doing, they were also inescapable in the records I was studying of grants made and, equally important, grants that were not made.

Writing *Private Power for the Public Good* and *The Politics of Knowledge* provided me with a profound education in politics, which enabled me to approach history with questions I found compelling. If writing *A Generation of Women* made me a scholar, writing those two books made me a scholar with firmer, more considered political commitments. They helped me clarify what I wanted to say. I hope they also stand, totally apart from that, as useful works that consider a tremendously important but still woefully understudied aspect of American governance. Once again, therefore, my research and writing fulfilled both subjective and objective needs.

"THE PLURAL WORLDS OF EDUCATIONAL RESEARCH"

During the five years since *The Politics of Knowledge* was published, my writing has taken yet another turn. It is now more clearly centered in education. Of course, I have always written about education. Because promoting education was the objective of both the Carnegie Foundation and the Carnegie Corporation, I was writing about education even while writing the histories of those trusts. That said, it is also true that most of what I have written has had something of a dual focus–education *and* the lives of women, education *and* the politics of knowledge. Now what I write is, in a sense, more concentrated and undiluted.

To some extent this is a result of the subjects I have been treating. As I was finishing *The Politics of Knowledge*, wondering what my next project should be, it occurred to me that there had been very little historical writing about education as a field of research. It also occurred to me that if I were to turn to that topic next, I could build on the work I had done in the history of philanthropy while also drawing on some of the new works in intellectual history that set ideas within their social contexts. For these reasons, I sought and won a grant from the Spencer Foundation to underwrite a multiyear study of "the social history of educational research." My plan was a broad investigation of this topic but not necessarily another book. At the time, I was feeling quite written out.

Having secured a wonderfully open-ended hunting license, I decided to begin by writing an article about John Dewey. I had already read a lot of Dewey, but I wanted to read more and to learn more about him as a person. As I read, I discovered that Dewey was infinitely more human and complicated than I had anticipated, and I became especially fascinated by what he had tried to do at the Laboratory School that he and his wife had founded in the 1890s at the University of Chicago. Although I was not (yet) writing about the Lincoln School, which was started a little later at Teachers College, I was clearly adding the third topic I had noted on the first page of my copy of the *Transformation of the School* to the two I had already taken up.

After completing an initial article, "The Plural Worlds of Educational Research"–arguing that even though Dewey had formulated a distinctive approach to educational study while at Chicago, that approach had had much less influence than the very different one developed by Edward L. Thorndike–and another article, which was an intellectual biography of George S. Counts, I had to put this project temporarily on the shelf. Having long since moved into a regular faculty appointment at Teachers College, I had very heavy teaching and committee obligations and, in addition, was director of the Institute of Philosophy and Politics of Education and, in January of 1990, became editor of the *Teachers College Record*. I had agreed to take on the *Record* for a number of reasons, the most relevant here having been that I wanted the challenge of confronting educational issues and writing about them on a regular basis. I need not have done this; previous editors had written editorials intermittently or not at all. But, once again, I found myself intrigued by the possibility of speaking out and, since then, have produced four essays a year on topics ranging from university reform to parental involvement in education. Obviously, the opportunity opened to me via the editorship of the *Record* also helped focus my work.

Last but hardly least, my current direction was profoundly shaped by experiences I had during the 1991–92 academic year, when I was a fellow at the Center for Advanced Study in the Behavioral Sciences in Stanford, California. Deciding to go to the center was not easy. Because my husband's law practice was (and is) in New York City, he could not move with me for the year (instead we enjoyed the dubious pleasures of a transcontinental "commute"); nor could our son come to Stanford since he was beginning college that fall. Going to the center therefore meant living alone, which was not a prospect I relished, though, as things turned out, I found being on my own, mid-career, mid-life, interesting. It made me more appreciative of the life I have chosen.

At the center, I finally had time to return to my study of the social history of educational research. I read a great deal about the history of psychology, wrote and junked a number of book outlines, and, feeling less and less written out as the year went along, finally developed an outline that made at least initial sense and began drafting the first chapter.

In addition to rekindling my enthusiasm for writing, my year at the center clarified my sense of profession. Although I was working very hard, I had time to get to know many of my "fellow fellows," all of whom were accomplished and engaged scholars in one or another of the so-called behavioral sciences. We ate lunch together, sat in the sun, went for walks, drank wine, played tennis, went swimming, and found our way to lots of restaurants in San Francisco. In the process I learned a lot about how different people, in different disciplines, work, write, and think.

As an historian, I had lots of company at the center–there were about a dozen of us. As a scholar of education, I was unique–various circumstances had prevented the other people in education who were meant to be there from coming. Being unique within such a methodologically self-conscious setting was enlightening. I learned to appreciate the rigor of social science models, although I realized that their abstraction from the "mess" of reality was unsatisfying to me. If this confirmed my identity as an historian, conversations with those of my "fellow fellows" who were also historians made me aware that my interests tended to be a little different from theirs. For better or worse, the educational focus of my work gave it a somewhat more "applied" cast. I was more directly concerned with the relevance of my work to contemporary issues and problems than they were inclined to be.

Thus confronted with a central and relatively distinctive aspect of the special field of history with which I am affiliated, I also became even more aware than I had been of the discount under which those of us in education labor. I remember being asked why I identified myself as a scholar of education since I could simply say I was an historian. I also remember the vehemence with which one of my "fellow fellows" declared that she was *not* an historian of education, even though many of her best writings had been squarely within that field. She obviously thought *educational* history as opposed to history was déclassé. And I remember, too, how intrigued some people were by educational questions once they were exposed to them, which led many to remark that it had never occurred to them that education could really be interesting.

For reasons I did not examine carefully at the time, my year at the center left me a more education-oriented educational historian than I might have otherwise been. Pondering that as I now write this essay, I think that was because my time there made me see that, at least for me, being in education and doing education can be and is political. For most of my "fellow fellows" who are historians, doing history was an end in itself; for me, it is primarily a method, a way to think. Whether reconstructing historical ideas, traditions, practices, and problems, or writing more directly in support of teachers, public education, and comprehensive educational policies, I hope to enrich contemporary and future educational possibilities. Education is not a panacea. It cannot alone insure that we will have greater economic and social equality, fuller racial integration, and more participatory forms of governance. But it can help move us in those directions. Clearly, therefore, in trying to enhance this society's understanding of education and, hence, its capacity to deliver effective education to all people, I am speaking publicly and independently about issues that matter greatly to me. I am acting as the women I wrote about in *A Generation of Women* did earlier, as a person I have struggled and wanted to be.

When I was a graduate student, Larry Cremin gave me a book with the phrase "scribere est agere" (to write is to act) written on the front page. It was one of his favorite mottoes and one he used often to inscribe books. At the time, I liked the phrase although it did not then really resonate with my experience. Now it does. Writing is my way of being the person I have chosen to become.

"A SUBJECTIVE NECESSITY: BEING AND BECOMING AN HISTORIAN OF EDUCATION"

As I have sat in my study writing this essay, I have realized anew that writing about my experience helps me understand and configure it in ways that can be both illuminating and energizing. However, I have also often found myself wondering how and why, whether and when narratives of personal experience can serve educative purposes for other people. Put otherwise, I have wondered about their "objective" value.

In the abstract, the answer is clear: Narratives of personal experience can educate if and when they connect, in a myriad possible ways, with the experience of those other people who will be one's readers. I was such a reader when, as a graduate student, I happened upon a collection of autobiographical essays by women scholars, writers, artists, and scientists called *Working It Out*, edited by Sara Ruddick and Pamela Daniels. Although none of the contributors had a situation identical to mine, their experiences meshed sufficiently with my own so that they could provide a frame of reference that was very helpful in understanding the social sources of the personal conflicts I was feeling. Their public reports of the deeply personal and individual ways they had combined the different elements of their lives, in a sense, socialized what I was still much too prone to understand as "my problem." *Working It Out* reinforced what I was also learning by reading Jane Addams. "Objective" circumstances often have "subjective" manifestations and consequences, even though our most characteristic ways of thinking, especially the formal ways of thinking most congenial to scholars, tend to obscure that. If this essay can, in turn, illuminate that connection for other people, I will be more than satisfied. Once again, I will have advanced my own education, a subjective necessity, while also contributing to something objectively worthwhile.

After I finish the book I am now writing about John Dewey and the history of educational scholarship, I want to write a book called *Creative Communities* that will consider the social sources of creative work. What will it and I be about? Having written this essay, I am more and more curious and hope that, with time, I will be lucky enough to find out. Scribere est agere.

NOTES

1. See Lagemann, 1981, 1983a, 1983c, 1985.
2. Henry S. Pritchett to Andrew Carnegie, November 16, 1905, Carnegie Foundation Archive, New York City.
3. See, for example, Furner, 1975; Haskell, 1977; Larson, 1977; Starr, 1982; and Brumberg and Tomes, 1982. See also Hawley, 1974a, 1974b; Sklar, 1988; McConnell, 1966; and Alchon, 1985.

BIBLIOGRAPHY

Addams, Jane. 1910. *Twenty Years at Hull-House, With Autobiographical Notes*. New York: Macmillan.

Alchon, Guy. 1985. *The Invisible Hand of Planning: Capitalism, Social Science and the State in the 1920s*. Princeton, NJ: Princeton University Press.

Bachrach, Peter. 1967. *The Theory of Democratic Elitism: A Critique*. Boston: Little, Brown.

Brumberg, Joan Jacobs, and Nancy Tomes. 1982. "Women in the Professions: A Research Agenda for American Historians." *Reviews in American History* 10 (June): 275–296.

Cremin, Lawrence A. 1961. *The Transformation of the School: Progressivism in American Education, 1876–1957*. New York: Knopf.

Cremin, Lawrence A. 1970–1988. *American Education*, 3 vols. New York: Harper and Row.

Dewey, John. 1927. *The Public and Its Problems*. New York: Holt.

Dewey, John. 1935. *Liberalism and Social Action*. New York: G. P. Putnam.

Flexner, Abraham. 1910. *Medical Education in the United States and Canada, Bulletin No. 4*. New York: Carnegie Foundation for the Advancement of Teaching.

Friedan, Betty. 1963. *The Feminine Mystique*. New York: Dell.

Furner, Mary. 1975. *Advocacy and Objectivity: A Crisis in the Professionalization of American Social Science, 1865–1905*. Lexington: The University Press of Kentucky.

Haskell, Thomas L. 1977. *The Emergence of Professional Social Science: The American Social Science Association and the Nineteenth Century Crisis of Authority*. Urbana: University of Illinois Press.

Hawley, Ellis W. 1974a. "Herbert Hoover and American Corporatism, 1929–1933." In *The Hoover Presidency: A Reappraisal*, Martin L. Fansold and George T. Mazuzan, eds. Albany: State University of New York Press, 102–119.

Hawley, Ellis W. 1974b. "Herbert Hoover, the Commerce Secretariat, and the Vision of an 'Associative State,' 1921–1928." *Journal of American History* 61 (June):116–140.

James, William. 1892. *Psychology*. Cleveland, OH: Fine Editions.

Lagemann, Ellen Condliffe. 1979. *A Generation of Women: Education in the Lives of Progressive Reformers*. Cambridge, MA: Harvard University Press.

Lagemann, Ellen Condliffe. 1981. "Education as Exchange: A Perspective Derived from the History of Women." In *Educating an Urban People: The New York City Experience*, Diane Ravitch and Ronald K. Goodenow, eds. New York: Teachers College Press, 29.

Lagemann, Ellen Condliffe, ed. 1983a. *Nursing History: New Perspectives, New Possibilities*. New York: Teachers College Press.

Lagemann, Ellen Condliffe. 1983b. *Private Power for the Public Good: A History of the Carnegie Foundation for the Advancement of Teaching*. Middletown, CT: Wesleyan University Press.

Lagemann, Ellen Condliffe. 1983c. "Women's History." In *Historical Inquiry in Education: A Research Agenda*, John H. Best, ed. Washington, DC: AERA.

Lagemann, Ellen Condliffe, ed. 1985. *Jane Addams on Education*. Classics in Education, No. 51. New York: Teachers College Press. Republished as Jane Addams, *On Education*, with a new introduction by Ellen Condliffe Lagemann (New Brunswick, NJ: Transaction, 1994).

Lagemann, Ellen Condliffe. 1989. "The Plural Worlds of Educational Research." *History of Education Quarterly* 29 (Summer):185–214.

Lagemann, Ellen Condliffe. 1992a. *The Politics of Knowledge: Philanthropy, Public Policy, and the Carnegie Corporation*. Chicago: University of Chicago Press.

Lagemann, Ellen Condliffe. 1992b. "Prophecy or Profession? George S. Counts and the Social Study of Education." *American Journal of Education* 100(2):137–165 (February).

Larson, Magali Sarfatti. 1977. *The Rise of Professionalism: A Sociological Analysis*. Berkeley: University of California Press.

McConnell, Grant. 1966. *Private Power and American Democracy*. New York: Knopf.

Pateman, Carol. 1970. *Participation and Democratic Theory*. Cambridge: Cambridge University Press.

Ruddick, Sara, and Pamela Daniels, eds. 1977. *Working It Out: Twenty-Three Women Writers, Artists, Scientists and Scholars Talk About Their Lives and Work*. New York: Pantheon.

Schwab, Joseph J. 1978. *Science, Curriculum, and Liberal Education: Selected Essays*. Chicago: University of Chicago Press.

Sklar, Martin J. 1988. *The Corporate Reconstruction of American Capitalism, 1890–1916: The Market, the Law, and Politics*. Cambridge: Cambridge University Press.

Starr, Paul. 1982. *The Social Transformation of American Medicine*. New York: Basic.
Walzer, Michael. 1980. *Radical Principles: Reflections of an Unreconstructed Democrat*. New York: Basic.
Wolin, Sheldon. 1960. *Politics and Vision: Continuity and Innovation in Western Political Thought*. Boston: Little, Brown.
Woody, Thomas. 1929. *A History of Women's Education in the United States*. New York: Science.

* CHAPTER 9 *

Accident, Awareness, and Actualization

Nel Noddings

MY PROFESSIONAL LIFE, like that of many other women, has not been the result of linear projection and orderly plan. Rather, in the words of Mary Catherine Bateson (1990), it has been "composed." It is largely the result of various accidents and an awareness of opportunity. Between awareness and actualization, of course, there has been something else–discipline, hard work–and I suppose lots of other external and internal factors. However, much can be explained in terms of accident and awareness, and important features of my philosophical work can certainly be traced to key accidents and the chains of awareness and action they triggered. All of the accidents recounted here involve love or led to love, and these loves, like bits of colored sea glass, are the elements from which my life has been composed.

The first wonderful accident happened in second grade. My family had moved the year before, and I had found myself in a strange and much more demanding academic environment. I remember that, at least twice in first grade, the school principal drove me home "ill." I wasn't ill; I was scared and suffering a loss of confidence. Beyond the feelings of fear and confusion, I have little memory of that year. Then, in second grade, the teacher invited me to join the top reading group, and the girls in the group welcomed me happily. I never knew the teacher's first name. She was Miss Christ, and I think she was old. But who knows? All adults seem old to second graders. She was special to me, and shortly after her recognition of my reading ability, I started to read *The Prince and the Pauper*. School became my home, and teachers–year after year of them, with occasional incompetents–provided the major part of my emotional and intellectual support.

It is not surprising that I now put so much stress on teacher-student relationships. However analytical my work in this area is or becomes, its foundation is in personal experience. What if Miss Christ hadn't been there?

Learning from Our Lives: Women, Research, and Autobiography in Education. ISBN 0-8077-3593-0 (pbk), ISBN 0-8077-3594-9 (cloth).

What if all my teachers had been like my first, third, and fourth grade teachers? They weren't bad, mind you, but they were not Miss Christ. I think of all the children whose parents, through no fault of their own, cannot give them intellectual support, and all the children who need an emotional anchor, and, sadly, all the teachers who are now encouraged to concentrate solely on academic skills and, thus, never form the relationships kids really need to grow. I wonder, also, how many young teachers who enter the profession because they want to make a difference in the lives of students become discouraged because the structures of schooling prevent their doing so.

The six years spent in my newly beloved school were stable and productive. It was a rich environment with lots of art, music, drama, sports, and projects. I was very active in sports–probably because I spent so much time with boys. My family lived in a second-floor apartment above relatives, and a male cousin was my most frequent playmate. He was forever "training" me in the skills of baseball. Naturally, he hogged the glory of batting time, and I did the fielding. But all the running, throwing, and catching made me a successful participant in every sport available to elementary school girls.

Besides the ordinary work of school, which, somewhat perversely, I enjoyed–I loved the neat look of everything done exactly right–I particularly enjoyed music. We had weekly assemblies. At most of these, we sang, and I still remember odd tunes such as "Captain Jinks" and "A Capital Ship." But there were also the lovely songs of Stephen Foster, Schubert's "Serenade," and Gounod's "Lovely Appear." At some assemblies we listened to the Damrosch concerts–programs of classical music specially arranged for young audiences. These contributed to my lifelong passion for classical music.

I enjoyed music mainly as a listener, although I did learn to play the piano, and my sister and I sang together. She had (and still has) an exceptionally fine voice; mine, with very limited range and volume, was adequate to supply the harmony. On the performance side, I was far better at math than at music, and my third-grade teacher, who thought only the arts were worth real effort, warned my mother that I would probably become a math teacher. The implication was that I should be watched carefully lest the warning signs deepen and increase.

It was also in these years that another lifelong interest developed. We lived next door to my grandparents, and my cousin, sister, and I had the run of two large yards and extensive fields behind them. I came to love the trees, shrubs, and flowers on these properties, and I can still walk around those yards in my mind: I can see the tall lilacs lining the driveway, the huge black walnut trees that almost always harbored caterpillars, the blackberry jungle into which I often crawled with a rope around my waist to retrieve a baseball (my cousin would stand unscratched outside holding the rope so that, at least, I would not be forever lost in the brambles), the majestic maples guarding my grandparents' house from the street, the hollyhocks that sprang unbidden every year and attracted swarms of bees, the raised flower gardens in both yards. My school contributed to this love, too. Every year we got to sell seeds, and the packets themselves were lovely and filled with promise. My mother shared this love with me as I have with my children and as they are now doing with theirs. What would spring be like without those packets of pansies, petunias, nasturtiums, zinnias, and marigolds? And what is a school like if its students are never asked to do something for it?

SCHOOL AT THE CENTER OF LIFE

In the summer before seventh grade, my family moved again. This was just before World War II, and the depression was still on. My parents had little money but wanted a home of their own, and so they bought a tiny "shell" home in the Raritan Bay area of the north Jersey shore. They had to build the entire interior–walls, ceilings, insulation–and they had to complete the foundation to keep the winter winds from freezing the pipes and chilling the floors.

The move was a potential disaster for me. I went from a progressive, academically advanced school to a four-room school in which seventh and eighth grades were in one room. My beloved former school had band and glee club, a terrific art program, school plays, and well-directed team sports. I had been popular with those lovely kids who first welcomed me to the advanced reading group, and I hated to leave them, my cousin, and my grandparents. I hated to leave the maple trees, and the bramble thicket, and the hollyhocks and the lilacs.

There were just two bulwarks against the flood of despair. First, there was Raritan Bay, that arm of sea along which I roamed all year round and in which I learned the delight of salt-water swimming. The bay was clear and beautiful then, and it was the center of recreation for us kids. It was rumored that even Sunday School might be scheduled according to the tide. None of us knew then that in just five short years the bay would be hopelessly polluted and the beaches deserted except by lonely beachcombers and thinkers like me. World War II and the dramatic growth of industrialization it induced destroyed the bay and its environment. Even today the beaches are only for walking, not for swimming.

The second bulwark against despair was my seventh-grade teacher. She was very young and very beautiful. There was nothing in my life but the sea and study, and since my prowess at studies seemed to please her, I studied everything she set out for us. By today's standards, it was pretty dull stuff–the three cases of percentage, the names of rivers, mountain ranges, cities, and countries, lots of dates, grammar–including infinitives, gerunds, and gerundives (but not, thankfully, diagramming–a technique I was never exposed to). I astonished my teacher by getting practically everything right. I wasn't really interested in the geography of Asia, but I got 100 on a hundred-question test on Asian geography. Awareness of what this teacher meant to me encouraged a form of discipline that has lasted a lifetime. How does one get through hard times? By thinking, reading, and studying. I spent the summer before and after seventh grade (when I wasn't swimming) drawing maps of Africa and South America–learning all the countries, capitals, rivers, and mountains. Study became both a pleasure and an anodyne. It became an effective drug against pain, one with no bad side effects. It still serves that function for me.

That four-room school at which I attended seventh and eighth grade had nothing but its four rooms equipped barely with chalkboards, desks, and–in our room–one bookcase. There was no music, no art, no counseling, no extracurricular activities; the playground was unusable when the septic tank overflowed. There wasn't even an office–just a small room that served as teachers' lounge, sick room, and place to keep records. Without Miss Baker, that place would have been horrible.

I had hoped, of course, for two years with Miss Baker, but the following year, the school went on double sessions. Eighth grade was scheduled in the afternoon, and the principal was assigned to teach us. I was devastated. The man was totally incompetent. He taught sitting down, usually with his hand across his mouth so that those of us in the back of the room could not possibly understand him. I chose a seat in the very back next to the door so that I could at least see my beloved Miss Baker as she walked by to leave for the day. What misery! The only saving grace was that my seat was also next to the bookcase. While the teacher mumbled on, I read several of James Fenimore Cooper's *Leather Stocking Tales*, and I especially enjoyed his *The Last of the Mohicans*. (I was outraged when I saw the recent movie and found the tale distorted beyond recognition.) I also read several of Albert Payson Terhune's dog stories and, I think, *Black Beauty*, but that may have been somewhere else. Mercifully, the year is blotted out in a blur of treasured reading.

Sometime toward the end of the year, our class underwent the usual standardized testing–a full battery covering all the subjects. After the results were in, the principal just happened to bump into my father on a bus. He told my father that he had never seen such test scores as mine in his forty years as a teacher. Shaking their heads, both of them said, sadly, that it was a shame I wasn't a boy. So far as I know, that was the last notice either took of my scholastic development. But Miss Baker followed my high school career with pride, and she came to my graduation. By then she had been somewhat displaced in my affections by my high school math teacher, but she was still important to me. Although I know I delivered the valedictory address at graduation, I have no idea what I said; what I remember is that *she* was there. This is a bit unfair to my parents. They did have a lovely party, and lots of relatives came. But what mattered to me is that *she* came. Looking back on those events now, I am led to extend my work on teacher-student relationships.[1] To do well in school, children need not only a *loving* adult in their lives but one who can also serve as a model of an educated person. My parents had had little education, and they could not serve that function for me. I needed my teachers. Suppose I had suffered that dreadful principal for both seventh and eighth grades. How many kids today suffer such teaching or worse?

Next came high school. Many kids hate high school and can't wait to grow up. I loved high school. From the first day, I felt there was something special in it, and I wanted it never to end. Two high school accidents of fate are worth mentioning because they have so greatly affected my life and work. When I got home after my first day in high school, my mother wanted to know all about it. After hearing all about the fascinating new subjects, Latin and algebra, she had to prompt me on people. Had I met anyone new? Well, I said, there was this boy. He was blond, blue-eyed, and wore a royal-blue shirt. He was about my height. My mother thought this was pretty funny. In high school, one was supposed to meet big, brawny guys. But we were only thirteen then. At age twenty, when we married, Jim was seven inches taller.

Now, of course, there is a long story to be told about the years between thirteen and twenty and many more stories to be told about the years since then. For present purposes, I want to reflect on the worries I had in high school about my womanhood. I would not have put it that way then, of course. Indeed, I would not have admitted a concern. I often said that I would never marry–that I definitely would not unless I was so much in love that I couldn't help myself. This was largely to cover up the nagging fear that girls like me–girls who were good at math and Latin–simply could not attract boys. So I vacillated in my attitude. There was ample evidence that I could attract boys. In my sophomore year, I attended school dances and had a good time. Jim and I "went together"–which in those days meant that he sent me notes in classes (sometimes on the wings of paper airplanes) and that we danced together at school events. In my junior year, however, I became quiet and somewhat withdrawn and just concentrated on my studies. If I showed my true self, could I still attract boys? I was unsure. And so it went for several years. When I married, after rushing through college in three years, it was certainly for love, but it was also to quiet those internal and external voices that wondered whether I was a true woman.

Another casualty of those years was my love of sports. "Real" girls, my friends assured me, could not play baseball, football, and basketball, and so–as quickly as I had given up saying "ain't" some years earlier–I gave up baseball and pretended to be a "real" girl. I got a respectable B in physical education, our teacher told me, because I always had a clean gym suit. Well, if you never sweat, it's easy to stay clean. And real girls did not sweat in those days.

I also found a way to compensate for getting so many A's. I became a ringleader in mischief. Girls like me did not engage in sex, or drink, or smoke, and I was no exception to the hard and fast rules against these activities. We just didn't do these things. Our mischief was far more innocent. A friend and I spent an entire evening carefully painting little square dog biscuits in beautiful pastel shades. We covered them with candy sprinkles, placed them in boxes lined with waxed paper, wrapped the boxes, and presented them (anonymously) to three of our male teachers. We were even careful to check that the paints we used were harmless. And when we had finished our artistic work, we laughed ourselves purple as we envisioned our teachers smiling in anticipation, attempting a bite (we hoped they wouldn't break a tooth), and licking the color from their lips in bewilderment. If only we could be there! Because I treasured my A's, I never skipped classes, but I did skip study halls, and it was during these "free periods" that my friends and I lived on the wild side. We were well supplied with books of hall passes (which I swiped from our history teacher's desk), and I could do pretty good forgeries of several teachers' signatures. We also studied our teachers' habits and knew how best to annoy them and, at the same time, to protect ourselves from retribution.

For example, we knew that our math teacher, Mr. Shea, would often step into the long coat closet at the rear of his room and, on tiptoe, look through the closet vent at activities in the hall. He often caught illegal wanderers this way. Because the vent was so handy for his surveillance activities, he usually left the sliding doors of the closet open. So, one day my friends and I dumped a whole bag of marbles through the vent and then ran like hell. Friends who were in the class at the time described a scene of chaos: marbles clattering everywhere, Mr. Shea trying to run from the window side of the room to the door to catch the culprits. But running across a room flooded with marbles is not easy. Meanwhile my friends and I safely escaped to the basement and enjoyed the scene in our imaginations.

I could tell many more such stories–fake firecrackers placed for mere visual effects, aliases always at the ready for unsuspecting substitutes (I was usually Mary Lou Alstein, sometimes Carolyn Swift), teachers' record books "borrowed" for careful inspection–but the purpose of the stories is achieved if the reader understands that a girl in those days had to compensate somehow for being genuinely interested in Cicero and geometric proofs.

Girls still suffer some of those anxieties today, and part of our work as feminist educators is to include such issues in our research and in the school curriculum. Most well-educated young women no longer suffer the "true woman" syndrome by the time they reach graduate school. Instead they suffer the "true professional" syndrome. Many ask whether it is possible to have both a profession and family life, and often highly successful women tell them that it is not. What such women mean is that it is not possible to plan a professional life in the single-minded, linear way of masculine tradition and still marry and raise children. Indeed to admit longings for home and family raises suspicions about one's professional commitment. But who says that the traditional masculine way is the only path to professional success? And, for that matter, why should success be defined in terms of money and percentile rankings? Life can turn into a dull and drab composition if it is planned with only competitive goals in mind.

The second influential accident in high school was the effect my math teacher had on me. I had the same teacher for four years. (Yes, he is one of those who received the dog biscuits, and it was he who ran the gauntlet of marbles.) I learned later that he knew very little mathematics, but that was unimportant. I guess I was on one of those Freudian searches for a father, and this man spoke precise and elegant English, went to church, played the violin, and was interested in drama. Older than my own father, he presented—without intending to do so—a very different picture of fatherhood and manhood.

The relationship between me and my math teacher was also very different from the earlier one with Miss Baker. Aside from acknowledging my mathematical ability, he paid no attention whatever to me. The interest, love, fascination, idolization, were all and entirely on my side. That was my good fortune, because the relationship could not have supplied what I needed if it had not been one-sided. What did it supply? Martin Buber, in *Between Man and Man*, puts it this way:

> Trust, trust in the world, because this human being exists—that is the most inward achievement of the relation in education. Because this human being exists, meaninglessness, however hard pressed you are by it, cannot be the real truth. Because this human being exists, in the darkness the light lies hidden, in fear salvation, and in the callousness of one's fellow-men the great love. (p. 98)

The analysis of relationships—especially those peculiarly one-sided yet reciprocal relationships that characterize teaching and parenting—is central to my work today. I know now that however important subject matter is, it is not the heart of teaching, nor is technique. It is that presentation of what Buber called the "effective world" that comes through the teacher himself or herself.

That math teacher, Mr. Shea, still affects my work. Although I loved him deeply and the affection was, in later years, reciprocal, I have to face the fact that many students hated him, and, worse, that their hatred was at least understandable–perhaps even justified. He was rigid in his methods, overly strict in his classroom management (which made playing tricks on him a great sport). Grading was viciously competitive; only 10 percent of us could get A's, and our entire grade depended on the results of timed tests. When 10 percent of the class had finished a test, everyone had to stop! It may not surprise readers to hear that class enrollment went like this: 52 students in algebra one, 40 in geometry, 26 in the first half of algebra two, 15 in the second half, 6 in solid geometry, and 3 left in trigonometry–my future husband, a boy who later got a Ph.D. in biochemistry, and me. Predictably, our grades were A, B, and C. I got the A. I think it is clear that Mr. Shea was not a good teacher for most kids, but he was right and terribly important for me.

Again, it is perhaps not surprising that much of the work I do today in mathematics education emphasizes well-informed freedom and steady support for students rather than uniform requirements and high expectations.[2] I think my beloved math teacher was dead-wrong in his insistence on speed, right answers (no partial credit), and competition.

However wrong he was for others, his instruction increased my own love of mathematics. As nearly as I can remember, I never got a word problem wrong in all of high school, and I liked problem solving and proofs better than anything else. It seemed to me then that problems and proofs could always be worked out and that there were ways to check one's answers so that no mistakes should go undetected. In contrast, more manipulative exercises could induce errors, and checks by repetition (and who had time for this?) were not foolproof. Some of my work even today focuses on problem solving.[3] Then, as now, I liked to do things my way. I can remember Mr. Shea asking once in exasperation, "Can't you ever do things the way they're taught?" Well, I should have said (but of course didn't), what fun would that be?

Today I am also convinced that we make a sad and deep error when we try to convert all teachers to a particular way of thinking or to a particular set of methods.[4] Instead we should help teachers to do the best they can with their own educational philosophies and their own beliefs. We should help them to build on their own strengths, just as we hope that they will build on the strengths of their students. A genuine pedagogical pluralism ought to be encouraged in our schools. Engaged in dialogue, encouraged to reflect on their own practice but allowed to keep their own beliefs, teachers might well begin to revise their methods and extend their pedagogical repertoires. Because I got to know my math teacher so well in later years, I am convinced that more respectful methods of supervision would have induced him to discard the most harmful of his methods. He would still have resisted conversion to a progressive, Deweyan model, but he would have been a better version of his own ideal.

In college, I majored in math, largely because I wanted to return to my old high school and do my student teaching with Mr. Shea. I did exactly that, and it was clear even then that I would be a very different kind of teacher. He let me be.

STILL IN LOVE WITH SCHOOL: NOW A TEACHER

When I finished college, no high school teaching jobs were available. Luckily, I had obtained an emergency elementary certificate, and so I was given a position teaching sixth grade. This was one of the most fortuitous accidents of my career as an educator. I thought I would hate teaching all that baby stuff. After all, I was trained as a high school math teacher, and I wanted to teach geometry and trigonometry. A wonderful thing happened. All the reading that started with Miss Christ and continued ever after became directly useful. All the fascination with Greece and Rome, with explorers and colonists, with maps and dates and charts and details swept over me in a great wave of childhood revisited. For example, in Miss Baker's seventh grade, I had written a play-script for Dickens's *A Christmas Carol.* I looked it over and found it adequate to direct my sixth graders in the school Christmas play.

These kids and I had such a good time that we stayed together for seventh and eighth grades. Each year we did the school play. We started a school paper and a safety patrol. We had class elections and planned activities democratically. Jim often stopped in after school and played basketball with the boys. Three of my boys were fatherless, and Jim went to Boy Scout father and son dinners with them. We taught the kids to dance. We went on hikes with them. I taught them to sing in parts. We did loads of art work. We read "Evangeline" and memorized quotations from it and from a host of other sources. The father of one of my boys greeted my husband on the train one morning with, "The pen is mightier than the sword!" I know I taught them math, too, but it was dull stuff compared with the other things we did. So far as I can tell after years of reflection, I wasn't really like any of my beloved teachers. Without giving up the enormous love I had for them, I was still doing things my own way and learning from my husband (an engineer who is terrific with kids) and from the kids themselves.

How did my first students do on achievement tests? Of course the school authorities were concerned about this. Was this group of children deprived because they did not go to junior high as all the other children in the district did? Apparently not; their achievement scores were the same as those of the junior high kids. However, their special teachers (they spent half a day a week at the junior high for classes such as shop, home ec, art, and music) rated them far higher on every affective measure. They were more cooperative, happier, friendlier, and more creative than their junior high peers. Both those years I was disappointed that they didn't do *better* than the junior high kids on the achievement tests but, with a fuller awareness now, I realize the results were just fine.

At the end of those lovely years, when Jim and I were about to move back to our childhood community with our first daughter, and I was preparing to take a high school job, I applied for a permanent teaching credential. I was told by a bureaucrat in the state department of education that I could not have one because my elementary credential had been good for only one year. She said, "You should not even have been paid for those two years." That woman knew nothing of my experience in those two years. She didn't even ask; she thought she was protecting the children of New Jersey from the sure evils that accompany teaching without a proper credential. Perhaps it is not surprising that today I have little interest in "professional" standards, teacher accreditation, and the host of stuffy, silly, and rigid regulations endorsed in the name of accountability.[5] What a weak word that is anyway! When you teach kids for several years, you take on *responsibility* not only for their academic growth but for their growth as whole human beings. To induce that sense of truly awesome responsibility in teachers, we must give teachers respect and freedom and allow them to experience the joy that goes with the responsibility. That joy arises out of continuous learning and out of the reciprocal relationships in which both teacher and students grow.

Next, in the chain of fateful accidents that structured my life, came parenthood. Our first child was, in many ways, like me. She turned the house upside down with intellectual curiosity–books, science experiments, artwork, and creative writing everywhere. In her college years as a math major, she would often start telephone conversations with, "Mother, consider the following." And there would follow a mathematical problem of some kind, not a recitation of the week's social events.

However, we did not have just one child. We had five, and then we adopted five more. There were several influences in this decision. Believe it or not, we were deeply influenced by *Cheaper by the Dozen*, the story of the Gilbreth family. We, too, wanted a large family, but we became concerned with the population explosion (to which we had already contributed) and decided to extend our family by adoption. Jim had spent almost two years in Korea while he was in the army and came to love Korean kids. Both of us were greatly impressed by Pearl Buck and her work with Amer-Asian children. Thus, over a period of time, three Amer-Asian boys joined the family.

And somewhere along the way, two teenage girls just "joined up" and became part of the family, too.

Experience with a large family of very different kids reinforced what I had started to learn with my sixth graders: People have widely different talents and interests. I had, for most of my early life, valued academic talent above all others. After all, consider what I had to do to earn my A in high school math! I think that, with some encouragement, I could have become an intellectual snob *magna cum laude*, but I was saved from that fate by a wonderful bunch of kids–kids who loved animals, played the piano, trumpet, and clarinet, danced, drew and painted, composed poetry, repaired old radios, made dresses and draperies, cooked, and played poker. We had an Eagle Scout and a couple of boys who would not even consider scouting. We had math majors and kids who hated math. We had two kids who demonstrated against the Vietnam War and one who joined the Air Force at that time (but, fortunately, did not go to Vietnam). They argued with one another about duty, decency, and democracy and brought home to us literally and forcefully how reasonable and decent people can differ and how lack of tolerance for ideological differences can lead to tragedy. Jim and I were both deeply opposed to that stupid and destructive conflict (the Vietnam War), but we also had great sympathy for the young men–just boys really, as in all wars–who felt that serving was their duty. I don't see how anyone could raise a large, diverse family without learning a lasting appreciation for the breadth of human talent and without acquiring a tragic sense of life. No cause but life itself could be great enough to sacrifice the beautiful possibilities in these young lives. When one comes to such a realization, there are no "sides"–just kids killing one another, kids who, through a different accident of fate, could have been members of my family or my sixth grade.

Again, it is no surprise that, in my current work, I urge educators to consider the full range of student capacities and ethicists to consider the full range of human response.[6] Human beings are not just rational mechanisms. Indeed, as Miguel Unamuno (1954) pointed out:

> Man is said to be a reasoning animal. I do not know why he has not been defined as an affective or feeling animal. Perhaps that which differentiates him from other animals is feeling rather than reason. More often I have seen a cat reason than laugh or weep. Perhaps it weeps or laughs inwardly–but then perhaps, also inwardly, the crab resolves equations of the second degree. (p. 3)

Thus, although I believe that designing new and better curriculums for science and math education is an important task, I am disheartened when colleagues see nothing more urgent and even embrace the dreadful goal that our children must be "number one" in math and science by the year 2000.

When kids are killing one another, when children are bearing children with no sense of how to raise them, when one in ten (or perhaps one in seven) children is on welfare, what can we be thinking in urging such a concentration on math and science? I am reminded here of Jerome Bruner's modest and insightful observation after the structure of the disciplines movement, in which he played such an important role, had produced so many rich and creative curriculums. Looking at the plight of our inner cities, he said simply, "Curriculum is not the answer."[7] This does not mean, of course, that curriculum cannot be *part* of the answer, but curriculum theorists and designers today must look beyond the rigor, beauty, and internal structures of their disciplines. Schooling must address the real problems of contemporary life.

Much of what we are striving for today in education is guided by a well-intentioned but deeply flawed conception of equality. Because academic math has for so long been a gatekeeper for higher education, many of us believe all students should be exposed to it. Policymakers are not satisfied with counseling and granting opportunities. They want to prove their commitment by forcing all kids to take algebra and geometry. A few see that most adults do not in fact use algebra in their professional or private lives, and so they talk about a "new" algebra–mathematical study that will have relevance and induce an admirable, analytic habit of mind. But surely there are other subjects that might also induce admirable habits of mind if students were allowed to immerse themselves in them. Why not question math's status as a gatekeeper instead of forcing everyone to study it?

There are at least two strong arguments against forcing all students to take algebra. (Notice that I say "take," not "study" or "learn," because one cannot force people to study or learn.) Both arise, for me, out of the personal experiences I have been describing. First, many kids–probably most–are just not inclined toward serious mathematics. Common sense should direct us to memories of our own school days. How many of our friends really liked math? How many understood it? As a teacher, I could always get some honest achievement out of most of my students, and good teachers all over the country do this year after year. But probably only 20 to 30 percent of our students really understand what it's all about, and 10 percent or so should be studying math in far greater depth than we allow now. We are so bound and determined to achieve equality that we ignore reality, and, paradoxically, we commit a great sin against equality itself. We confuse equality with sameness.

Human talents are wonderfully broad, and, if we are really concerned with equality, those talents should be treated with equal respect. Students need to understand what it means to live in a mathematicized world,[8] which means that they need to know something about the political and social uses of mathematics, but it is not clear how much mathematics they must be able to do in order to achieve this understanding. Indeed they might learn the mathematics they need better through the study of social problems that really interest them.

At bottom the present crusade for equality is deeply, although not intentionally, disrespectful. It aims to cast all students in the mold of a traditional, successful, white male—of a hypothetical male really, for most actual, even affluent, boys have not fitted the mold comfortably. In talking this way, I seem to be in the minority today, but prominent educators in the past urged us to think about what we are doing when we force the same curriculum on everyone. John Dewey, in *Democracy and Education*, said of education:

> The general aim translates into the aim of regard for individual differences among children. Nobody can take the principle of consideration of native powers into account without being struck by the fact that these powers differ in different individuals. The difference applies not merely to their intensity, but even to their quality and arrangement. As Rousseau said: "Each individual is born with a *distinctive* temperament. . . . We indiscriminately employ children of different bents on the same exercises; their education destroys the special bent and leaves a dull uniformity. Therefore after we have wasted our efforts in stunting the true gifts of nature we see the short-lived and illusory brilliance we have substituted die away, while the natural abilities we have crushed do not revive." (p. 116)

My perspective on aims and equality has been deeply influenced by the work of John Dewey, but it has also been formed by reflection on my life as a mother, student, mathematics teacher, and philosopher. The personal dimension has, perhaps, been more important than any philosophical argument.

LOVE DEEPENS: I BECOME A PHILOSOPHER

One more wonderful life-shaping accident occurred in 1969 when we moved our family from New Jersey to California. I had not wanted to go. I had been at our local high school for twelve years as math teacher, department chairperson, and assistant principal. With a master's in math, I also taught part-time at Rutgers, and I loved that work. But Jim had been offered a good job in Silicon Valley, and I guess—despite my objections—I, too, wanted a change. In my last year of high school teaching, I taught six classes, with five different preparations because I needed the intellectual stimulation. Union leaders said they wouldn't allow me to do that again, and I couldn't bear the thought of only two preparations. How was I to learn anything that way? Besides, all through these years I had enjoyed the experience of teaching some students—including my own first daughter—almost all their high school math. That experience, too, would be lost if I had to settle for two preparations. Continuity was, for me, still the heart of teaching.[9] It is perhaps not surprising that the daughter I taught for three years started her telephone conversations in the odd way I have described.

So we moved to California, and the full impact of what we had done hit me hard. "Now, what am I supposed to do?" I asked. "Well," said Jim, "you've always wanted to get a doctorate. Go to Stanford and get one." Oh, lucky ignorance! I knew nothing of Stanford and its great reputation. If I had, I would not have had the nerve to apply in the summer. Thus I rushed off to take the GRE summer special and applied to Stanford. Now all those years of reading and math teaching, combined with something that might be called specific test-taking ability, paid off handsomely. I was admitted, and my life changed dramatically.

All the glories I had dimly perceived in earlier years with Miss Christ, Miss Baker, and Mr. Shea became real. Imagine a place where one could occupy a whole library table all afternoon and evening if one wished, where the staff treated students as respectable persons, where becoming lost in thought was not regarded as an abnormality, where the written word–even in psychology!–was treated as an art. I stayed away from math (except for set theory) and tried to swallow a lifetime of philosophy in a few years.

I had to finish quickly. After all, there were all those kids to support and educate. Like high school, graduate school went too fast. Although I loved it and went through on a "high," I was not untouched by its dark side. I think it takes most people four or five years to regain a genuine voice and a decent style after writing a dissertation. Quite a few of my brightest peers found graduate school an ego-destroying experience. I was fortunate indeed. Again, I was drawn to philosophy first by the person teaching it, and later it became a passion in itself.

There came a time, eventually, when reflective awareness made it possible to bring my hard-earned analytical skills to bear on issues that, given my life experience, seemed really to matter. Surely, to be able to do that in one's work is one form of actualization.

The loves that rose up in my schooling–of plants, of music, of the sea, of teaching, of studying, and of particular people, my husband, teachers, friends–are with me still. My continuing love of the sea, for example, recently led me to a passage in *The Mirror of the Sea*, by Joseph Conrad, that expresses something beautiful for educators as well as sailors and beachcombers. Referring to an article on yachting, Conrad wrote:

> For the gist of that article, written evidently by a man who not only knows but *understands*–a thing (let me remark in passing) much rarer than one would expect, because the sort of understanding I mean is inspired by love; and love, though in a sense it may be admitted to be stronger than death, is by no means

> so universal and so sure. In fact, love is rare–the love of men, of things, of ideas, the love of perfect skill. For love is the enemy of haste; it takes count of passing days, of men who pass away, of a fine art matured slowly in the course of years and doomed in a short time to pass away, too, and be no more. Love and regret go hand in hand in this world of changes swifter than the clouds reflected in the mirror of the sea. (p. 21)

In our search for scientific methods, treatments, and techniques in education, we often forget the simple truth that kids will do things for people they like and trust. They are inspired by a form of love. Similarly, teachers who really care about their students and their subjects are inspired by dual loves to make themselves ever more competent. I see the striving–a striving out of love–in my youngest daughter who teaches math and in my son who brings such love to his principalship. However, subject-matter competence is not all that is required. Teachers must also share their quest for wisdom and disclose enough of their personal experience to give students a sense of possibility, tragedy, and wonder.

Emphasis on understanding and wisdom, an appreciation for spiritual and everyday life, has also become a part of my work, and I believe it should guide our teaching.[10] At the conclusion of his life's story–one of adventure and duty and wonder in the air above the Mediterranean, the South Atlantic, the Sahara, and Madrid–Antoine de Saint Exupéry wrote:

> To come to man's estate it is not necessary to get oneself killed round Madrid, or to fly mail planes, or to struggle wearily in the snows out of respect for the dignity of life. The man who can see the miracles in a poem, who can take pure joy from music, who can break his bread with comrades, opens his window to the same refreshing wind off the sea. He too learns a language of men.
>
> But too many men are left unawakened. (p. 239)

We cannot force people to awaken, however. Instead we have to invite them, share with them the miracles and joys we have experienced and listen to theirs. This approach makes education both easier and far more complex–easier because we will not be forever forcing things on students "for their own good," more complex because we will not always know exactly what our students are learning. In many cases, it could be years before we learn the real effects of our work, and in some cases, we may never know. But there are signs along the way: Students may express themselves more articulately, they may approach problems with greater patience and sophistication, they may read more widely and discuss more freely, they may treat one another (and us) with greater kindness and respect, they may reveal in continuous dialogue that they are acquiring impressive stores of information, and they may show in their daily lives that they are gaining some self-knowledge. How do we know such things? By talking with our students, by living with them. Among other things, students may learn that a life can be composed out of loves and that accidents–fortunate and unfortunate–can be turned toward actualization.

NOTES

1. I later wrote about teacher-student relationships. See Noddings, 1984, 1986, 1988a, 1992, 1995.
2. See Noddings, 1993b, 1993d, 1994.
3. See, for example, Noddings, 1988b.
4. See Noddings, 1991, 1992.
5. See Noddings, 1991.
6. See, for example, Noddings, 1984, 1989.
7. From Bruner's 1971 address to the Association for Supervision and Curriculum Development.
8. A number of writers have made this point, as have I in Noddings, 1994.
9. I was later to write about this. See Noddings, 1992.
10. See Noddings 1993a, 1993c; also Witherell and Noddings, 1991.

BIBLIOGRAPHY

Bateson, Mary Catherine. 1990. *Composing a Life*. New York: Plume.

Bruner, Jerome. 1971. "*The Process of Education* Reconsidered." *Association for Supervision and Curriculum Development Annual Conference Address*. Alexandria, VA: Association for Supervision and Curriculum Development.

Buber, Martin. 1965. *Between Man and Man*. New York: Macmillan.

Conrad, Joseph. [1906] 1988. *The Mirror of the Sea*. Marlboro, VT: Marlboro.

Dewey, John. 1916. *Democracy and Education*. New York: Macmillan.

Exupéry, Antoine de Saint. 1939. *Wind, Sand, and Stars*. New York: Harcourt Brace Jovanovich.

Noddings, Nel. 1984. *Caring: A Feminine Approach to Ethics and Moral Education*. Berkeley: University of California Press.

Noddings, Nel. 1986. "Fidelity in Teaching, Teacher Education, and Research on Teaching." *Harvard Educational Review* 56(4):496–510.

Noddings, Nel. 1988a. "An Ethic of Caring and Its Implications for Instructional Arrangements." *American Journal of Education* 96(2):215–230 (February).

Noddings, Nel. 1988b. "Preparing Teachers to Teach Mathematical Problem Solving." In *Research Agenda for Mathematics Education: Teaching and Assessment of Mathematical Problem Solving*, Edward A. Silver and Randall Charles, eds. Hillsdale, NJ: Lawrence Erlbaum, 244–258.

Noddings, Nel. 1989. *Women and Evil*. Berkeley: University of California Press.

Noddings, Nel. 1991. "The Professional Life of Mathematics Teachers." In *Handbook of Research on Mathematics Teaching and Learning*, Douglas A. Grouws, ed. Reston, VA: Macmillan and NCTM, 197–208.

Noddings, Nel. 1992. *The Challenge to Care in Schools*. New York: Teachers College Press.

Noddings, Nel. 1993a. "Beyond Teacher Knowledge: In Quest of Wisdom." *The High School Journal* 76(4):230–239.

Noddings, Nel. 1993b. "Caring and Constructivism." In *Schools, Mathematics, and the World of Reality*, Robert B. Davis and Carolyn A. Maher, eds. Boston: Allyn and Bacon, 35–50.

Noddings, Nel. 1993c. *Educating for Intelligent Belief or Unbelief*. New York: Teachers College Press.

Noddings, Nel. 1993d. "Politicizing the Mathematics Classroom." In *Math Worlds: Philosophical and Social Studies of Mathematics and Mathematics Education*, Sal Restivo, Jean Paul Van Bendegem, and Roland Fischer, eds. Albany: State University of New York Press, 150–161.

Noddings, Nel. 1994. "Does Everybody Count? Reflections on Reforms in School Mathematics." *Journal of Mathematical Behavior* 13:89–104.

Noddings, Nel. 1995. *Philosophy of Education*. Boulder, CO: Westview.

Unamuno, Miguel De. 1954. *Tragic Sense of Life*, trans. J. E. Crawford Flitch. New York: Dover.

Witherell, Carol, and Nel Noddings, eds. 1991. *Stories Lives Tell: Narrative and Dialogue in Education*. New York: Teachers College Press.

CHILDREN'S LITERATURE CITED

Cooper, James Fenimore. 1919. *The Last of the Mohicans*. New York: Scribner's.

Cooper, James Fenimore. 1985. *Leather Stocking Tales*. New York: Viking.

Dickens, Charles. 1900. *A Christmas Carol*. New York: Scribner's.

Gilbreth, Frank B. 1963. *Cheaper by the Dozen*. New York: Bantam.

Sewell, Anna. 1952. *Black Beauty*. New York: Dell.

Twain, Mark. 1901. *The Prince and the Pauper*. New York: Harper and Row.

* CHAPTER 10 *

First Words. Still Words.

Patricia J. Gumport

I BEGIN THIS ESSAY feeling extremely tentative in my search for words. My professional socialization and family upbringing caution me against disclosing the personal, speaking about what is presumed to be private. To do so is to risk tainting an intellectual autobiography with indulgence in a reflexivity that is surely to be dismissed by traditional scholars.

Nonetheless, I will do just that. I sit at my computer in my home office at the edge of the Stanford University campus. I am an assistant professor of education in my fifth year of the tenure track. That tenure clock ticks loudly today. It counts a rhythm that urges conformity. They tell me that I should use my time wisely. That is, I should write articles for the most highly regarded refereed journals. They tell me that I'm not supposed to be wondering/wandering in my writing now. They tell me I'm supposed to be producing.

I begin to write this essay wondering why I even accepted the editors' invitation. Clearly, it is not with tenure in mind. For that, I need to present myself as a scholar. Appearing as a human being in a publication (in a book chapter, no less) is not valued in my current work context. Nor do I begin in anticipation of the joy of speaking in a personal voice, for this sort of disclosure is awkward if not fundamentally uncomfortable. Just as clearly, it is not for the satisfaction of public revelation, for what I select to tell here is necessarily a partial accounting.

Yet, on another level, I am drawn to the task, viewing the invitation as a rare opportunity to step aside from the formal scholarly voice and to consider how to connect in a more genuine, human way. With that in my mind, my goal in this short piece is to join my colleagues in reflecting on some personal aspects of our scholarly paths. Central to my path is a strong track record of professional accomplishments interwoven with a compelling strand of per-

Learning from Our Lives: Women, Research, and Autobiography in Education. ISBN 0-8077-3593-0 (pbk), ISBN 0-8077-3594-9 (cloth).

sonal reflections on two persistent themes: my interest in the social construction of "what counts" and my growing awareness of the reality that "what counts" has implications for "who counts." I know now that my life would have been easier if I had taken for granted "what counts."

A QUICK LOOK BACK

The first words on my curriculum vitae reveal, as is commonplace, the degrees I have earned: a bachelor's in philosophy from Colgate University in 1980, two master's degrees (one in sociology, one in education) and a Ph.D. in education from Stanford University by 1987. Printed starkly on the page, those degrees signal my achievement of a certain kind of legitimacy. Yet, on my own terms, legitimacy is more complex and less easily bestowed. The discrepancy between the two lies at the heart of the matter.

Perhaps recalling some childhood memories will serve as an appropriate anchor. The youngest of three children, I was born in 1958, eight years after my brother and five years after my sister. I was an easy target for teasing from my siblings. When I was very young, they threatened to throw me out with the trash on garbage collection day. As I got older and achieved academic success, a state of grace they placed less value upon, they kept their distance from me and I from them.

Both of my parents worked outside our home, which was in Westchester County, New York. My father was the gourmet food buyer and manager for Bloomingdale's, while my mother worked in the library at a local elementary school. The family came together at dinner (which my mother called "supper" in order to lower my father's expectations of what would be served). We ate at the kitchen table, even though we had a separate dining room; that area of the house, along with the plastic slipcovers on the dining room chairs, was saved for company.

Dinner-table talk was both educational and intended to reinforce family values. Sometimes my father taught us simple things, like how to remember the colors of the rainbow (Roy G. Biv); other times he talked to us about unusual food (quail eggs, turtle soup, and French cheeses). My father had been an English major in college; every Sunday he did the *New York Times* crossword puzzle in ink. A stickler for precision with words, he encouraged us to use the dictionary not only for spelling but also for pronunciation. He took every opportunity at supper to correct our speaking: "going to" instead of "gonna," "because" rather than "'cuz," vacationing on a cruise "ship" rather than "boat," and, in preparation for answering the telephone, "This is she" rather than "This is me." Certain basic rules were made clear in the subtext–to speak clearly, correctly, and above all politely. On one occasion, my sister made the mistake of swearing, and she got her mouth washed out with soap. I learned early that there were great rewards for getting it right and penalties for not respecting the boundaries.

In this context, as an adolescent, I often chose the privacy of my room, where I explored a deeply introspective world. I became an excellent student. Throughout my teenage years, I read widely, choosing authors–Sartre, Camus, and Hesse–who spoke most eloquently to my youthful existential ruminations. I filled spiral notebooks with daily journal entries.

I also became a long-distance runner and ran competitively on the boys' cross country, winter track, and spring track teams. (There were no separate girls' teams yet.) As road races became popular in the early 1970s, I regularly went on fifteen- to twenty-mile training runs. I cannot recall exactly what I was running from or toward; I was just out there pounding the pavement, yet in my own inner world. It wasn't that I was always preoccupied by fundamental truths. Sometimes, it was pretty mundane. I recall one race in particular, when I was a high school sophomore enrolled in a typing class; as I completed the hilly terrain of the 25 K Thanksgiving Day Turkey Trot, I practiced my homework by typing every one of the words in my thoughts on an imaginary typewriter keyboard. Selecting words, placing them in sentences, and doing this imaginary typing became a suitable way to pass the time in the journey to the finish line. Much to everyone's surprise, my first publication emerged from these running experiences in a 1975 article in the *New York Times* that was entitled "2,000 Toes–A Race Odyssey." There is a persistent lonely quality to long-distance running that I am reminded of during sustained periods of research and writing.

Immersed in what seemed at the time to be a rich inner world, I preferred being by myself. I liked locating myself on the edges as an observer rather than being in the center of activity. I thought in my own peculiar disciplined way that I had mastered detachment, self-sufficiency, and objectivity. I thought this was the safest place to be. I thought it was up to me.

Yet that turned out not to be the case. What my family thought about me still mattered. I didn't want to be dismissed as the youngest, or labeled simply as a good daughter or a good student. And it was in this context that I faced an uncomfortable truth: I wanted their approval, their recognition that I mattered.

External approval was significant to me on some level, but not enough to guide my decision making. For, despite my making Phi Beta Kappa, my choice of a philosophy major in college became a sign to them that I had opted out of the real world. Getting two master's degrees, a Ph.D., and later faculty positions in graduate schools of education (UCLA, Stanford), confirmed for them their hunch that I would never get a "real job."

While I have waited for them to take me seriously, I realize that to this day my parents have waited for me to get serious. Just what serious is remains somewhat mysterious. I get hints. According to my father, my brother's successes are a source of pride in the family for "he leads men" as an executive in the sales division of a computer company.

In this sense, my interest in individuals' struggles for approval has an autobiographical basis. I easily translated this interest into research on legitimacy; that is, how and why areas of knowledge–and the people in them–become differentially valued. The need for approval and legitimacy, why I/we care, and how our lives are shaped by that valuation are central to my work and my life. External approval has dogged my steps but not shaped my path.

STRUGGLES FOR LEGITIMACY

In my professional life and academic career, I have developed these interests into an ambitious scholarly agenda. I was fortunate in college to find philosophy, a comfortable academic home for my questions about epistemology, metaphysics, and ontology. In a glimpse of things to come, I wrestled with my philosophy advisor over what constituted appropriate coursework to supplement my major. He assessed as a waste of academic credits the one course offered in the newly emerging field of women's studies. He also discouraged me from taking courses in the education department. I took them anyway to obtain a secondary school teaching credential in English, and I convinced him that this was acceptable as a vocational component to my liberal arts degree.

I continued to puzzle over what counts as worthwhile to do and to know as well as who decides. Graduate school began my immersion in the classical social theory of Weber, Durkheim, and Marx. I began to understand the complex mix of social structure and human agency that contributes to determinations of what counts as knowledge. Since I viewed colleges and universities as a natural setting in which these dynamics get played out, it seemed appropriate to specialize in the study of higher education. Much to my frustration, my early contact with higher education revealed a field that was divided into such finite topic areas as curriculum, students, faculty, finance, and governance. My interests didn't fit neatly into any one of these areas, which led a professor of higher education to deem my interests trivial and me intractable.

In any case, I found other scholarship for inspiration and for development of my thinking: Foucault on knowledge, power, and discourse; C. Wright Mills on the sociological imagination; radical structuralist interpretations of Weber; and feminist reflections on marginality and standpoint epistemology. I know that I would not have pursued this line of research or any academic career had it not been for a sociology professor, Ann Swidler, who offered a keen intellect and a respect for those inclined to ask big questions as well as to think hard about theory and practice. Her affirmation of my interests was crucial to my emerging sense of place in the academy.

With that support, I felt a measured confidence to venture forth into dissertation research on knowledge legitimation within the domain of higher education. My initial avenue into this topic was to examine how a new field emerges at the intersection of institutional and individual commitments.[1] I used feminist scholarship as a contemporary case study to show how knowledge legitimation lies at the intersection of organizational, political, and intellectual contexts. I also sought to show the ways in which socially legitimated knowledges and academic identities may be generated, in part, from an autobiographical basis.[2] Over the next decade, I would come to study the changing organization of academic knowledge through different frames: disciplinary reproduction, graduate education, and academic program reduction, all dynamic processes worthy of inquiry within the context of broader changes in the political and economic structures supporting higher education.[3]

In order to pursue these questions from an interpretive orientation in the sociology of knowledge, it soon became clear that I was stretching into new terrain. It involved talking with people, and writing about people, as well as documenting patterns of structural change. Since using multiple kinds of data sources along with explicit interpretive analyses was a nontraditional approach to scholarship in the field of higher education, the research process itself would prove challenging.

INTERVIEWING: DATA COLLECTION AND RECOLLECTION

The field research led me into new territory beyond my comfortable stance as a detached observer. The kinds of research questions I pursued led me to an essential next step for which I felt unprepared–to negotiate ways of observing and, at the same time, to adopt an attendant stance of attachment and detachment.

As a doctoral student, I knew early on that my dissertation research would lead me onto university campuses to interview faculty, students, and administrators. Required courses on methodology focused on number crunching for descriptive and inferential statistics. In the early 1980s, there were few courses on field research in educational settings or on interviewing as a research technique within a phenomenological or *verstehen* tradition. And, since I was busy completing required courses, I had no training in what to expect using this approach "in the field," beyond what I read in my spare time from assorted library books. Initially, I felt most apprehensive about asking people for the time to be interviewed. Once I began the interviews, there were two main surprises. First, there was the exhaustion of doing back-to-back interviews for weeks at a time. And cumulatively, I realized that there were unexpected pleasures in connecting with people I interviewed. My experience doing two studies illustrates these dimensions well.

My dissertation research entailed doing in-depth intellectual autobiographies and career histories with women faculty. My relative youth and student status seemed to be grave liabilities. Yet once I got through that, and my uncertainty about what to wear (!), my "informants" were extremely candid in their retrospective accounts of their struggles to find a place in the academy. Their stories were filled with insights about reconciling tensions between the personal/intellectual, the political/academic, the emotional/rational, and how these tensions all served as fuel for genuine creativity in their work and meaningfulness in their lives. As the research progressed, despite my aim to take a scholarly stance (whatever that meant), I gained much respect and compassion for them and their work.

I puzzled over the mutuality in the interviews. There seemed to be a healing dimension that pleased me and them. I tried to listen well, and they hoped to be heard. A few women even declared that our meeting had been "better than therapy." I felt sure that I had gotten "great data" in these sessions, though I wasn't sure of their acceptability. But I knew I had gotten an even more precious gift: Each interview helped me to refine ways of being attached, even though I sensed these attachments were not likely to be sustained over time.

In another study, entitled "Fired Faculty," that I recently completed, I had a similar opportunity. Connecting rather than distancing was my goal for understanding the meaning of being laid off during university fiscal crises and ensuing budget cuts. In this case, the fired faculty with whom I spoke were in a much more fragile state, emotionally raw. Many of them spoke of the shock of being laid off and how they were coping. In some cases, I was the first person with whom they had had the opportunity to reflect verbally on what it meant to have their positions "dis-established"; the people I talked with likened this to an early death, in the process of being evaluated for tenure.

In order to facilitate the interview process, I revealed to them that I was in the same field (education) as well as on the tenure track. This contributed to a level of intimacy and a sense of shared vulnerability that gave way to moments of profound reflection in the interviews. I found the research both revealing and depressing. I felt drained emotionally with the recognition, in the words of Holly Near, "it could have been me but instead it was you." In a way, these interviews revisited my earlier existential ruminations on life, knowledge, and work. But this round was markedly different: The reflections were shared with others, in a flow of spoken words. The exchanges enabled me to be more confident with people in emotionally and intellectually difficult times, and more comfortable relating from our authentic selves rather than revealing only a prescribed persona.

My purpose in highlighting these real-life threads is to offer some personal reflections on the research process that we don't often choose to reveal. The relationships I have had with people in interviewing gave me permission to try out ways of being attached and gave me deeper human experiences, with words as the medium for genuine understanding. As I write this, it occurs to me that I am treading on dangerous scholarly ground, or at least ground far from the objectivity ideals of social science. I hesitate yet persist, asserting that my experiences as interviewer have helped me become a fuller person, if not a better researcher. It is on this level that I have experienced both the real and semantic gulf that presumably exists between "human" and "researcher."

I have come to see words as central to our exchanges in many arenas of my professional life. In my classroom teaching, especially seminars with graduate students, it is so apparent that we use words as scholars as well as human beings in relation. I have also come to see words in this way through my research in the relational opportunities that present themselves at every turn in the conduct of our research and writing–if we look for them. It is this recognition of potential for communication and understanding that frees me to proceed with inquiry. Time and again, it is this recognition that comes to life in the daily practice of my work, whether teaching, interviewing, or writing.

It is clear to me this recognition is not supposed to be central to my scholarship. In an effort to be taken seriously by those who judge me, perhaps I have misread some cues. After all, unlike my family of origin, reviewers are judging my scholarly work/output rather than me per se. (At least that's what I'm told.) As for the people I interviewed, I am deeply grateful for their time, involvement, forthrightness. And keeping them in mind, I retain the part of my research agenda where I have sought to make sense of their experiences. I believe that learning how and why different areas of knowledge get constructed and valued is central to higher education and the future of our knowledge-based society. As we restructure universities and the organization of academic units, I believe we need to carefully consider what and who get dismissed as dispensable. At the same time, we need to consider where to make investments, knowing full well that as we change our minds we also deem some knowers and their knowledges more valuable for future generations.

INTO PRINT: AM I AUTHOR/ITY?

At this point in my academic career, I have done over 400 interviews with people in universities and related higher education organizations around the country. The interviews have been integral to constructing an interpretive understanding of the complex mix of social structures and human agency that shape what counts as knowledge.

Unlike my experience with the flow of spoken words and safe silences that I helped create in many interviewing relationships, framing these as data, analyzing them, and translating them into written text became, and continues to be, a more formidable challenge. At this point, I am not daunted by the difficulty of creating written representations of what I learned in the field or critically analyzing what I saw and heard about life in universities. I find those dimensions of writing to be energizing and filled with creativity. Where I struggle now is with authorship. The primary issue of publishing is the difficulty of determining to whom am I writing and with what purpose(s). I know now that written words (in particular, well-placed publications) are the currency for career advancement. I now approach writing with ambivalence, and a tendency to slip into worry rather than to proceed with wonder.

Individuals' accounts reside in my interview transcripts and field notes. I use the words of my informants/subjects to make sense of the changing nature of higher education. As I reread transcripts and code them in analysis, I take pieces and assemble them in ways to bring new meanings, which may in turn become academic currency in the world of educational research. In this sense, I am aware that I use them for publications, a process of moving from sense-making to currency-making, which is at once a powerful privilege with the potential for exploitation.

As I prepare publications, I wrestle with past mandates from senior scholars and assorted editors whose admonitions echo in my head: "Select from the transcript only the most poignant phrases," "Take yourself out of it," "Write as if what you know is timeless." What I make of these cautions is to follow the traditional social science dictum to erase the human presence in the research. Although it might be an easier route to conform to the mandates, I find it antithetical to the nature of the endeavor of understanding our social worlds and unacceptable to trade a fuller understanding for approval.

This approach to authorship comes at great cost. In the article "Fired Faculty," I wrote about the research process in the text in a self-disclosing way. I illuminated details of the research process and the research site. In working with the interview data, I used a phenomenological approach, taking individuals' accounts of "what is" as a starting point for the narrative analyses. I also explicitly stated some methodological, ethical, and political concerns that emerged in the course of my field research.

Although graduate students loved the piece in its draft form, my colleagues on campus gave it mixed reviews. On the side of praise, some students said it inspired them to research knowledge legitimation, invited them to think about academic identity, and gave them permission to speak about emotionally hot topics. Similarly, a few colleagues saw it as "cutting edge" for its insight, narrative analysis, and postmodern perspective. On the other hand, a fellow researcher said the article "gave me the creeps." Another senior colleague said, "I don't know what this is, but don't do any more of it." The draft became known by a few local critics as "that piece that shall remain nameless." Those words wounded me and reminded me of my continuing struggle to follow my own inclinations or to seek traditional approval.

STILL WORDS

Although words once came easily to me, at this point in my life they do not. The words that have the most professional value do not come easily, when I sense the cost is trading approval for understanding. The stakes are higher than ever.

When I sit down to write for publication, I resist the accounting: First words; words are the hardest. Words sit still. Still words remain daunting. Once in print they are static, positioned, and given away for others to accept or to dismiss.

How I am working with words is the clearest signal for me of how I am managing the gaze of external reviewers. Either words flow or they don't. When they flow, writing is pleasurable; I get out of my own way and yield to the momentum. When they don't, faltering cannot be helped by personal admonitions to work harder or to think more clearly.

I have learned that words are not only a vehicle through which we present ourselves and our work for subsequent judgment. In my family upbringing, self-presentation was all-important, leaving unexplored the potential for words to illuminate experience or to foster intimacy. In my professional life, I have been fortunate to learn that words can be a medium for interpersonal connection and understanding. Some visionaries have even urged us to embrace self-revelation as central to our professional commitments. As Audre Lorde has forcefully argued in *Sister Outsider*, "Your silence will not protect you. . . . What are the words you do not yet have? What do you need to say? . . . We can learn to speak and work when we are afraid in the same way we have learned to work and speak when we are tired. For we have been socialized to respect fear more than our needs for language and definition, and while we wait in silence for that final luxury of fearlessness, the weight of that silence will choke us. . . . [I]t is not difference which immobilizes us, but silence. And there are so many silences to be broken" (pp. 41–44).

To the extent that I choose between making sense and seeking approval, I choose making sense. Approval matters but not enough to move me off my path. And so I write this essay for this book, speaking with authenticity yet awaiting approval, well aware of those who dismiss this reflexivity as either mere or excessive navel-gazing. So be it.

At a fundamental level, knowledge is developed and carried on by people in various discourse communities. With this in mind, I wonder if we can alter the function of words in academic publications, since they are not the best forum for reflecting on where we have been. As educators, researchers, teachers, mentors, and colleagues, we are brought by our daily work lives face to face with opportunities to redefine the parameters of our conversations. We are offered opportunities to acknowledge how some past experiences have shaped our work, made us more teachable, kept us humble. Yet, when such reflections are expressed as still words among scholars, there is a cost. In a world where approval and what we most care about are not at odds, the form of our lives and our work will be richer reflections of ourselves.

POSTSCRIPT, AUGUST 1996

As with all autobiographical writing, the perspectives that we offer from a point in time convey some of the essence of our specific social and historical locations. It may be helpful for the reader to know that I wrote this chapter in the summer of 1994. In April of 1995, I received tenure and promotion to Associate Professor at Stanford. During the 1995–96 academic year, I became Principal Investigator of a 5-year, $12.5 million grant from the U.S. Department of Education to establish the National Center for Postsecondary Improvement. As Executive Director of this Center, my daily work now includes management in addition to ongoing research and teaching at Stanford. I hope that the reader's knowledge of these recent achievements will not diminish the impact of the chapter.

NOTES

I appreciate thoughtful comments on a draft of this manuscript from Estela Bensimon, Maxine Greene, Barbara Gumport, Anna Neumann, Penelope Peterson, and Brian Pusser.

1. See Gumport, 1987, 1990.
2. See Gumport, 1988, 1989.
3. See Gumport, 1991a, 1991b, 1993a, 1993b, 1993c, 1993d, 1994.

BIBLIOGRAPHY

Gumport, Patricia, J. 1987. "The Social Construction of Knowledge: Individual and Institutional Commitments to Feminist Scholarship." Ph.D. diss., School of Education, Stanford University.

Gumport, Patricia J. 1988. "Curricula as Signposts of Cultural Change." *The Review of Higher Education* 12(1):49–62 (Autumn).

Gumport, Patricia J. 1989. "Postsecondary Organizations as Settings for Life History: A Rationale and Illustration of Methods." In *Aging and the Life Course through Personal Histories*, Gail Livings and David Unruh, eds. *Personal History Through the Life Course*, Vol. 3, Zena Blau, ed. Greenwich, CT: JAI, 175-190.

Gumport, Patricia J. 1990. "Feminist Scholarship as a Vocation." *Higher Education: The International Journal of Higher Education and Educational Planning* 20(3):231–243 (October).

Gumport, Patricia J. 1991a. "*E Pluribus Unum*?: Academic Structure, Culture and the Case of Feminist Scholarship." *The Review of Higher Education* 15(1):9–29 (Autumn).

Gumport, Patricia J. 1991b. "The Research Imperative." In *Culture and Ideology in Higher Education: Advancing a Critical Agenda*, William G. Tierney, ed. New York: Praeger, 87–105.

Gumport, Patricia J. 1993a. "Graduate Education and Organized Research in the United States." In *The Research Foundations of Graduate Education: Germany, Britain, France, United States, and Japan*, Burton R. Clark, ed. Berkeley: University of California Press, 225–259.

Gumport, Patricia J. 1993b. "Graduate Education and Research Imperatives: Views from American Campuses." In *The Research Foundations of Graduate Education: Germany, Britain, France, United States, and Japan*, Burton R. Clark, ed. Berkeley: University of California Press, 261–293.

Gumport, Patricia J. 1993c. "The Contested Terrain of Academic Program Reduction." *Journal of Higher Education* 64:283–311.

Gumport, Patricia J. 1993d. "Fired Faculty: Reflections on Marginalization and Academic Identity." In *Naming Silenced Lives: Personal Narratives and the Process of Educational Change*, Daniel McLaughlin and William Tierney, eds. New York: Routledge, 135-154.

Gumport, Patricia J. 1994. "Graduate Education and Research: Changing Conduct in Changing Contexts." In *Higher Education in American Society*, 3rd ed., Philip Altbach, Robert Berdahl, and Patricia J. Gumport, eds. Buffalo, NY: Prometheus, 307–331.

Lorde, Audre. 1984. *Sister Outsider: Essays and Speeches*. Trumansburg, NY: Crossing.

* *CHAPTER 11* *

Multiple Dimensions of Reality: Recollections of an African American Woman Scholar

Linda F. Winfield

I BEGIN THIS CHAPTER in a traditional scholarly voice because during most of my career that was the "only voice" I had. However, I realized very early that there were many other dimensions to my "real self" as an African American woman who had "no voice" in this society. In general, African American females in America have not been valued for their femininity or their scholarly work, making issues of personal and scholarly identity problematic. I myself have found few self-affirming images of scholarship, beauty, or success for women of color.

Previous scholarship indicates that the presence of black women in the workplace has generated an alternative to traditional views of femininity.[1] Historically, black women have been portrayed as "beasts of burden"—as laborers in a society where ideals of femininity emphasize domesticity, fragility, pureness, and being not too intelligent. African American feminist scholars have provided alternative perspectives on the traditional notion of femininity.

For example, Joyce Ladner indicates, in *Tomorrow's Tomorrow*, that in some ways black womanhood has always been at the very core of what American womanhood is attempting to become. Writing about black women and women's liberation groups, she says:

> [W]e have always been "free," and able to develop as individuals even under the most harsh circumstances. This freedom, as well as the tremendous hardships from which Black women suffered, allowed for the development of a female personality that is rarely described in scholarly journals for its obstinate strength and ability to survive. Neither is its peculiar humanistic character and quiet

Learning from Our Lives: Women, Research, and Autobiography in Education. ISBN 0-8077-3593-0 (pbk), ISBN 0-8077-3594-9 (cloth).

> courage viewed as the epitome of what the American model of femininity should be. (p. 280)

Recent scholarship on black women supports Ladner's conceptualization and refutes previous myths about and distortions of black femininity.[2]

In reshaping traditional images of American femininity, African American women have encountered a major question and challenge–how to integrate discrepant parts of their lives. African American women in university workplaces have had to address the particularly difficult question of how to develop professional identities that do not interfere with personal development or ethnic identities. The following quote, from Ann Wilson Schaef's *Meditations for Women Who Do Too Much*, is especially significant to African American females struggling to integrate these often conflicting facets of their lives:

> Life is a process. We are a process. Everything that has happened in our lives has happened for a reason and is an integral part of our becoming. One of the challenges of our lives is to integrate the pieces of our lives as we live them. It is sometimes tempting to try to deny huge periods of our lives or forget significant events, especially if they have been painful. To try to erase our past is to rob ourselves of our own hard-earned wisdom. (March 17)

The socialization of most African American women includes the fostering of ideals of nurturance, caring, collaboration, and service to others, including one's family and community. Though these values are an integral part of our past, they are not congruent with the value system of academia where individualism and competition are the norms.

In my life, certain threads are interwoven between personal and professional identity; however, the integration has not been easy and sometimes nonexistent, for often these threads were totally separate. Very early, I developed multiple dimensions within my reality that allowed me to function simultaneously as wife, mother, scholar, Sunday school teacher, choir director, and in other roles in the community. One might think that the whole equals the sum of its parts, but what is missing from this equation is the dimension of a self separate and apart from the multiple dimensions. I would often (at least in my own head) make a conscious and deliberate distinction between my profession (or what I do) and who I really am. This allowed me to have some semblance of a "self" that operated independently of my profession. There was never adequate time to fully appreciate or develop this "self," but nevertheless it was there waiting to be revealed and rooted in the strong spiritual beliefs of my Cherokee and African American heritage. This distinction also allowed me to exist in a reality larger than academia and thus avoid acquiescence to mainstream academic values or to alienation. Whenever I encountered disappointments, rejection, marginalization in academic pursuits–and it occasionally happened–I was not totally devastated, because my sense of who I was was not entirely dependent upon being accepted and rewarded by my peers and colleagues in academia. Conversely, when chaos and confusion occurred in my personal life, I shifted to the professional realities of my existence, and to my spirituality.

My values for family, spirituality, and community were shaped very early in watching a mother work outside the home, remain active in church, cook, clean, and raise two children. An early interest in reading was fostered by my father, who, having never finished high school, appreciated the value of education and walked us every Saturday morning to the free public library. Growing up in the 1950s and 1960s, I was imbued with the ideas of commitment, excellence, and social consciousness, both in our segregated schools and in my home. We were admonished, "You have to uplift the race, . . . you have to be twice as good." Mrs. Henry, my sixth-grade teacher, often reminded me, "Time is precious and whatever you do, don't waste it, . . . whatever you do, get wisdom."

My mother's ideals of courage, commitment to God and others, and excellence were demonstrated in how she lived her life. One example comes to mind. When I entered a newly integrated junior high school after leaving the segregated elementary school, I along with my African American friends was placed in the lowest track class. I was having fun, listening to the older guys who had repeated several grades "play the dozens," and began repeating "bad" language at home. The teachers did not assign homework because most of the students could not read the seventh-grade textbooks. I was the exception. My mother, who actively monitored homework, began to wonder about the origins of my new vocabulary and why I never had homework to complete. She sensed that something was not quite right. She came to the school and spoke with the principal who, of course, defended the placement. She went to my classes and met with each of my teachers, finally encountering a science teacher who knew I was capable of comprehending the textbook. She returned to the principal with evidence in hand, and I was moved to a higher section within two days. My mother was extremely intelligent but never had the opportunity to finish high school. However, she was not distanced from knowledge and power. Her knowledge of relationships and how society works was based on intuition or "motherwit," and was part of a collective identity of being African American and a woman.[3] Very early, I learned from her the relationship between knowledge and power: that whatever knowledge you obtain cannot be taken away, has intrinsic value, and, most important, can be used for survival and advancement.

My life was both easier and more difficult than my mother's. She often worked as a domestic or store clerk during a period when concerns about professional identity/ethnic identity for African American females were nonexistent. Her work schedule was fixed: Once she got home, it was her time for family activities, homework, etc. Although my hours as an academic are flexible, affording me opportunities to be with my children, the demands of the academic life have required me to bring work home and to stay up very late, hours after everyone has gone to sleep. To remain competitive in a field where women and minorities were underrepresented and undervalued required additional hours of my personal time alongside the added responsibility of "uplifting the race," which I continued to take very seriously.

DOING IT ALL—ALL THINGS ARE POSSIBLE

At the beginning of my academic career–during my undergraduate years–the threads of commitment, caring, and courage were tightly woven into my multiple realities of being a student, mother, wife, and worker. Though I was an honor student and had some scholarships, I rebelled against my parents after completing high school and refused to go on to college. Instead I worked in private industry, enrolled in a cooperative program with a business college, and took university-level classes at night. It took a lot of courage, after six years, to leave a secure job in private industry to matriculate as a full-time undergraduate student majoring in psychology, especially so with my responsibilities as wife and mother to a one-year-old son. And since I was married, I was ineligible for financial aid, so I worked part-time in a day-care center. Sheer determination and commitment–the energy and idealism of youth–kept me going. I was determined and committed to continue my education. Most individuals I met, of course, thought that what I was attempting to do was pure craziness–which, at times, it was. But I was young, idealistic, and convinced–I could do it all, and I did, with God's help.

As an undergraduate, I focused on child psychology and language development. I was convinced of the importance of early childhood education, and as a first-time mother, I wanted to learn all I could about how children develop. As I plunged deeper into readings and research, I discovered, much to my chagrin, deficit theories, stereotypes, pejorative notions about black children and families. I began to question where knowledge and theories come from, how these are derived. I asked, "Who is the knower and conceptualizer?"–a question that would resurface throughout my career. I remember the influence that Stephen and Joan Baratz's article, which describes bias in much of the research and social policy related to African American children, had on my thinking.

My undergraduate internships were important in determining my later research interests. An observational study of aggressive behavior in African American children, which I designed as a sophomore, confirmed for me the importance of considering who the "knower" or "observer" is in research. I earned an A–as well as praise and encouragement–from my psychology professor. Another internship in which I examined black English vernacular led to a paper for a national conference. The project involved considerable mentoring from Joel Gordon, my psychology professor, later my undergraduate advisor, and to this day one of my very best friends. He saw potential in me and encouraged me to apply to graduate school in psychology and educational psychology. As the first in my family to attend college, I did not know anything about the process.

What sticks out most in my mind about experimental studies during this time was the language, which was quite biased. Most studies used Caucasians as subjects. When you did an experiment, unless it was cross-cultural, you were told that race was a "nuisance variable" and that including other ethnic groups "contaminated" the sample. Intuitively, I questioned how one could generalize to ethnic populations without having them represented in a sample. As an undergraduate, I was curious about epistemological and methodological issues. I had many questions about the research process, as well as the theories that research generated concerning African American children, the relationship between language and thought, and social policies. Since I was never thoroughly convinced of the validity of research findings on ethnic populations, I felt I needed to understand how such findings were derived. My initial interests reflected a focus on child development and language development because, during this time, I had a preschooler. I did not realize it at the time, but my vision was to become the "knower," to produce credible research, and not merely to be part of populations "to be known by others"–that is, by researchers standing outside these populations.

In spite of my part-time job, caring for a preschooler, and family concerns, I completed the requirements in psychology in four years and graduated with honors.

I CAN DO IT ALL BUT SOMEONE HAS TO SACRIFICE . . .

Often in two-career families, or in families with children or aging parents, women are the ones who compromise or sacrifice. My first dilemma was where to go to graduate school. Although I was accepted into the Harvard Graduate School of Education, I chose to stay within commuting distance because of my family. A minority fellowship to the University of Delaware provided tuition plus a stipend, so I could give up the part-time job at the day-care center and become a research assistant.

A flashback: I was in the university library reviewing literature for a study and came across a book by the superintendent of the Wilmington Public

Schools in the early fifties. I looked it up and began reading about the "poor disadvantaged colored children in the segregated school on the east side, the poor health, language and test scores and what to do about 'the problem.'" I remember thinking, "She's writing about me–I was in that cohort." I remembered that over half of my first-grade class went to the speech therapist to learn how to pronounce words properly. I thought to myself, "Growing up I never once thought of myself as poor and disadvantaged, or as living in a ghetto." These so-called problems were someone else's conception of me. The issue of who is the knower, observer, and producer of knowledge reemerged in my consciousness. I was the "known" becoming the "knower." Again I questioned the accuracy of what was known from the past as well as how that was derived. The focus and identification of "the problem" as residing inherently within the population studied was typical of the educational writings of that period. More importantly, I was coming to understand that though logical positivism emphasizes objectivity, the conceptual frameworks of research studies are inherently subjective because they come out of human consciousness. Thus I was further motivated to become the "knower" and to provide an alternative perspective.

Graduate school at the University of Delaware contributed four things to a successful academic career:

1. *Expansion of my views of research*. From early work with my graduate advisor, Richard (Dick) Venezky, I moved toward exploring the school achievement and academic performance of low-income as well as African American students.[4] Dick would always say, "Whenever there's a problem, people point a finger, and then they end up studying the finger rather than the problem." Much past educational and psychological research on race and ethnicity focused on "the students" as "the problem." An alternative and unexplored view considered the classroom, school, or society/environment as possible sources of "the problem."

Dick turned my conception of school learning from a focus on what is "inside the individual's head" to a focus on what is "inside the school." He viewed teaching as paramount in what children learn: If teaching is inadequate, learning at a high level will not occur. This scenario, he felt, was particularly true for students coming from lower socioeconomic backgrounds where, many times, support for learning is not available. Blaming the students, their parents, and their language is equivalent to "studying the finger."

Before encountering this new way of thinking, I was thoroughly indoctrinated in experimental methodology. Dick strongly encouraged that I change paradigms–that I adopt naturalistic methods to study what occurs in classrooms and schools. The shift was not easy because within the new paradigm, the research process was very different. I was frantic, since there were no variables to manipulate or control, no statistical inference to determine significance. I was "the instrument." I struggled with the process of going from field notes and observations to generalizations and results. I had learned in experimental methods to pay no attention to my intuition. I had learned not to become involved, to remain detached. However, in qualitative research, particularly participant observation, the researcher's intuition, involvement, and attachment are important because the researcher is the direct knower. At that time, this methodology was just beginning to be used and understood.

My shift in methodology, my expanded conception of learning and development, and my inclusion of schools as objects of study coincided with my son's entrance into formal schooling. As a researcher and parent, I was interested in understanding what factors within schools influence achievement, and what constitutes "good" instruction.

2. *Socialization into the profession*. My role model, Dick, was extremely prolific, intelligent, humorous, and caring, and a demanding taskmaster. I did not experience ethnic identity conflicts in working with him. We developed a mutual respect for each other's expertise and unique perspectives. Often we appeared as the "odd couple" walking undauntedly through high-poverty urban areas, on our way to various schools. We once sat together on a curb in a high-crime area of North Philadelphia eating hoagies. Local residents must have thought we were crazy. Of course, the opposite also occurred. Once when attending a meeting on City Line Avenue, we sat in an upscale bar, and the waiter served Dick but did not want to serve me until Dick insisted he do so. We were ready to walk out. Sharing such experiences was important in my socialization.

3. *Professional training*. My graduate program was nontraditional, in that students had to demonstrate competence by compiling portfolios reflecting activities like writing literature reviews, presenting at conferences, and publishing papers. Methodology, both quantitative and qualitative, was not only required but heavily emphasized. Classes and engagement in research and data analysis using structural equation modeling, path analysis, ethnography, and so forth, were commonplace. I felt well prepared to conceptualize, design, and conduct either quantitative or qualitative studies, and I learned methodological pragmatism–that is, that methodology changes depending on the research problem.

4. *Development of a research focus*. During my graduate school years, I was interested in urban schools and how factors within schools facilitate reading achievement. Some of my writing at this time–in particular, an article entitled "Teachers' Beliefs Towards Academically At-Risk Students in Urban Schools"–led to a career-long interest on the effects of categorical and compensatory programs on student achievement. The article presented a typology of teachers as tutors, custodians, general contractors, and referral agents. Some of the language was, I am sure, unconsciously inspired by my renova-

tion, at the time, of a one-hundred-year-old Victorian house: I had a general contractor who shifted responsibility for specific tasks (as well as for delays and mistakes) to subcontractors. I observed a similar process in classrooms whereby teachers indicated that the responsibility for improving student achievement was not primarily theirs but that of "reading teachers" or other specialists. Like the general contractor, the teachers failed to take responsibility.

I CAN STILL DO IT ALL, AT LEAST I THINK I CAN

Over the next four to eight years, my research interests were continually redirected or broadened by professional situations. I surmised I would never be like academics who focus very narrowly on one specialization.

The dilemma of career versus family reemerged as I searched for an academic position after completing graduate school and having a baby. Most positions required relocation. I chose family over career and spent three years in local school district research and evaluation. My research in school effectiveness and improvement translated into pragmatic issues, including evaluation of Chapter 1 programs, testing and assessment, and students' opportunities to learn the subject matter on which they are assessed (often referred to as "opportunity to learn"). I was motivated primarily by the need to inform teachers and principals of what was occurring (or not) in classroom instruction of Chapter 1 students. This work led a local civic group to give me an award for "commitment and caring in research."[5]

My work during this period involved generating reports for schools and districts responding to a desegregation mandate. However, I presented some of these studies at annual meetings of the American Educational Research Association (AERA), and some were eventually published.[6] I also maintained active memberships in professional associations like the National Council on Measurement in Education. Through these organizations, I developed networks of colleagues and was appointed to numerous committees, including the National Institute for Education Study Group on Schooling and the Joint Committee on Standards for Educational Evaluation. These committees provided me with collegial contacts and intellectual stimulation. Many of my new colleagues were encouraging and offered assistance in publishing or wrote recommendations. I met one professional colleague and mentor through the "blind review" process. Richard Allington reviewed one of my articles on opportunity to learn of Chapter 1 students. He asked the editor to forward a message to me, and so I called him. We eventually worked together on issues of reading and literacy in disadvantaged populations.[7]

More important, encounters with colleagues beyond my own work situation helped me see the value of the knowledge I was developing–for example, through observations of schools and classrooms and through interactions with school personnel. Unlike the knowledge developed by many of my academic colleagues, my understanding of schools and learning was grounded in the reality of practice. I also realized that to have an impact on educational policy and practices, I would have to leave the local level and pursue a position in higher education.

Even though we are scattered across the country and see each other only once a year at professional meetings, my colleagues from this period and I formed a core support group. We celebrate and commiserate in each other's joys and traumas in academia and personal life.[8] Some seven or eight years later, some of us would collaborate on a monograph on African American youth.

CAN I DO AND HAVE IT ALL?

For the next five years I confronted daily the question of whether I could maintain an academic research career, a family, and my sanity. Imagine commuting an hour and a half, leaving at 6:00 A.M. for Princeton, New Jersey, where I was appointed Visiting Scholar with the National Assessment of Educational Progress (NAEP), conducting data analysis with NAEP data, and coming home between 6:30 and 7:00 P.M. to a rambunctious three-year-old, an adolescent with raging hormones, a husband, three loads of wash, cooking, and on and on. Fortunately, I did not have to go in every day, and my commuting partner and former graduate school colleague, Irwin Kirsch, Director of Adult Literacy Assessment, usually did the driving. Our conversations during our long commutes–about literacy assessment–would later be reflected in grants and research on high literacy-proficient black young adults.

During this period (1985) most districts and state departments around the country were spending millions of dollars to implement minimum competency tests. These measures reflected erroneous assumptions about how children learn; they were, primarily, accountability mechanisms. There was little or no empirical evidence that the tests would have an impact on achievement. I therefore decided to use NAEP data to explore whether competency tests impact student achievement among various racial/ethnic groups. My experience with this study demonstrates the "fickle" nature of publication. I wrote an article that was rejected initially by two journals. Many researchers did not understand the measurement issues involved, nor did they understand the complexity of analyzing NAEP data. My study, entitled "School Competency Testing Reforms and Student Achievement: Exploring a National Perspective," was eventually published in *Educational Evaluation and Policy Analysis* and later won the AERA Palmer O. Johnson Award for distinguished contribution to research. I guess the long commutes, the wear and tear on my body, eventually paid off in terms of professional growth, development, and recognition.

The scenario of the commute, the kids, the husband, the profession continued for another six years. The only things that changed were the institutions in which I worked. It was becoming clearer that the multiple dimensions of my reality were becoming more disparate rather than more integrated. Joining the education faculty of an urban institution, I was rudely awakened to the horrors of being a junior faculty member in a department where, at the time, sexism and racism were rampant. As the only African American female, with an overabundance of doctoral students to advise, two graduate courses a semester, and one quarter of my time assigned to an interdisciplinary research center, I questioned the efficacy of academic pursuits. My supporter and mentor at the time, Jay Scribner, continually reassured me. I had been awarded grants from the National Science Foundation and the Rockefeller Foundation to study literacy among black young adults and had established a reputation as a competent scholar, researcher, and teacher. I had established extremely high standards for my graduate classes and advisees. However, it became increasingly clear that my contributions were not valued by my colleagues, and at my three-year review, I received a negative evaluation of my work. Although individuals in central administration were very supportive, I decided that the institutionalized racism and sexism within the department were larger than I. And I had other more pressing issues to face–a divorce after twenty years.

WHAT CAN I DO?

The next few years brought considerable questioning and reexamination of my personal life. My multiple realities were now those of single parent and scholar. I was recruited by Johns Hopkins University, Center for Research on Effective Schooling for Disadvantaged Students. Jomills Braddock, whom I respect and admire considerably, was director and largely responsible for my recruitment. For the first time in my career, I had African American colleagues like Jomills and Saundra Nettles who were working on similar issues; I also had as colleagues well-known scholars like Jim McPartland, Joyce Epstein, and Bob Slavin. Working at Johns Hopkins in a research position, I synthesized the research interests I had developed and maintained over the preceding decade. My research and experience with Chapter 1 came at an opportune time, since Congress was interested in funding studies regarding effectiveness to inform reauthorization. I was returning full circle to issues I had examined years back at the local school district level.

I was again back in schools conducting observations and interviewing teachers and students.[9] This research helped to take my mind off my personal issues, as I once again became absorbed in exploring how central administrative changes influence what occurs in classrooms in high-poverty urban schools. I learned a great deal about implementation and change from Perry Robinson, a former principal who at the time was manager of Philadelphia Schoolwide Projects, and his staff. I was well respected and trusted as a researcher. But more important, the colleagues with whom I worked at this time showed much concern about me as a human being undergoing transition.

This time, going into the schools, I was prepared for the methodological problem of how to work with "observers" and "knowers" who differ socially, culturally, and personally from those to be "observed" and "known." This would be a key issue in the training of field staff, many of whom were white and would be observing in predominantly African American and Latino high-poverty schools. Individuals' perceptions, beliefs, and attitudes about differences between self and other had to be worked out because each research team would be the "lens" through which snapshots of schools would be taken.

What I was not prepared for was seeing, up close, what poverty, unemployment, crack, and cocaine had done to some of the same neighborhoods and schools I had been in ten to twelve years earlier, and, more importantly, how these horrid social conditions affected the children constantly exposed to them. At one point, after conducting three days of observation in a classroom, I felt completely devastated and psychologically "burnt out." Reflected in the eyes of the children I was studying was a sense of despair, hopelessness, and disillusionment with life, some of which I felt within my own wounded psyche. I recognized, in them, feelings of pain, trauma, hurt, despair, anger, betrayal of trust, and confusion, and these mirrored what I felt as an adult going through a divorce.[10]

I felt it was time to return to the computer, again to do quantitative studies and crunch numbers, activities generally devoid of human emotions. However, before I did, I collaborated with other African American females in synthesizing some of what I had learned about urban schools' cultures.[11] During this time I also mentored Delois Maxwell, an African American female graduate student at Morgan State University. Some of these female colleagues would eventually provide the support system I needed to relocate away from what was then my home.

Another research area that captured my attention at the time was alternative assessment. From my past position in the school district and at NAEP, I knew there were many equity issues to be addressed, including the fact that students are not always given opportunities to learn the material on which they are being tested. An invitation for a paper on this topic from Eva Baker, Director of the Center for Research on Evaluation Standards and Student Testing (CRESST) at UCLA, allowed me to reflect on the meaning of "performance" and to review some studies, from the 1970s, regarding competence and performance of African American children. As many schools, districts, and states became engaged in the push toward performance assessment, national standards, and assessment, I developed a framework for addressing these topics in relation to equity and diversity. I eventually co-authored, with my colleague Michael Woodard, an editorial for *Education Week* and an article for *Educational Policy* on this topic.

Around this time, I gave the commencement address at my alma mater, the University of Delaware. As a result of what I was going through in my personal life, I began to examine what–other than my own inner determination and spirituality–had allowed me to persist in my life and career. The hurdles included my humble beginnings, outright discouragement from pursuit of an education (I had a guidance counselor tell me in high school that I would be wasting my parents' money to go to college, since I was just going to have babies anyway), encounters with racism and sexism, the need to juggle children and husband, and eventually a divorce and single parenting. In that speech in January 1990, I spoke about the need for courage, about the need for people to think deeply about how to solve social problems, and about the need to provide long-term, systematic, and ongoing supports for minority students to counteract instances of racism and sexism. In my own career, I had been fortunate to have "mentors," but this does not always occur for ethnic/minority students and should not be left to chance.

I did not realize it at the time, but this speech was the beginning of my research interest in the topic of resilience. The notion of resilience, as discussed in the health-care and psychiatric literature, connotes variations in individuals' successful responses to adverse conditions and circumstances. My interest is in uncovering protective mechanisms and processes within the environment that allow some children in urban settings, and with multiple risk conditions associated with high poverty, to adapt, persist, and eventually be successful in graduating from school and attending postsecondary institutions or obtaining further training.

Later that year, some of my AERA colleagues and I collaborated on a special issue of *Education and Urban Society*, focused on the topic of resilience, and I took the lead to develop the conceptual framework. In general, much of the research on African American, Latino, and other ethnic/minority students is based on the deficit model, which focuses on risk, psychopathology, and negative developmental outcomes. This literature typically "blames the victim" for risk conditions and identifying deficits to be remedied. A focus on resilience and successful coping shifts attention to sources of strength in the hope of designing better intervention models. My research on resilience represents a synthesis of ideas in my past work–for example, on successful schools, equity, and human development–but it also represents ideas emerging from reflection on my life. For positive change to occur, there must be beliefs, visions, and models of success that exemplify the highest forms of human potential and that demonstrate abilities to overcome adverse social conditions. My research on resilience attempts to get at some of the mechanisms for achieving this goal.

NEW BEGINNINGS

With fewer restrictions on my ability to relocate (though I had responsibility at this time for my ten-year-old son, another son was completing a dual degree at the University of Michigan/Morehouse College), I felt, for the first time in my life, that I could choose to go and be at any institution I desired. As an aside, my sons' well-being and achievements are not listed on my curriculum vitae, but as a mother, I feel they are equal to, if not more important than, my professional accomplishments. Finally, I could devote time to working on my professional career as well as to developing the self that was so underdeveloped.

An opportunity for change presented itself after the Los Angeles uprisings in April 1992 through my colleague, Eva Baker, who helped me acquire a visiting professorship in the Graduate School of Education at UCLA and a position in CRESST. In September 1992, I relocated to Los Angeles. Although the opportunity to address urban issues in education and the work with CRESST were real attractions, to tell the truth, I really wanted to be in the sunshine. I moved both for professional and personal reasons. Ruth Johnson and Michael Woodard, professional colleagues and friends already in Los Angeles, helped. My mentee, Delois Maxwell, obtained a postdoc at UCLA and provided invaluable support and assistance with child care. The support systems that I write about in the research on resilience were operating in my own life. I am continuing to grow, heal, and develop the self within a spiritual community in Southern California that is self-empowering, loving, and fostering of diversity among different kinds of people.

At the end of my visiting professorship at UCLA, I took a faculty position at the University of Southern California in the Department of Policy and Administration. Returning to an academic environment has allowed me to revisit the theme of "Who is the knower?" in the research process, and within a university setting. Universities are microcosms of society, but unfortunately few gains have been made in ethnic minority faculty appointments in many institutions. I realize the value of informing, not only the research process and knowledge production but also the process of higher education more broadly, from my unique perspective as an African American female. It is through my scholarly work that my concerns about "Who is the knower, and how does this person know?" and "Who are the known–and how are they known?" are becoming resolved.

NOTES

1. Dill, 1987.
2. See hooks and West, 1991, and Dill, 1987.
3. For a discussion of this phenomenon, see Wendy Luttrell's article on working-class women's ways of knowing.
4. See Venezky and Winfield, 1979.
5. The Wilmington branch of the National Association of University Women presented me the "Woman of the Year" award, May 20, 1984.
6. Examples of this work include Winfield, 1986a, 1987.
7. See, for example, Winfield, 1995.
8. Some of these individuals include Diane Scott-Jones, Sharon Nelson Le-Gall, Maxine Clark, Angela Taylor, Antoine Garabaldi, Walter Allen, Bill Trent, Bruce Hare, Valerie Lee, and Karen Wilson-Sadberry. I met Valerie and Karen while I was a Visiting Scholar at the Educational Testing Service, forming long-term professional and personal friendships with them.
9. I was involved, at this time, in two projects: research on implementation of Chapter 1 schoolwide projects in a large urban school district (see Winfield, 1991a) and the Urban Special Strategies for Educating Disadvantaged Students Project (with Mary Ann Millsap, funded by the Office of Planning, Budget and Evaluation, U.S. Department of Education).
10. The divorce process itself was traumatic, but for many years in that relationship I had also relived the trauma of the Vietnam War on a daily basis. My ex-husband was a former combat medic and survivor of the war.
11. This collaboration with Ruth Johnson and Joanne Manning resulted in two publications (Winfield and Manning, 1992; Winfield, Johnson, and Manning, 1993).

BIBLIOGRAPHY

Baratz, Stephen S., and Joan C. Baratz. 1970. "Early Childhood Intervention: The Social Science Base of Institutional Racism." *Harvard Education Review* 40:29–50.

Dill, Bonnie Thornton. 1987. "The Dialectics of Black Womanhood." In *Feminism and Methodology*, Sandra Harding, ed. Bloomington: Indiana University Press, 97–108.

hooks, bell, and Cornel West. 1991. *Breaking Bread*. Boston: South End.

Ladner, Joyce A. 1971. *Tomorrow's Tomorrow*. Garden City, NY: Doubleday.

Luttrell, Wendy. 1989. "Working Class Women's Ways of Knowing: Effects of Gender, Race, and Class." *Sociology of Education* 62:33–46.

Schaef, Anne Wilson. 1990. *Meditations for Women Who Do Too Much*. San Francisco: Harper and Row.

Venezky, Richard L., and Linda F. Winfield. 1979. *Case Studies of Schools That Succeed Beyond Expectations in Teaching*. Studies in Education, Technical Report No. 1. Newark: University of Delaware. ED 177484.

Winfield, Linda F. 1986a. "Do Chapter 1 Programs Promote Equity: A Review and Some Comments." *Journal of Educational Equity and Leadership* 6(1):61–71 (Spring).

Winfield, Linda F. 1986b. "Teachers' Beliefs Towards Academically At Risk Students in Inner Urban Schools." *Urban Review* 18(4):253–268.

Winfield, Linda F. 1987. "Teachers' Estimates of Test Content Covered in Class and First Grade Reading Achievement." *Elementary School Journal* 87(4):437–454 (March).

Winfield, Linda F. 1990a. "Graduates of the '90s: The Demand for Diversity of Talents." Commencement Address, University of Delaware.

Winfield, Linda F. 1990b. "School Competency Testing Reforms and Student Achievement: Exploring a National Perspective." *Educational Evaluation and Policy Analysis* 12(2):157–173 (Summer).

Winfield, Linda F. 1991a. "Lessons from the Field: Case Studies of Evolving Schoolwide Projects." *Educational Evaluation and Policy Analysis* 13(4):353–362.

Winfield, Linda F. 1991b. "Resilience, Schooling and Development Among African American Youth: A Conceptual Framework." *Education and Urban Society* 24(1): 5–14 (November).

Winfield, Linda F. 1995. "Change in Urban Schools With High Concentrations of Low-Income Children: Chapter 1 Schoolwide Projects." In *No Quick Fix: Rethinking Literacy Programs in America's Elementary Schools*, Richard L. Allington and Sean A. Walmsley, eds. New York: Teachers College Press, 214–235.

Winfield, Linda F., Ruth Johnson, and JoAnn B. Manning. 1993. "Managing Instructional Diversity." In *City Schools: Leading the Way*, Patrick B. Forsyth and Marilyn Tallerico, eds. Newbury Park, CA: Corwin, 97–130.

Winfield, Linda F., and JoAnn B. Manning. 1992. "Changing School Culture to Accommodate Student Diversity." In *Diversity in Teacher Education: New Expectations*, Mary E. Dilworth, ed. San Francisco: Jossey-Bass, 181–214.

Winfield, Linda F., and Michael D. Woodard. 1992. "Where Are Equity and Diversity in Bush's Proposal 2000?" *Education Week* (January 29):31.

Winfield, Linda F., and Michael D. Woodard. 1994. "Assessment Equity and Diversity in Reforming America's Schools." *Educational Policy* 8(1):3–27 (March).

* *CHAPTER 12* *

Learning Out of School and In: Self and Experience at Home, School, and Work

Penelope L. Peterson

I HAVE AN IMAGE that has been with me for more than forty years. It is of a five-year-old girl with straight brown hair and huge brown eyes, standing by a tall, blank, brick wall that stretches upward into the blazing blue sky as far as the eye can see. Standing next to the girl is a woman, whose dark hair and eyes mirror her own. The image is accompanied by the sights and sounds of a joyous spring as it bursts through the stillness of the dead midwestern winter. Shining far overhead, the sun casts a golden glow, and fluffy clouds keep time to the music of the birds, happy to be home from their sojourns in the South. Suddenly, the little girl's eyes fill with tears, and she begins to sob quietly. The woman bends over her as if to seek the source of the girl's distress. Between sobs and hiccups, a quavering voice whispers, "I don't want to go to school any more!" Stiffening with surprise, the woman asks, "Why?" The girl replies, "Because I've learned it all." Seeming to have heard the girl's words, the woman responds matter-of-factly, "But you *have* to go to school. Come–I'll go with you." Taking the girl's hand, the woman leads her to a small door in the brick wall that had been hidden heretofore, she opens the door, and the two disappear inside. While outside, the world blooms, buzzes, and sings with the wonder of growth and change.

No doubt I have embellished this image over time. I have constructed and reconstructed it from fragmentary recollections and from Mother's retelling of the story over the years. Interwoven into the creation and recreation of this image are my experiences as I have developed from that sloe-eyed serious child to an even more serious dark-eyed woman, who, looking back on her experiences at home, school, and work, wonders about the learning she has done in her life. She is I; and I am she. She is me.

Is it only coincidence that I have spent the last two decades of my life

Learning from Our Lives: Women, Research, and Autobiography in Education. ISBN 0-8077-3593-0 (pbk), ISBN 0-8077-3594-9 (cloth).

doing research on learning? I wonder. Or is it more? I think back to my fellow graduate student who studied with me at Stanford University; he proposed to do his dissertation on how teachers' explanations facilitate learning yet never finished because he could never explain his dissertation to his committee. I recall a fellow faculty member in the Department of Educational Psychology at the University of Wisconsin–Madison; he conducted extensive studies of depression in adolescents while he continued to battle clinical depression in his own life. I can't help but wonder how a researcher's research may reflect the questions of his or her life, and I wonder how my research reflects the questions of my own. Was I only fortunate in my life to have been able to do research on what interests me most–learning? Or did I choose to become an educational psychologist who studies learning because that is what has always puzzled and interested me most?

What is "learning" anyway? And how do we come to know it? Who helps us come to learn, and how do these significant others frame our learning experiences for us and help us make sense of them? How do we construct ourselves as learners to make sense of learning in multiple contexts? How do we help others construct themselves to learn in meaningful ways in multiple contexts?

EXPERIENCING LEARNING—MY STORY

I was born as part of that fortunate baby-boomer generation of the late 1940s and early 1950s who grew up in a time of prosperity when "women didn't have to work." Ours was the kind of family later immortalized on the early TV sitcoms by "Ozzie and Harriet." My father had a full-time office job, and he was gone from 7:00 A.M. to 5:00 P.M. every day. My mother's job was to take care of the house and to raise me and my brother. My job, as I was to learn, was to live up to my parents' expectations for me: to work hard, be good, do my best, be "smart," and achieve at the highest levels at everything I did whether at home, school, or work.

Learning at Home

As is the case for most of us, I first experienced learning from the "student's" side of the table. In my case my mother was my first "teacher," and my learning began at home. Two decades later researchers were to document how well middle-class homes provide a literacy environment that prepares the middle-class child for school.[1] Mine was such a home. My mother had a college degree in English. She filled the house with Golden Books when I was little. Every time I went to the grocery story with my mother as a toddler, my mother bought me a Golden Book. They cost twenty-five cents at the time. We had a houseful of them. My mother read to me every day before my nap and every night before I went to bed. My earliest memories are of my mother's voice chanting "I think I can; I think I can" as she read to me from *The Little Engine That Could*.

My mother's voice, her interactions with me, and the activities we did together all prepared me for the experiences I was to have later in kindergarten. At home, I was expected to listen, respond to questions when asked, and follow directions. It was a warm, encouraging place as well. I always knew I was secure. My parents had high expectations. But there was also a culture of learning as transmission. I learned that I was expected to learn what more experienced others like my teachers and parents already knew. In this way, my mother helped me begin to frame for myself what was "learning."

In addition, my parents communicated several other messages about learning. First, trying hard to learn and doing your best were important, and I–as a learner–could control that. My parents thus communicated to me a sense of agency that I internalized. Second, school and education could make an economic difference in your life. It was important to do well in school. Third, my parents communicated to me a sense of mutual responsibility and that I was loved and valued. They were responsible for me but I was also responsible to them.

My parents believed in the power of education because it had worked for them and brought them into the middle class. My father was second generation, Swedish. As the last child in a family of seven, my father was living proof of how you could pull yourself up by your bootstraps by doing what you were told, applying yourself diligently to your work, completing high school, getting a good job, and working hard at it. While my father's siblings remained farmers, laborers, and vagrants, my father rose to become chief industrial study engineer at one of the largest farm implement companies in the Midwest. I often ponder how he managed to do this, and now that my father is dead, I regret that I did not ask him. But I think my father thought he achieved as he did through hard work, not by learning. He never saw himself as particularly intellectually talented, and he wrestled constantly with an inferiority complex because he had never completed college.

During his whole life, my father compartmentalized the learning that he did at school, work, and home. He had learned all his teachers taught him in school in the 1930s, but what he learned wasn't enough for the world and job in which he found himself in the 1980s. Suddenly, my father was chief industrial engineer in a world of computers, enhanced communications, and cutthroat industrial competition where sheer hard work and task orientation were just not enough. My father was little prepared to learn in new ways and create the new knowledge that he needed to survive as a leader in a major agricultural corporation. So my father took the "golden handshake" he was offered and retired, only to die a year later, ostensibly of cancer, but also perhaps because he felt he had ceased to be valued for the work that had given his life meaning.

Learning at School and Home

Twenty years after my father attended public school, so did I. Not surprisingly, little had changed since my father had been to school. The desks were still in rows, we still sat and listened while the teacher talked, and we still learned reading out of little primers with words like "Look Jane look. See Spot run." We learned how to be quiet, do your own work, get the right answer, and raise your hand when you wanted to speak.

It was no wonder that at first, I found it to be a pretty boring place, and I preferred to be at home where I could read books to my stuffed animals and dolls. I figured these were pretty easy lessons, and I had learned them all. I didn't need to go to school anymore. I was puzzled when my mother didn't think so too. Since my mother had always been right before, I decided that she must know something I didn't know, so obediently I returned to school. That was the beginning of sixteen more years of learning in school.

My mother helped me frame my early experiences of "learning" at home in ways that served me well in school. Her talks with me about school also helped me frame my experiences there. With my mother's encouragement and assumption that I could do it, I became not only a good student, I became the best student, eventually graduating as valedictorian of my high school class. But it all began in first grade where I was the best student in the top reading groups. I was good at reading the texts that my teachers chose and responding with the appropriate interpretation. I was good at doing the mathematics problems my teachers selected and responding with the appropriate answers. I always worked very hard, believing that I could achieve because my mother told me I could. I did very well at school and so after kindergarten, I began to like it more and more. Holding my mother's hand, I got past the brick wall of school, and slowly the wall that had separated my learning in school and out crumbled. Because of my mother's encouragement and tutelage, my experiences of learning at home and in schools became seamless in many ways. I did well on academic tasks at school and my parents praised me for these same kinds of tasks at home.

At school, my teachers' only negative comments about me were that I seldom smiled. I think I didn't smile at school because I wasn't paying attention to other people, I was concentrating on my own inner thoughts and reflections. In my own reflective life, I chose the texts and I created the contexts for my learning. I didn't talk much either at home or at school, usually preferring to listen to my mother or the teacher and then reflect on what had been said in my own thoughts.

Weekends and summers were times when my reflective life expanded to include my whole day. These were times of reading and playing with dolls with my best friend, Vicki. One summer, when I was in fifth grade, I read every book about dogs and horses in the children's section of the Rock Island library. Other summers I explored other literatures, but I created and participated in multiple worlds through my reading. Vicki and I also created and explored other worlds in our doll playing. In our play with dolls we posed and acted out real-life problems. The most difficult one was: What happens when Betty, a school teacher, gets married and has children? Will she have to give up her job or will she be able to manage a job and raise a family too?

Learning at Work and School and Home

In junior high school, I began thinking that I might become a schoolteacher when I grew up. When I was growing up, I didn't know many adult women who worked, and those I knew were often schoolteachers. I thought I could be a pretty good teacher. I knew I was good at schoolwork myself, and I thought I could teach others to do the kinds of things I was learning in school. It wasn't until I got to college that I started imagining myself as a university professor. The academic life seemed to bring together my secret life of reading and reflection and my more public life of learning that I had done in school and with my mother. Professors seemed to get paid for engaging in all the kinds of activities I most enjoyed and excelled at–learning from texts, reading, reflecting, and exploring the imaginary world of ideas. The fact was that I liked the idea of working in the academic world because it seemed to me like the world of school, not like the world of work, particularly the world of work in business and industry as I saw it through my father's experience as an industrial engineer with a firm that made farm machinery.

At the same time, I worried that living in a realm of ideas was not enough–these ideas need to be connected somehow to real life. I remember being profoundly moved by reading Herman Hesse's *The Glass Bead Game*. In this text, Hesse envisions a world where scholars spend their days playing a game that involves moving musical and mathematical ideas around in *n*-dimensional space. At some point in the story, the protagonist realizes that playing the glass bead game is not enough and that he needs to focus on what it means to be a teacher and to help others experience learning. The protagonist ends up leaving the world of the glass bead game to enter into the real lives of those he hopes to educate. I wondered: Is this the only way to repair such a divide in a scholar's life or are there other ways?

In this way, I first began to peer into a potential divide in my own life. The work of academics is often viewed as a mysterious "ivory tower" to lay people. To the day he died, my father had only a fuzzy idea of what professors like me did, even though I had been a professor for fifteen years by that time. As an industrial engineer, my father always wanted to come in and do a "time study" of my work and figure out how much time and money it was costing to produce each of the products I created. My father would look perplexed whenever I pointed out to him that my products were harder to identify and quantify than the tractors built by the company where he worked. How do you really assess the look of insight that comes into a student's face when a professor has truly helped her understand a new idea? How do you measure the worth of teaching a student to understand a powerful mathematical idea such as "function"–one that will help her see relationships among variables in multiple-problem situations for the rest of her life?

After graduating at the top of my class from Dubuque Senior High, I attended Iowa State University (ISU) where I did the same. At ISU, I conducted my first study of teaching and learning in an experimental psychology class where our professor assigned us to apply electrical shock systematically in order to condition a goldfish to swim to one side of its tank. At the time, I was an undergraduate psychology major at ISU in Ames, Iowa. The year was 1967, and "dust bowl" empiricism was alive and well in Ames–the place where "split-plot" and "factorial designs" had been invented years before. Researchers created these experimental methods because they wanted to investigate the effects of different variables, such as soil type or fertilizer, on crop yields in experimental corn fields. "Teaching" the goldfish was my first experience with the idea of manipulating independent variables or "treatments" (the duration and timing of the shock) in order to study the effects on dependent variables (the "learning" of the goldfish to swim to one side of the tank to avoid the shock). It also was my first experience with trying to get another organism to "learn" to emit a certain behavior. The idea conveyed to us by the professor of experimental psychology was that a goldfish could be "taught" to engage in certain behaviors upon specific occasions by manipulating stimuli and reinforcers that control these behaviors. As a "good student," I "learned" this principle well, and consequently I got an A on my write-up of this laboratory study, an A on the multiple-choice test of principles of learning, and an A again in my experimental psychology course. At the time I asked no questions. It was only later that I began to wonder: What did I really learn from this study?

After graduating from Iowa State, I applied to four graduate schools–Stanford University and three others. One was the University of Texas at Austin because I was still attempting to compose a possible life with my boyfriend who thought he might consider leaving the farm and going there to law school. I remember most vividly my interview with the chair of the Educational Psychology Department at the University of Texas at Austin because he looked at my perfect 4.0 undergraduate grade point and said, "That could indicate that you are a real conformist." I ran out of that interview because I was angry, but I was also worried that he might be right.

Acts of overt rebellion and public questioning of authority were hard for me then. I had always experienced learning at home and learning at school within the relationship of an "expert" other. In the beginning, the expert was my mother, then the experts became the texts and the teachers at school. I found it difficult to question directly these experts, particularly when I had done so well by not questioning them explicitly or confronting them directly. I had always achieved so well by either working publicly within the experts' standards and the relationships they constructed for me or working privately in my own reflective life where I could question.

My major act of rebellion occurred when I decided to go to Stanford University for graduate school–a place that was halfway across the country from my parents. It was an act of courage for a mild-mannered, shy, twenty-one-year-old girl who had never been west of Sioux City, Iowa. One reason I decided to attend Stanford was that I had read a description of the Program for Research on Teaching at Stanford in which Dr. Richard Snow talked about doing research on "heuristic teaching," or teaching that gave birth to learning. I didn't know what it was, but it sounded like an interesting frame within which to explore learning. A second reason I chose to go to Stanford is that the director of the Program in Research on Teaching, Dr. Nate Gage, called and offered me a position as a research assistant in the program. This was important because I didn't want my parents to pay my way in graduate school as they had in college.

It turned out that Dick Snow and Nate Gage had rather different frames for thinking about teaching and learning, and trying to put these two frames together presented a major problem of learning for me. Gage focused on behavior in teaching and learning; Snow focused on cognitive abilities underlying behavior. Snow argued that the effects of different teaching approaches depend on the individual learner, whereas Gage asserted that effective teaching approaches could be found that would improve learning for *all* students without regard to individual differences among learners. I puzzled about my professors' different ideas about learning and how to make sense of them. I wondered how to reconcile these differences. I wondered about how to relate my developing ideas about learning to those of others, including my professors, while still maintaining my own ideas and my own identity as a learner.

How does one learn with others while not always agreeing with them? How does one create relationships and communities within which participants respect and value each other's opinions while also tolerating disagreement and diversity, but yet each person learns with and from one another?

Although I had engaged in collaborative imagining with Vicki and other girlfriends, most of my learning prior to graduate school was either of the solitary sort or gleaned from an "expert other." In the collaborative "envisioning" I had done with playmates as a child, we engaged in imaginary play about our work and home, but typically these collaborative conversations were not around intellectual ideas. In graduate school, I became aware of the power of collaborative discourse and learning of intellectual ideas with peers. I worked closely with a team of graduate students (Chris Clark, Ron Marx, and Phil Winne). We became a research community. Together we conducted a number of studies of teaching and learning that led to new ways of thinking about teaching in our field.

In one famous experimental study, Chris, Ron, Phil, and I worked with Dr. Gage to examine the effects on student learning of different levels of teacher structuring, soliciting, and responding.[2] Each teacher administered each of six treatments to counterbalance for the effect of teacher on students' learning (that is, each teacher taught all six treatments). We were thinking of the teachers as "memory drums." Retrospectively, I came to believe that this was an unfortunate metaphor because it actually helped reify what I think was a misleading assumption–that all teachers can be considered alike if they are given scripts and engage in scripted behavior. From our research, we found evidence that this was patently false. No matter that we scripted teachers' behavior, and teachers trained and practiced to perfection–we still found whopping teacher effects that accounted for a significant proportion of the variance in students' learning. What accounted for these effects?

In retrospect, I would say that teachers interpreted and "read" the scripts differently, and the meanings that teachers made of the scripts shaped the way they thought about their teaching and taught their students. Teachers are not just technicians or robots; they are human beings. There was a personal side to the different kinds of relationships these teachers developed with their students even as they were teaching the script. One teacher remained quite formal while another exuded warm enthusiasm that enveloped her students in learning. At the time, however, I merely questioned whether a teacher's actions were sufficient to explain what goes on among learners and the teacher. Representing teaching and learning as a technical activity was clearly inadequate for capturing the teaching-learning experience. Just as I tried to convey to my father, the job of any educator or teacher was more than could be measured in dollars or cents or scores on a test. The creation of new knowledge, whether in research or in the mind of a learner, is not the same as creating a tractor or a widget in manufacturing. At some point, a technical model simply breaks down and does not apply.

The experience of collaborative learning with graduate-student colleagues made explicit for me the power of critically questioning oneself and others in the generation of new knowledge. Conversations and collaborations among Christopher Clark, Ronald Marx, and me resulted in our embarking on extensive research on teachers' thinking during our several years together as graduate students. In doing research on teacher thinking, we were really questioning the dominant research paradigm in the field, which still focused on teachers' behavior and did not probe teachers' thoughts or beliefs. Our alternative approach to representing teaching did not go unnoticed. Chris Clark and I subsequently received the Palmer O. Johnson Award from AERA for a study of teachers' thinking that we did together as graduate students at Stanford.[3]

Elsewhere I have described my learning from my research, beginning with the original study we did at Stanford, so I will not describe it here.[4] What I have not described before is the personal side of my life during graduate school and thereafter.

While the connection between school and work merged for me in graduate school, I struggled with the connection of these to the home and family life I hoped to create. My imaginary childhood play as Betty, the schoolteacher caught between job and family, seemed to continue unresolved. As a graduate student, I took a course from Sandra Bem in the psychology department at Stanford. She was talking about a new idea–being "androgynous" rather than masculine or feminine. Bem referred to androgyny as "flexibility of sex role." This idea helped me create a new image of my personal and professional roles. I began thinking: Maybe my husband and I could develop a new kind of family relationship in which we collaborated in raising our kids, somewhat like the way I had collaborated in doing research with my colleagues. In this way, we would share responsibilities for our children and the household.

As a graduate student, such an image of a family relationship seemed remote to me. I found Sandra Bem to be as adroit as other scholars at playing the glass bead game–creating and manipulating abstract ideas. Moreover, she described how she was enacting these ideas in her own parenting with her husband and fellow psychologist Darryl Bem. Yet I still couldn't envision how I would create these abstract ideas about family life in my own practice as a parent. I had never experienced such parenting myself. Such flexibility of sex role seemed to require a special kind of husband, much different from my own father or any man I had ever met.

When I met another graduate student, Patrick Dickson, I began trying to ground the theoretical idea of merging work and family in some everyday reality. We fell in love and quickly developed a wonderful relationship, except for one major stumbling block. Patrick loved children and wanted to have six. I, on the other hand, didn't think that I could have any if I also wanted to have a career as a professor of educational psychology. It was a difficult time for me as a young woman struggling to be a "feminist" and thinking about career and family. I tried to imagine how this would work and how we would create this new collaborative parenting relationship. Could Patrick and I learn flexibility in the ways that would be required to blend our lives and balance home and work? Could I learn to parent along with Patrick while each of us was still learning to become a professor and an educational researcher?

LEARNING EXPERIENCE: THE STORY OF ANDREW AND ME

Patrick and I did get married, and we compromised by having three children. Collaboration, flexibility, and negotiation framed our learning to parent. The way we eventually created our family revolves around an idea of flexibility of roles that we change and negotiate continuously as the situation requires. The one thing I always did was carry the babies until term and breastfeed them (although I know that Patrick would have loved to do this). Meanwhile, Patrick always dealt with electronic and mechanical failures around the house (he had gone to Georgia Tech, whereas I had never taken a physics course nor lifted a hammer, even though my father was an expert carpenter by avocation). But otherwise Patrick and I move in and out of traditionally masculine and feminine roles. Learning, flexibility, and negotiation have been key to our survival as a dual-career couple with three children.

I am not sure that my colleagues in educational psychology knew what to make of me when I arrived in Madison in 1976. First, I was a woman, and the department's only other woman had left after a messy divorce from another professor in the department.[5] Second, I was the only person in the department other than Herbert Klausmeier who did research on learning in real classrooms; everyone else did laboratory studies of learning. A final puzzle to them was that I was the first person in the department to have a baby while she was an assistant professor.[6]

Learning at Home

It's interesting that although what I learned at home prepared me well for school, it prepared me less well for motherhood. Having a baby when I was twenty-nine began the gradual change in the way I thought about the relationship between home and work. Even though I had taken multiple courses in developmental psychology, I hadn't learned how to be a real mother to a real baby. I wasn't prepared for Andrew.

My son Andrew was a puzzle to me. When he appeared on the scene in March of 1979, he wasn't at all what I had expected. Patrick, who has a Ph.D. in child development, is fond of quoting a famous developmental psychologist who quipped that before he had children, he had five theories of child development; after he had children, he had none. No theories of child development that I knew about seemed to help me understand Andrew. Nor did I find particularly useful the findings from positivist empirical research studies. Those studies with their decontextualized research findings seemed to apply to large numbers of nameless and faceless other children. I couldn't see how a particular statistically significant result applied to Andrew or to me.[7] Andrew seemed to me a unique individual. I found that I needed to understand Andrew's own personal thinking and experiences.

Andrew learned to read by writing when he was three. This perplexed me because it wasn't how I had learned to read. At the time, I was doing quantitative research in the positivistic empirical mode. I wasn't sure what to make of such a "case" of learning as Andrew. Andrew's invented spelling intrigued me, but in 1982 I didn't know what to make of it. I became fascinated by how Andrew seemed to be learning to write when he couldn't "read," at least according to a simplistic literal definition of reading as decoding text. My entry into this was through ideas I was developing about mathematics learning as a constructivist activity. I had begun working with colleagues who were studying addition and subtraction in mathematics, and I was wrestling with the idea that students "construct" knowledge.[8] In the context of my practice of mothering Andrew, I began to understand what it really meant to say that individuals "construct meaning."

Just as my mother had framed my experiences for me in the way she construed learning and communicated what was important to me, I found myself doing this with Andrew, sometimes consciously and sometimes unconsciously. Patrick and I have encouraged Andrew to ask questions, such as "Why?" and "How?" We vowed that we would never say to Andrew, "Because I am your parent, and I say so." We agreed that we would always explain the "why" behind our responses to Andrew. We encouraged him to talk a lot and write a lot, and to play with objects visually and physically. He always had a roomful of Legos, Tinker Toys, "constructs," and "transformers." He began playing and typing on a computer when he was eighteen months old.

Just as my early teachers framed for me how I thought about learning and knowledge, so too did Andrew's teachers. We chose to send him to a private Montessori school from ages two and a half to seven. The teachers in Andrew's Montessori school also assumed that children construct meaning. They taught Andrew writing by asking him first to dictate "stories" and then writing these stories down for him. Soon Andrew was writing "stories," a series of symbols and letters, that he then "read" back to me when he brought his story home from school. Thus, from the day Andrew began school, his teachers helped him see himself as the author of his own texts and the composer of his own learning.

To this day, Andrew remains convinced that it was the best schooling he ever had. All schooling since then has been a mere shadow by comparison. When Andrew looks back at his learning journal from kindergarten in Montessori school, he notes that he was doing advanced subjects like multiplication because his teacher encouraged it, but also because, as a learner, Andrew got to choose his own learning activities and plan his own daily course of learning. Andrew puzzles as to why his school and teachers now don't give him such choices and encourage him in independent learning and thinking.

Learning at Home and School

Andrew puzzles his teachers as well; sometimes he is even a "pain in the ass." Why? Perhaps it is because children construct knowledge in school, but they also construct knowledge outside of school, and frequently children (unlike many teachers) do not see the need to keep these separate. Andrew brings a lot of knowledge and experience to any learning situation, so the questions he asks are good ones. When Andrew asks a question, he doesn't settle for just an answer, he wants to know why. As one of the new generation of kids who have grown up with computers, video games, and instant access to information and technology of all kinds, he often "knows more" about these than his teachers.

Teachers often know little about the learning experiences of today's students, so these teachers often remain in the dark as to how to relate to their students' home learning experiences. In Andrew's case, such experiences center around role-playing games and computers. Andrew dares to question, and the questions he asks are hard ones. Next to computers, Andrew's favorite activity at home is role-playing games such as "Dungeons and Dragons." He enjoys being the "master" who tells the story and constructs the contexts and problems for the characters. Through playing narrative adventure games over the last seven years, Andrew seems to have developed literacy abilities not only in oral story telling but also in creative writing. He is an expert at figuring out the winning strategy for any game, particularly adventure games.

For Andrew, this became an issue in eighth grade when his teacher had the whole class play a game called "Discovery," a social studies simulation of the discovery and colonization of America. Andrew quickly figured out what you needed to do to win the game but consequently found the game frustrating in its simplicity. He was disappointed that the rule book (which was held by the teacher) was only three pages thick. The rules in typical role-playing games go on for pages and pages and are quite complex. Moreover, the learners (rather than a teacher) control the game in "authentic" adventure games. Andrew pointed out to his teacher that some rules didn't make sense. For example, when you bought rifles in "Discovery," you didn't gain any more "strength" in battle; all you could do was "trade rifles to the Indians," and "the Indians hardly ever asked for rifles." Andrew and his sophisticated adventure-game-playing classmates suggested changes in the rules, but the teacher wouldn't hear of it.

As Andrew told it, the only interesting simulation occurred in another class because "Mrs. Anderson made it more like a role-playing game." She let her students change the rules, and Mrs. Anderson embellished the rules too. "Mrs. Anderson said, 'O.K., it's time to collect taxes.' And one of the groups in her class said, 'We're not paying you.' So Mrs. Anderson brought the British troops over, and they began fighting the colonists, trying to get their money. And then the Revolutionary War started."

Although Andrew was disappointed because the simulation became so boring in his class, he didn't blame his teacher. He realized that she saw her expertise in social studies, not in English, and she actually had less expertise in role-playing adventure games than did Andrew and his colleagues. But what is curious to me is why Andrew's teacher was not able to turn the situation into a learning experience for her students as Mrs. Anderson did. Why wasn't she able to listen to and learn from and with Andrew and his friends?

Learning at Work, Home, and School

Andrew combines his expertise in narrative and writing with his technological acumen and mathematical ways of thinking. For Andrew a key to learning is authentic learning activity. He taught himself a computer programming language through engaging in the authentic activity of constructing an adventure game on the computer that he could then play with his friends. As a fifteen-year-old, Andrew works in the communication technology laboratory on the Michigan State University (MSU) campus, engaging in the authentic activity of learning design and programming while doing real work for which he is paid. He is in an apprenticelike situation where undergraduates, advanced graduate students, and a professor engage in the same activities. The key for Andrew here is that he is performing work that is valued and that counts in real ways. In our society we provide adolescents few such contexts, certainly not in school or at home.[9] It used to happen in earlier days when, in an agrarian society, children and youth were needed to work and help on the farm. Their work really mattered.

One way of thinking about Andrew as a learner is to situate his learning within the particular historical context in which he has grown up. My son Andrew was on a computer keyboard when he was eighteen months old.

When he was four years old, Andrew and our family were written up in the cover story of *Family Computing* magazine with the headline, "Is two too young?" The reference was to the age at which a child should learn to play/learn on a computer. Now, thirteen years later, it seems a moot question.

The question now is: Are we as educators in schools prepared to deal with the Andrews of the world? I often wonder. Not really, I usually reply. And yet I am one of those educators who is supposed to be doing research that makes a difference in the learning and teaching of children in our schools. But I am also Andrew's mother and, as such, have encouraged him to construct meaning, to ask questions, to seek for and justify knowledge for himself. As Andrew's mother, I want him to learn freely, but as a teacher educator and researcher of teaching, I also see the problem of reform from the teacher's side of the street. What can I do?

As I finished a first draft of this paper in spring of 1994, I had to stop in midstream on a Friday afternoon in order to attend to Andrew's latest concern about learning in school. Andrew was finding little of academic interest or inspiration in his classes at the local high school. Having met a Michigan State undergraduate who went through a "home-based" schooling approach to high school, Andrew was intrigued by this idea. He persuaded me to drive him to Ann Arbor, sixty miles away, to explore the home-based schooling program that is run out of Clonlara, an alternative school there. In talking with the Clonlara's assistant director, we learned that Andrew could design his own learning experiences and readings and materials for his courses as long as he met the requirement of twenty-two credits in each of several subject areas. Andrew was excited by the prospect of having choice and flexibility as he had had in his Montessori school days; he was and is a motivated learner. Andrew pointed out to me that while this approach would not work for everyone, he saw himself as self-directed enough to carry it off. I pointed out that his father and I couldn't be home to work with him closely, as a teacher would on a daily basis. Part of me felt guilty that I couldn't "quit work" and do this; the other part realized my own limitations. I was torn. I was not sure how to negotiate this latest dilemma as a mother, a scholar, an educator, a learner. Part of me wanted to take the easy way out and send Andrew back to East Lansing High School. Then I flashed back to the image of the little girl crying by that brick wall of the school, and I remembered, but this time I was the mother asking, "Why?"

LEARNING EXPERIENCES: REVISING OUR SENSE OF OURSELVES

While considering my son's dilemma, I came across the book *Peripheral Visions* by Mary Catherine Bateson. In this autobiographical account of herself as mother, teacher, and anthropologist, Bateson writes about her experiences of teaching and learning across multiple cultures and contexts with her daughter, Vanni. In the end, Bateson's message is one of revising our sense of selves even as we experience the multiple contexts of learning. As Bateson puts it:

> It is a mistake to try to reform the educational system without revising our sense of selves as learning beings, following a path from birth to death that is longer and more unpredictable than ever before. Only when that is done will we be in a position to reconstruct educational systems where teachers model learning rather than authority, so that schooling will fit in and perform its limited task within the larger framework of learning before and after and alongside. The avalanche of changes taking place around the world, the changes we should be facing at home, all come as reminders that of all the skills learned in school the most important is the skill to learn over a lifetime those things that no one, including the teachers, yet understands.
>
> It may be that withholding commitment and retaining skepticism even in the classroom is the wisest course, for we cannot tell our children with conviction that the civilization we know will always be right and true. We know it must change. . . . You will always be acting under uncertainty. You will know the future when you get there. Only then can you make it your home. (pp. 212–213)

Just as Andrew has strived to create a sense of himself as a learner, so too have I struggled to do so as a student, mother, researcher, and educator. Andrew's success, like mine, will depend on developing a capacity to make sense of similarities and differences in experiences across contexts, to improvise under uncertainty, and to learn across a lifetime.

Forty years after I cried as I faced the brick wall of school, what have I learned? One thing I learned is that in one way, my mother was right: I hadn't learned it all. I did have a lot more to learn. But what I had to learn probably is quite different from what my mother had in mind at that time, most noticeably because the world was quite a different place forty years ago when there were no xeroxes or FAX machines, or computers, and the world had not yet heard of the cold war, let alone experienced the downfall of Communism. So a second thing I learned was to think about learning and knowledge in new ways quite different from those my mother had in mind. And a third thing I learned is that school is only one of many significant situations in which we learn.

Fifteen years after having my first child, I realize that I have been striving all this time to live a life and learn through participation in a seamless web of experiences. In my "re-vision" of my life, my experiences with my children and husband at home merge and blend with my experiences with colleagues and students at work. There are common discourses and texts that cross the multiple contexts of my life–for example, my concern about problems of learning both at home and at school. My children face such problems, struggling to learn in school and out, and often I have tried to solve these problems by using my knowledge drawn from the research literature. This has shown me the limitations of research and has highlighted for me areas where we, as educators, need to do more research. But it has also led me to think about research, knowledge, and learning in new ways. I have begun to think of the findings of my research as a recounting of my personal learning experiences, and the findings of others' research as a recounting of theirs.

I try not to compartmentalize knowing and learning, for I realize that these are alive in the multiple settings in which I live my life (and others live theirs). Because of this I have difficulty imagining how one might bring together a positivistic, narrowly quantitative, research-based approach that separates the person and her life from the researcher. That's not to say it wouldn't work. It worked for Gary Price, my colleague in child development who systematically set about applying research findings to raising his child.

But for me, it worked in reverse–I learned as part of experiences with my children. My children made me human and in becoming human, somehow the decontextualized "dead" research findings and *t* tests of research no longer had meaning. What took on meaning for me was marveling at my children's first words as they struggled to communicate in spoken and written language. Then I had to figure out what kinds of research findings made sense. And what made sense were case studies of children constructing mathematical meaning, or case studies of teachers helping learners want to read, write, and speak for a purpose and an audience and in ways that are meaningful to them.

Another way I have interwoven my personal and professional lives is that I have brought my children into my professional life. For example, I often discuss with my children the paper I am writing or what I have just seen in my research in classrooms in California. I have had my son, Andrew, speak to my classes of teachers on "Learning in School and Other Settings." Teachers in my classes have interviewed my children for their projects on trying to understand learners' experiences in school and out. I am always on the lookout for others with whom to have conversations about how to bring together my lives at home, school, and work in a more seamless way.

Similarly, Bateson writes that she "believes it is important to provide a vocabulary that allows men and women whose lives do not follow the compartmentalized model of a successful career that our society has developed to value their achievement. Life is not made up of separate pieces. A composer creates pattern across time with ongoing themes and variations, different movements all integrated into the whole, while a visual artist combines and balances elements that may seem disparate" (pp. 108–109).

For me, the metaphor for my life is one I learned from my son Andrew, the technology wizard. It is one of multitasking. I imagine myself sitting at my Macintosh computer with twelve different "windows" open–each one running a different application. Within each window then, I participate in a different ongoing electronic discourse with someone, create a different text, experience a different representation of reality, or work within a different problem space. The tricks I use to do this are all ones I learned in relationship with my mother–the power of individual agency, the importance of interpretations created among others, and the significance of constant care and sustained effort. My mother's voice reminds me that as a learner, I am the one with my fingers on the mouse. With sustained and coherent effort, I can effectively manage what's going on in all the windows. And while more windows will open and there will always be more to learn, there will always be those to help me–those in whose company I can experience the world anew, create reflective spaces, and continue to learn along the way.

NOTES

Work on this article was supported in part and at times by my parents, Betty J. and LeRoy "Pete" Peterson; my husband, W. Patrick Dickson; my children, Andrew, Joshua, and Elissa Peterson Dickson; and my many professional colleagues and students. Their mentoring and their love have helped me–the author–immeasurably, and their ideas have contributed to this paper. But the opinions expressed here are those of the author, and not necessarily of her supporters.

1. See, for example, Hess and Shipman, 1968, and Heath, 1984.
2. See Clark, Gage, Marx, Peterson, Stayrook, and Winne, 1979.
3. The study is Peterson and Clark, 1978.
4. Peterson, 1994.
5. I arrived to find that another new Ph.D. had been hired who was also a woman. Her name was Louise Cherry, later to become Louise Cherry Wilkinson. Louise and I became great friends, colleagues, and supporters of one another. We often have said to each other that we never could have survived our four years as assistant professors without having each other to talk with about our research and about departmental politics.
6. I was told when I was hired that to get tenure I would need to develop my own program of research and have the "baker's dozen" of publications (that is, thirteen). These publications should preferably be single-authored, but if not, then co-authored with my grad students where I was the first author. They should be in peer-reviewed journals that were first rate (for example, journals published by the American Psychological Association or the American Educational Research Association). Collaboration with other faculty was actively discouraged for a beginning assistant professor. Being one who knew how to conform to the norms, I did what I was

told, and I made it. In four years, I had tenure, in two more I was a full professor, and by age thirty-five I had been awarded a chaired professorship. During the same year, I began a six-year term as editor of one of AERA's major journals, the *Review of Educational Research*. Two years later I was awarded the Raymond B. Cattell Early Career Award by AERA for my programmatic research on teacher effectiveness and student mediation of instruction. But that's only part of the story.

7. The only person I know who has been able to apply consistently the results of quantitative research directly to his own parenting is our friend and colleague, Gary Price. The year before our first child was born, Gary and his wife, Lanette, had a son. Like my husband, Gary has a Ph.D. in child development and did his dissertation on mother-child interaction with Robert Hess at Stanford. A reflective and thoughtful individual, Gary set out to directly apply the results of his research to raising his son. He taught his son language and information systematically, based on the kinds of questions he asked in his dissertation and the way researchers had found middle-class parents to interact. He read the research on infants' physical development and then systematically did physical "baby" exercises with his infant son every day to strengthen his muscles.

8. This research on children's construction of mathematical knowledge and the implications for teaching resulted in several publications including Peterson, Carpenter, and Fennema, 1989, and Peterson, Fennema, and Carpenter, 1991.

9. Some educational researchers are arguing for the creation of more such contexts for authentic learning both in school (Collins, Brown, and Newman, 1989) and out (Heath, 1994).

BIBLIOGRAPHY

Bateson, Mary C. 1994. *Peripheral Visions: Learning Along the Way*. New York: HarperCollins.

Clark, Christopher M., Nathaniel L. Gage, Ronald W. Marx, Penelope L. Peterson, Nicholas G. Stayrook, and Philip H. Winne. 1979. "A Factorial Experiment on Teacher Structuring, Soliciting, and Reacting." *Journal of Educational Psychology* 71(4):534–52.

Cohen, David, and Deborah Ball. 1990. "Relations Between Policy and Practice: A Commentary." *Educational Evaluation and Policy Analysis* 12(3):249–56.

Collins, Alan, John S. Brown, and Susan E. Newman. 1989. "Cognitive Apprenticeship: Teaching the Crafts of Reading, Writing, and Mathematics." In *Knowing, Learning, and Instruction: Essays in Honor of Robert Glaser*, Lauren B. Resnick, ed. Hillsdale, NJ: Lawrence Erlbaum, 453–494.

Heath, Shirley Brice. 1984. *Ways With Words: Language, Life and Work in Communities*. Cambridge: Cambridge University Press.

Heath, Shirley Brice. 1994. "Play for Identity: Where the Mind Is Everyday for Inner-City Youth." In *Creating Powerful Thinking in Teachers and Students: Diverse Perspectives*, John N. Mangeri and Cathy C. Block, eds. Fort Worth, TX: Harcourt Brace, 215–229.

Hess, Robert, and Virginia Shipman. 1968. "Maternal Influences Upon Early Learning: The Cognitive Environments of Urban Preschool Children." In *Early Education: Current Theory, Research and Action*, Robert D. Hess and Robert M. Bear, eds. Chicago: Aldine, 91–103.

Hesse, Herman. 1969. *The Glass Bead Game*. New York: Bantam.

Peterson, Penelope L. 1990. "Doing More in the Same Amount of Time: Cathy Swift." *Educational Evaluation and Policy Analysis* 12(3):277–296.

Peterson, Penelope L. 1994. "Research Studies as Texts: Sites for Exploring the Beliefs and Learning of Researchers and Teachers." In *Beliefs About Text and About Instruction With Text*, Ruth Garner and Patricia Alexander, eds. Hillsdale, NJ: Lawrence Erlbaum, 93–120.

Peterson, Penelope L., Thomas P. Carpenter, and Elizabeth L. Fennema. 1989. "Teachers' Knowledge of Students' Knowledge and Cognitions in Mathematics Problem Solving: Correlational and Case Analyses." *Journal of Educational Psychology* 81(4):558–569.

Peterson, Penelope L., and Christopher M. Clark. 1978. "Teachers' Reports of Their Cognitive Process During Teaching." *American Educational Research Journal* 15: 555–565.

Peterson, Penelope L., Elizabeth L. Fennema, and Thomas P. Carpenter. 1991. "Using Children's Mathematical Knowledge." In *Teaching Advanced Skills to Disadvantaged Students: Views From Research and Practice*, Barbara Means, C. Chelemer, and Michael S. Knapp, eds. San Francisco: Jossey-Bass, 68–101.

Resnick, Lauren B. 1987. "Learning in School and Out." *Educational Researcher* 16: 13–20.

CHILDREN'S LITERATURE CITED

Piper, Watty. 1990. *The Little Engine That Could*. New York: Putnam.

* *CHAPTER 13* *

Learning from Research and Everyday Life

Anna Neumann and Penelope L. Peterson

IN LOOKING BACK AT THEIR CHILDHOOD, adolescent, and early adult years, the authors contributing to this volume refer often to the rhythms of their daily lives, both the "high moments and memorable ones" and the "banal" (as Maxine Greene defines these), both the continuities and discontinuities in the composition of life (as Nel Noddings explains). Greene, for example, describes her efforts to create and maintain a home and family life—"what with an infant to care for, cardiographs to give, x-rays to administer, phone messages to take, food to prepare." Concha Delgado-Gaitan writes of daily "household struggles due to poverty" and frequent reminders that "the system 'couldn't be trusted.'" Penelope Peterson writes of the disjunctures she felt between learning freely at home and in more constrained ways at school, and of her realization, later in life, that "school is only one of many significant situations in which we learn."

The significance of the everyday in these writers' lives becomes especially clear when daily settings shift—when how a person knows the everyday is lost, when everyday existence must be recrafted. Nel Noddings, for example, tells of moving from home and school settings that were rich in learning, exploration, and play to a new everyday life that, with few exceptions, represented a "flood of despair" and the solitary wanderings of "lonely beachcombers and thinkers like me." For each of the writers in this volume, the particularities of everydayness constitute much of their lives.

As these examples suggest, daily life presented unique challenges to each woman—and each addressed these challenges in equally unique ways, often seeking to re-present what she found as "given" in her life.[1] Though each woman remained acutely aware of and responsive to the demands and expectations of others in her everyday life, each tried, at various times in her life, to "re-present" everydayness. This might happen through withdrawal (for example, into reading or into relationships that foster learning). Or it might happen through connection and commitment to a social endeavor (for example, through advocacy or teaching). Amidst the x-rays, cardiographs, phone messages, and family care that comprised her everyday life, Maxine Greene made time to write novels and to join with communities of writers, artists, and activists. In this way–slowly–she began to re-present her life as connected to communities of her own choosing. Amidst the boredom and feelings of powerlessness that marked her early life, Concha Delgado-Gaitan created visions of possibility as she learned to advocate for herself, her family, and her community, whether on her own or with others. Amidst the loneliness of "hard times" in a new environment, Nel Noddings created opportunities for connection with special teachers who provided, in her words, "the major part of my emotional and intellectual support." From her early frustrations with school and her fascination with learning outside school, Penelope Peterson created, in her adult years, responses that allow learning in one setting to incite learning in the other. In each of these cases, a woman encountering the constraints of the life in which, literally, she found herself also found ways to re-create that life–to re-present it to herself and others–at least in part. For some of these women, these re-presentative efforts–initiated in childhood, adolescence, or young adulthood–turned into research as an activity of their adulthood.

In this concluding chapter we consider how the authors contributing to this volume encountered the everydayness of their lives, and how, often, they tried to re-present their own (and others') experiences of the everyday, including through their research. We also consider the nature of re-presentation as an activity in a life, and the implications of these women's re-presentative efforts for their own learning and for the learning of others–their readers and the educational community at large.

RE-PRESENTATIONS OF SELF AND EVERYDAY LIFE

The preceding chapters suggest that a person's efforts to re-present her everyday life reflect a deeper impulse to know and learn authentically–from her own questions, concerns, and understandings–rather than to assume unquestioningly the perspectives of presumably more knowledgeable others. Maxine Greene, for example, presents herself as wanting to do more than merely respond to the immediacies of her everyday existence. She sought to create a broader range of connections to foster her own developing thought, and thus she chose to research and write on her own and to return to school amidst the demands of mothering and "proper partnering." Concha Delgado-Gaitan refused to accept her placement in a low-track high school

English class, and "confident that [she] could do better work because of [her] previous success in college preparatory classes," she asserted her interests to school authorities. Similarly, Nel Noddings refused to surrender to the boredom produced by uninspired teachers, and she worked hard to create alternative relationships with special teachers and with authors who would inspire her learning. As a young girl, Penelope Peterson would not resign herself to learning just in school, and with her mother's support, she created ways to learn beyond school (a pattern she continues in her adult life in supporting her own son's efforts to learn in a variety of settings). Though differing in content, these four authors' re-presentations of self and everyday life reflect a common thread that winds, as well, through the other writings in this volume: Each author assumes a point of view–on self and world–that differs in personally important ways from the reality in which each "found herself" as a child or young woman or, at times, later in life. Each author acts willfully in her attempts to foster her own developing (and differing) point of view amidst everyday demands and expectations that often threaten to overwhelm it.

For some of the women writing in this volume, research is an extension of their personal efforts to re-present their lives and their inherited worlds. For others, research marks the beginning of their personal re-presentative efforts. Virtually all the writers describe their scholarship as attempts to rethink or remake what has been "handed down" to them–to re-create their inherited, predefined realities to be more just, more open, more considerate, more tolerant of diversity, more conducive of learning, more representative of what education might be. But as we have just noted, these authors' re-creative efforts manifest themselves variously at different times in their lives and with varying effects, and their efforts to re-present themselves and their worlds reflect the diverse selves and worlds in which their re-presentative efforts are situated. As we describe in the remainder of this section, each author conducts and focuses her re-presentation in unique ways–Maxine Greene through reimagination of self and everyday life, Concha Delgado-Gaitan and Gloria Ladson-Billings through reconstruction of self and community, Kathryn H. Au and Anna Neumann through remembrance of self and time, Ellen Condliffe Lagemann and Martha Montero-Sieburth through re-creation of self and voice, Nel Noddings and Patricia J. Gumport through relation to self and other, Linda F. Winfield and Penelope L. Peterson through repair of self and contexts.[2]

Reimagining Self and Everyday Life

Maxine Greene portrays the making of "alternative realities"–including her research–as the creation of new knowledge and discourse. For Greene, this has meant locating and joining communities beyond those that frame her day-to-day existence. She recalls that in her youth "what [she] chose to like" was often "what [her] family spurned," including concerts and lectures that "opened doors to some alternative reality." Greene became part of "an eager, committed audience" whose members appeared consistently (and to her, surprisingly) at the lectures, exhibits, and concerts she attended. She had stumbled onto an invisible community within which she could think and create in ways that diverged from her more mundane and restricted everyday endeavors.

Just as in her life, Maxine Greene strives in her scholarship to create and join–to draw from–alternative communities offering her (and others) alternative discourses–alternative opportunities to reimagine more restrictive everyday existences. She also does this in her teaching–for example, as she encourages her students to "look from a number of vantage points at the same phenomena" so that they may "pose more and more probing questions." But Greene herself learns through this experience as well: She continuously re-creates her courses, "remaking [them] as I go, . . . rewriting the original book so as to come to terms with critiques of the canon, with contextualism, with gender and class and ethnic concerns."

Greene says, "I wanted (and I still want) people to become 'wide-awake' . . . to refuse passivity, to refuse to be mere clerks or functionaries." She describes herself as striving to create a citizenry that will be able "to look at things 'as if they could be otherwise' . . . [to break] through the rigid structures, the exclusions, the constraints that prevent people from envisaging possibility." Greene pursues these lifetime commitments through her research.

Reconstructing Self and Community

Concha Delgado-Gaitan and Gloria Ladson-Billings associate the idea of everyday life with existence amidst family and community, but their daily lives, both now and in the past, reflect conflicting forces. Delgado-Gaitan describes her life as a "'tinkling' dance in which I have hopped between two clanking bamboo sticks, skillfully avoiding getting a foot severed as I jumped in and out." In her youth, Delgado-Gaitan skillfully maneuvered between the cultures of home and community, and the cultures of schools disconnected from home and community life. This theme resonates with Gloria Ladson-Billings's description of her graduate school experience as, initially, a "pleasant divergence from the cares of the world . . . like having a day at an amusement park" quite apart from everyday life. But when Ladson-Billings tried to bring these worlds together (for example, by studying aspects of African American cultures, initially through methods and perspectives that cannot apprehend them), the differences became barriers. Rather than dividing their lives among diverse, competing communities, these researchers have tried to create what

Delgado-Gaitan (borrowing from Gloria Anzaldua) describes as a "borderland"–"a space where multiple cultures, multiple consciousnesses, and multiple possibilities exist–where a border is dissolved . . . mak[ing] room for borderlands to configure." But in addition to reconstructing notions of community, Ladson-Billings and Delgado-Gaitan have sought to reconstruct *themselves* as being of more than one or another community. In Ladson-Billings's terms, "My identity is not an either/or proposition . . . it is both/and."

These researchers' struggles to create synthetic spaces within which they might reconstruct previously divided images of self and community are reflected in their research. To do this, Gloria Ladson-Billings has convened a "research collective" of successful teachers of African American students. The collective has grown at the juncture of competing communities–divided by race, or by commitments to research or practice; it has sought synthesis (and reconstruction) through dialogue among persons of diverse understandings and commitments. Ladson-Billings quotes Patricia Hill Collins in explaining her dialogic approach to research: "Dialogue implies talk between two subjects, not the speech of subject and object . . . a humanizing speech . . . that challenges and resists domination" (p. 212). She adds that "[the] give and take of dialogue makes struggling together to make meaning a powerful experience of self-definition and self-discovery (recovery) . . . the hallmark of my investigation." Similarly, Concha Delgado-Gaitan says that her work in the Latino community of Carpinteria has given her "an immense opportunity to understand and reconcile ethnic, intellectual, and political borders"–that the study of Carpinteria has been "my borderland, providing me with the 'time' to work through academic, interpersonal, and political problems in a protracted way."

Delgado-Gaitan's and Ladson-Billings's efforts to transform divisions between diverse communities into altogether different "borderlands" have served both self and community. Ladson-Billings draws parallels between her efforts to reconstruct community and her efforts to integrate her own "personal, public (sociocultural/civic), and intellectual interests." Delgado-Gaitan explains that her studies of Latino communities have "stretched [her] consciousness theoretically, politically, and personally" and that the emerging "unity of ideas and praxis . . . constitutes a [personal] borderland" for her.

Remembering Self and Time

Kathryn H. Au and Anna Neumann portray their modern American lives–in which both were "schooled" and "credentialed"–as shielding internal (at times unvoiced) cultural existence among mothers, fathers, aunts, uncles, and grandmothers whose lives were formed in other places and at other times.

They attempt to apprehend and articulate aspects of the past that reach silently into their lives today, in this way reviving aspects of the "selves" that their modern American schooling and their acquired professionalism have absorbed. They strive to reconstruct their everyday lives today in relation to the everyday lives of their pasts. Kathryn Au describes herself as "a Chinese American . . . in the fourth generation of my family to live in Hawaii" and as having "always had an interest in family history, particularly in the lives of my grandmothers . . . consciously gathering information about my family's past." In her chapter, Au recalls stories of her grandmothers' lives, and their efforts to learn, that she has purposefully pursued over the years, and she explains how these memories and stories shape her life and her ideas about the learning of literacy today. Anna Neumann describes herself as reaching beneath the securities and opportunities of her American life, struggling to apprehend her parents' experiences in the Holocaust and in its aftermath–whether by listening to stories her father and mother tried to tell or by pursuing bits of story they revealed without words. She describes herself today as pondering over what this listening, watching, and probing into their pasts has brought to her life and work–what she has learned, about learning itself, that otherwise she might not know.

Au's and Neumann's efforts to re-present their own–and others'–modern, everyday lives in relation to ways of life (and ways of knowing) that modernism has all but displaced are evident in their research as well. Kathryn Au describes how she and her colleagues developed talk-story–like reading lessons for young Native Hawaiian students. "These studies," says Au, "were among the first to verify the possibility of improving the academic learning of students of diverse backgrounds through the use of culturally responsive instruction, that is, instruction reflecting values and practices similar to those of the home culture." But, Au notes, the deep learning of one's own culture, alongside the learning of a more general culture, holds far more than instrumental value, an insight she gained from her own life: "Students of diverse backgrounds . . . will be encouraged to use their literacy skills not just to learn mainstream content, as I did in school, but to deepen their understanding of their own worlds. . . . I did not receive this opportunity in my own schooling and wish that I had."

Anna Neumann explores the substantive and methodological implications, for her research, of her attempts to uncover her parents' pasts. She describes herself as learning, from her efforts to know her parents' lives, that "with every text that's told comes a silence that cannot be converted into words," but also that often "in . . . silence . . . there exists a text to know and to tell." Neumann began her career by studying colleges and universities as social institutions, emphasizing the administrative and leadership discourses that formally define "institution" in higher education. She says that her work has changed and that now she attends to aspects of collegiate discourse that escape or defy institutional discourses (though often remaining influenced by them)–for example, among professors who strive to define themselves personally by means of their scholarly work. Neumann also describes how her continued learning about interview-based research draws on what she learned from being with her parents–"how little I can truly know of another person's experience" and how carefully inquiry into silence must proceed.

Though living different lives and pursuing different research agendas, both Au and Neumann describe themselves as retrieving–for their lives, their work, and their times–the almost-forgotten meanings of the pasts that formed their lives.

Re-creating Self and Voice

Ellen Condliffe Lagemann and Martha Montero-Sieburth write of their struggles to develop personally meaningful knowledge and to voice such knowledge in pursuit of socially worthwhile ends. However, they did not easily realize this dual goal in the courses of their lives: Lagemann describes herself as growing up in a world where "women might read the words of others, but neither write nor speak their own words in public." She says that in the past, she "had 'a room of my own,' a study to which I could and did retreat, but I had no reason to go there except to pay bills or write letters." Montero-Sieburth describes her hardships as an immigrant of Mexican and Costa Rican parentage struggling to join a new American society whose members seemed unable to hear or understand her voice. To survive, she acquired the skills of "a chameleon," learning when to "blend" and when to assert her "differences," learning to moderate her voice. Though living very different lives, both women struggled with limitations on their efforts to use and speak their minds in intellectual and public domains.

Though expected to attend to other people's definitions of who they were–whether as woman or immigrant–neither Lagemann nor Montero-Sieburth acceded long to imposed definitions; both turned to research to redefine themselves and to redefine, as well, the worlds and selves of others. Lagemann began her scholarly career by reconceptualizing historical institutions from within the experiences of women's lives–by "defin[ing] criteria of historical significance that could bring into fuller view the activities and institutions important to women as women," in this way illuminating "where and how women had acquired the skills, sensibilities, and ideas important to them." In her early research, Lagemann sought to achieve an aim of "objective" worth (defining women as active, historical beings) that simultaneously addressed her more subjective need to act and create as a woman of "scholarly ambitions . . . seriously intellectual, publicly articulate, independent minded, interested in public affairs, and deeply committed to work." "In writing *A Generation of Women*," she says, "I was searching for and finding examples of women who had been able to do the things I, too, wanted to do." In writing about the historical creation of women's public voices, Lagemann created her own public voice.

Martha Montero-Sieburth's search for self and voice unfolds differently, though (like Lagemann's) with benefits accruing both to others and herself. In her chapter, Montero-Sieburth defines herself as a researcher who seeks to "become an instrument to channel the unstated ideas, or words, or meanings people share when using their own voices." Her own experiences as a child and adolescent amidst people who did not know (or care to know) who she was inspired her research commitments to "hear and respect the voices of others" and "not [to] speak for 'them.'" She describes herself now as replacing "the notion of subject-object (the researcher studying the 'other')" with "one of subject-subject (the researcher becoming the 'other,' and the 'other' becoming the researcher)." In sum, Montero-Sieburth's experiences as a stranger who learned to attend to the dictum, "define yourself, before you are defined," shaped her conceptions of research: She views research as a means for the subjects of research to define and articulate their own identities and to develop their own voices. She explains that, "Today, the notion of teacher as researcher or community member as researcher is commonplace in my research repertoire."

Initially, Lagemann and Montero-Sieburth encountered communities that could not hear their thoughts and experiences or the thoughts and experiences of others like themselves. However, these scholars' personal and intellectual struggles within these encounters helped each to create herself as a public intellectual being.

Relating to Self and Others

Nel Noddings and Patricia J. Gumport describe their efforts to construct identity, initially alone but in time through connection with others. Nel Noddings describes how she came to think of her readings and her relationships with teachers as "bulwark[s] against despair," as sources of companionship not otherwise available to her. "I needed my teachers," she says, an early realization that followed her, years later, into her research. As she explains, "The analysis of relationships–especially those peculiarly one-sided yet reciprocal relationships that characterize teaching and parenting–is central to my work today."

Noddings has used a central issue in her life–her need as a young student to relate to teachers, and later as a teacher herself to relate to her students–to frame her research on teaching and learning. She studies teaching and learning from within her personal experiences of these relationships, in this way bringing the analytic powers of research to bear on a concern that is core to her life. "There came a time, eventually," she explains, "when reflective awareness made it possible to bring my hard-earned analytical skills to bear on issues that, given my life experience, seemed really to matter." "Surely," she adds, "to do that in one's work is one form of actualization."

Patricia Gumport also describes her distances from others—"I . . . chose the privacy of my room, where I explored a deeply introspective world . . . choosing authors . . . who spoke most eloquently to my youthful existential ruminations." As an adolescent, Gumport was "immersed in . . . a rich inner world." Avoiding "center[s] of activity," she positioned herself "on the edges as an observer," for she felt that in these spaces, she might achieve "detachment, self-sufficiency, and objectivity." Like Noddings, however, Gumport learned, in time, that attachment mattered to her.

Though learning early in life to be comfortable in "being by myself," Gumport soon realized that others' recognition and approval of her thoughts—her developing knowledge—were important to her. This realization and her subsequent struggles to understand what the need for approval meant in her life materialized in her research. "I easily translated this interest into research on legitimacy," she says, "that is, how and why areas of knowledge—and the people in them—become differentially valued." "The need for approval and legitimacy," she explains, "why I/we care, and how our lives are shaped by that valuation are central to my work and my life." In her studies of lives disconnected from mainstream academe (for example, "Fired Faculty"), yet often seeking connection, Gumport has herself found ways to connect.

Though struggling, each in unique ways, with conceptions of self among others, both Noddings and Gumport use their research to explore alternative representations of relationship, for self and others.

Repairing Self and Contexts

Linda F. Winfield and Penelope L. Peterson write about struggles to understand and appreciate learning within and across the diverse contexts of their lives, though their struggles manifest themselves differently.

Linda Winfield opens her chapter in a "traditional scholarly voice," noting that through much of her career, "that was the 'only voice' I had." But she adds that despite the prominence of this scholarly voice, her "real self"—apart from career—is far more complex and developed. She purposefully maintained two selves—two voices spoken in separate parts of her life—because she discovered, early in life, that "African American females in America have not [historically] been valued." Winfield shows how hard it was for her to bring the personal self that others hardly recognized–much less valued–into the public/professional realm of educational research.

A divided life made more sense to her; a divided life also let Winfield have the multiple facets of her self: "I would often (at least in my own head) make a conscious and deliberate distinction between my profession (or what I do) and who I really am," and she adds that this "allowed me to have some semblance of a 'self' that operated independently of my profession." This division, she explains, let her "exist in a reality larger than academia"; it also gave her alternatives: "Whenever I encountered disappointments, rejection, marginalization in academic pursuits," she says, "I was not totally devastated . . . Conversely, when chaos and confusion occurred in my personal life, I shifted to the professional realities of my existence, and to my spirituality."

Though the division between professional work and personal existence was helpful to Winfield initially, she began, in time, to bring these separate parts of herself into conversation with each other and, in this way, to question the utility of the sharp division she had constructed. Realizing that the professional literature on African American children did not match her own experiences, she asked: Who are the "knowers" in this research, who are "the known," and how does knowing proceed? What would happen if those who traditionally have been "the known" were to become "knowers" of their own culture and community? Much of Winfield's career has been devoted to epistemological repositionings of the educational literature–to the re-creation of research stances whereby "the known" and "the knowers" merge, as professional and personal facets of her life merge as well.

Penelope Peterson also writes about her struggles to join the separate spheres of her life, though her efforts materialized in very different ways. Peterson was aware of the division–between learning personally at home and learning more formally in the professionalized/institutionalized contexts of school–and she fought it for much of her life. The division, though real in her life, and though promoted by respected adults, was not something she made sense of easily. Unlike Winfield, however, Peterson did not need "the personal" to serve as an alternative to "the professional" (or vice versa); rather, she sought to learn freely in the multiple physical and social spaces of her life. Her reading, role-playing, and imagining in one locale (most often, home) were as valuable in her learning as anything she might do in school–at times, more so. As a young child, she believed that she had already learned all that school could offer and that the true challenges of learning lay in explorations and imaginings beyond school.

Peterson's childhood struggles to make sense of learning across multiple settings have materialized in her adult life–both in her relationships with her husband and children, and in her relationships with children and teachers in general in the context of her research. For example, Peterson, working collaboratively with her husband, W. Patrick Dickson, has been actively involved in helping her children exist in school as the learners that she, as a mother who cares deeply about their learning, knows them to be more naturally at home. At times, that has verged on (or resulted in) major logistical changes in their schooling–for example, following Andrew in pursuit of alternative schools aimed at extending the spirit of his earlier Montessori experiences. Peterson and Dickson have also fostered their children's learning at home–for example, encouraging Andrew's out-of-school narrative adventure games, self-initiated writing projects, and technological wizardry.

In pursuing her children's "natural" learning, Peterson has come to rethink learning as she conceived of it in graduate school and early in her career. However, in studying her own children's learning, she has also rethought the nature of research, which she presents as her learning about learning. "I learned as part of experiences with my children," she says. "My children made me human and in becoming human, somehow the decontextualized 'dead' research findings and *t* tests of research no longer had meaning. What took on meaning for me was marveling at my children's first words." She continues: "Then I had to figure out what kinds of research findings made sense. And what made sense were case studies of children constructing mathematical meaning, or case studies of teachers helping learners want to read, write, and speak for a purpose and an audience and in ways that are meaningful to them."

Though leading different lives in very different contexts, Winfield and Peterson seek to re-present the school and professional settings in which each finds herself. For both, the coming together of disparate worlds–and disparate selves–contributes to the "re/pairing" of divisions (literally, double visions) in their own and others' lives.

Re-presentation and Research

Each of the women writing for this volume has, in her own way, sought to re-present her self and the everyday life into which she was born or brought; moreover, each–in her own way and time–has created research that extends her personal re-presentative efforts. But what might we learn from these women's efforts at re-presentation? In particular, what might we learn about research as a means for researchers to re-present their own lives and worlds and to re-present, as well, the lives and worlds of others whom they care deeply about?

In analyzing these authors' reflections on their research in their lives, we realized two important patterns. First, as we have already noted, we came to see research as an extension of these authors' personal efforts to re-present their selves and their everyday lives. Second, we came to understand research as a means for these women to rethink and re-form their selves and their worlds in their adult years, a process that, for some, began in their childhood or adolescence. For example, Patricia Gumport's early efforts to balance a desire to be by herself with an emerging need for approval and connection materialized, in later years, as research on legitimacy—as studied considerations of whose knowledge counts. Martha Montero-Sieburth's efforts to identify herself in childhood and adolescence—to know and to be known by others around her—materialized, in her adulthood, as research on how marginalized communities may assert their identities among other social groups. We also came to see research as a site for "working out" personal puzzles and problems at the same time that it served as a site for "working out" larger social problems. For example, Concha Delgado-Gaitan's research on social "borderlands"—such as Carpinteria and other Latino/a communities—has illuminated the personal "borderlands" of her own life, including her struggles with health and family. Linda Winfield's struggles with "who is the knower? . . . and who are the known?"—and how the known may become the knower—appear to be concerns in her life inasmuch as they are concerns in the populations she studies.

These patterns suggest that research, as personal as it is, nonetheless projects outwardly—for example, as writers probe the lives of subjects beyond themselves. But this is not where the story of "how research happens" ends: What researchers learn from research (about the subjects they study "out there") may return to the self of the researcher, as a form of personal learning. Thus as we have noted already, researchers may learn from their selves and from their everyday lives *for their research*. However, the converse applies as well: Researchers may learn much of personal value from their research *for their selves and for their everyday lives*. Research may return personal learning to the life from which it grows. But as we shall see in the following sections, this kind of self-oriented research—growing from self and returning to self—is not to be equated with self-indulgent or, more simply, selfish, research. Research that draws intentionally from the researcher's self, and that intends to fulfill researchers' personal needs to learn, may be more meaningful to others than more "selfless" research that seeks to mute the self of the researcher. We explore this seemingly counterintuitive assertion first by considering the nature of research as a form of personal re-presentation and second by examining the social value of this view of research.

THE NATURE OF RE-PRESENTATION: THE INTERTWINING OF SELF, RESEARCH, AND EVERYDAY LIFE

The women writing for this volume have sought to re-present their lives more authentically—more personally—than the demands and pace of their daily lives would typically permit. Their stories reflect moments stolen for personal thought, negotiated lives, courses of life diverging from the norm. Each has found her own way to frame her research in light of her needs to understand "things in particular" rather than assuming others' understandings as her own. Each in her own way has struggled to create what Maxine Greene calls her "alternative reality"–spaces in the flow of everyday life within which she has considered personally meaningful questions and puzzlements more freely, fully, and critically than life in the surrounding world allows. Viewed as an effort to experience moments of authentic thought, the creation of an "alternative reality" requires a turning away–a shift from unquestioning reliance on others' constructions of knowledge to studied reliance on self as creator of knowledge or, often, on self as creator of community within which new knowledge is constructed. Maxine Greene turned from images of herself among family to images of the self she created in the company of authors, artists, and lecturers whom she purposefully sought out–initially in "a secret, private garden" that later she expanded into her "alternative reality." Ellen Condliffe Lagemann turned toward the construction and articulation of her own thoughts, away from her family's view that women might not publicly express themselves. Gloria Ladson-Billings turned away from white mainstream ways of knowing to an African American community whose knowing became the source and subject of her research. Each woman turns from "given" constructions of everyday life in unique ways–whether through re-imagination, reconstruction, remembrance, re-creation, relation, or repair.

However, for each, this turning away from everyday life is, in time, "re-turned" to everyday life, her own and others'. For example, "re-turn" may occur as a woman teaches to others what and how she learned in the alternative moments apart from the "main stream" of everyday life–much as Gloria Ladson-Billings does when she shares the insights of the teachers with whom she explores the successful teaching of African American youth, or as Ellen Condliffe Lagemann does in her analysis of women's history, or as Maxine Greene does in her explorations of social imagination as a form of community education. "Re-turn" may also occur as a woman institutionalizes her personal efforts to create alternative realities within a socially recognized and legitimated research career–for in this way, she formally inscribes research within her everyday life, much as all these writers have.

But this distinction between everyday life and alternatives to it is not nearly as clear as it seems. A woman's alternative reality may eventually "return" to her everyday reality as she teaches, or as she assumes a research career that becomes the "everyday" of her life. *Everydayness, however, as a facet of life never disappears*, even within the spaces that a researcher creates as alternatives to the everyday. In searching (and researching) in alternative spaces in their lives, the volume contributors do *not* escape the hold of the everyday: Anna

Neumann, though searching her parents' pasts, returns to realities of her present-day life. Patricia Gumport, though exploring the meaning and power of delegitimized knowledges, returns daily to the legitimized routine of the tenure clock and collegial relations. Linda Winfield, though escaping momentarily from life to research–or conversely, from research to life–always turns to the other. Though these women may appear to depart from their everyday lives as they create "alternative realities," they do, in fact, always return to the everyday.

In a semantic sense, such return is unavoidable, for an alternative reality is defined *in reference to* and *in terms of* the everyday reality to which it exists as alternative. Without the everyday, that which exists as its "alternative" loses meaning. Thus, though intended as a departure from everyday life, the alternative is, paradoxically, captured and defined by everyday life. Moreover, a person who is formed–who thinks, knows, and learns–within a particular framing of everyday life is the same person who constructs alternatives to that framing. That is, she brings the person who was formed "out there" amidst the everyday–that is, in the contexts of relationships with others "out there"–to her alternative creations. Gloria Ladson-Billings, formed in part by the daily currents of a conflict-ridden and discriminatory white world, is also the Gloria Ladson-Billings who creates alternatives to that world–for example, in her teaching and research on teaching. Concha Delgado-Gaitan, shaped by a world in which the voices of Latino parents had little power in school and community, is also the Concha Delgado-Gaitan who represents Latino parents' presence and voice in schools. Kathryn H. Au, formed by a world in which her cultural heritage was ignored, is also the Kathryn H. Au who now strives to create opportunities for students to explore their own cultures even as she persists in exploring her own. Everyday reality inescapably infuses scholars' creations of alternatives to the everyday.

In these ways, we view alternative realities as existing within the everyday lives we seek to re-create. But the converse of this statement merits attention as well in that everyday life as "given" to us permeates the alternatives to it that we construct. Everyday life exists, as well, within alternatives to it. How might this be explained? Dorinne Kondo writes that selves (and as individuals, we each have multiple selves) form in the presence of others existing in our everyday lives. The person who creates an alternative reality brings to the making of that alternative space an array of "selves" (perhaps, a self-of-many-selves) formed in the company of others who, by interacting with her in everyday life, helped to craft how this person defines herself and her world. Paradoxically, the person who momentarily escapes the everyday life that has already formed how she knows herself brings the selves of her everyday life to the creation of her alternative reality.

But what is important is that *in the alterative space*, the researcher's self-of-many-selves–initially formed "out there" among those who comprise her everyday life–may be re-formed in the company of new companions whom she consciously and purposefully selects. The alternative space offers her more freedom in choosing her relationships, as opposed to accepting the inherited or otherwise predefined relationships of everyday life. In this alternative space, she is able to craft new and different relationships within which she may learn and change, though slowly, who she is, how she knows herself. She may form such relationships, as Greene describes, with authors or artists who evoke in her alternative images of herself and the world. Or borrowing from Noddings, she may form such relationships with selected teachers who, surprisingly, help her hear and appreciate herself in ways that others in her daily life do not. She may also form such relationships, as Gumport does, by choosing the human subjects of her research intentionally and with care (relative to what she hopes to learn from/with them) rather than randomly.

Most important, however, the researcher may form such relationships, reflexively, *with her own selves*. In an alternative reality, the relationships a researcher evokes with diverse aspects of her self–for example, as she reflects on her past thinking–may become contexts for formation and re-formation of that complexity of self. In an alternative reality, the diverse aspects of self (to which others "out there" have already contributed so much) can converse with and learn from one another. Internal conversations such as this (between self engaged with self) may help a researcher reach for integrity in a world that rarely allows her time to reflect on and "integrate" the multiple selves created amidst her everyday life.

Because our alternative realities reflect the relationships formed in everyday life, they are never solely about an authentic self untouched by external forces. But these alternative realities *may* represent times when we strive to be as much "of self" as we can be. These are times when we may converse with others whom we deliberately choose–colleagues, authors, artists, friends–and in whose presence we can, more self-consciously than otherwise, become our selves. These are also times when our own multiple "selves" may converse with each other. Though we may not be able to craft our selves directly, we may, through deliberate action, craft the relational contexts of our becoming. In these alternative spaces, we may rethink and re-create our selves in the contexts of our selves–our reflexivities serving as contexts within which we become *more* ourselves than we can be amidst the currents of everyday life.

The selves we re-present in this way–in our alternative spaces–return to everyday life, incompletely and imperfectly re-formed yet often with some deepened insight. We may return to the world with a different perspective or understanding, and we may then act in the world in ways that differ from what others have always expected of or exacted from us. We may also induce change (if only slowly) by teaching to others what we have learned from within ourselves, helping others see what we see–or better yet, helping them see from within themselves, from within their own creations of their own alternative spaces.

RE-PRESENTATION AS LEARNING *FROM* RESEARCHERS' LIVES *FOR* THEIR OWN AND OTHERS' LIVES

Research is often viewed as needing to be of benefit to persons beyond the researcher, and researchers often go to great lengths to cut themselves personally out of research–to make their work appear, as Susan Krieger points out, selfless–for example, by trying to excise their personal voices and agendas from their research in the hope of highlighting agendas deemed more socially worthwhile. The assumption in this practice is that attention to self may overshadow attention to others or to a larger social good. Our analyses of these autobiographies of accomplished educational researchers suggest that the muting, in research, of the researcher's personal needs to learn "things in particular" is neither possible nor necessarily desirable. In many of the preceding chapters, researchers describe themselves as engaging in research for personally meaningful reasons and as gaining insights of personal value from their studies: Ellen Condliffe Lagemann explains that she has used her scholarly writing to create the person she has become. Martha Montero-Sieburth describes herself as using her research to give voice to others; but in doing this, she works out her own needs for voice. Concha Delgado-Gaitan uses her research to learn how to create meaningful parent involvement in schools and communities viewed as "borderlands," but these efforts also feed her personal struggles to understand the blurring of borders in her life–between school and home and community, between research and practice, between physical endurance and faltering health. Patricia Gumport uses her research to understand what it is like to devote one's life to the construction of knowledge that does not (or cannot) meet with social approval; in doing this, she works at balancing her own needs for approval and connection.

We wonder (and worry) what would have happened if the eleven women writing for this volume had cut their personal interests and needs out of their research–if Gumport had decided not to probe the question of "whose knowledge counts?"; if Ladson-Billings had not committed herself to tackling the questions of her own ethnic community but had adopted the research questions of white mainstream academe; if Peterson had not allowed her learning from her children to question her methodological stances; if Neumann had not gained interest in probing the unspoken? We conjecture that diminishing the presence of the self in the research of the eleven women writing in this volume would be tantamount to losing their research–their thoughts and their voices–in education, including the knowledge they have constructed within their diverse fields, and the knowing and learning they have inspired. To mute the personal learning needs of these researchers, in their research, would not have created better studies; it would likely have obliterated areas of study. We suspect that what imbues these authors' research with social value–what makes their studies compelling to those for whom they write–is their framing of these studies from within their own experiences of the problems they pursue, as opposed to relying on the experiences of others. Their work then emerges as a more personal statement of their learning and thus as more open to personal connection with the learning needs of others.[3]

We wonder also why this is and suggest that these women's retreats into "alternative realities" (simultaneously "apart from" and "a part of" their everyday lives) provide them with rare opportunities to engage, conjecturally and critically, with their own selves, and to engage with others of their choosing on issues at the center of their everyday lives. Based on our analyses of these writers' accounts, we surmise that this kind of sustained self-reflection will not occur if the subject of reflection bears little personal meaning for the person who tries to reflect on it. Engaged self-reflection requires a subject of intense personal meaning and value to the researcher–one that will engage her in sustained and probing conversation with diverse aspects of her self, whether in solitude or among others with whom she chooses to converse.

LEARNING FROM EXPANDED RE-PRESENTATIONS: IMPLICATIONS FOR THE FIELD

In closing, we wonder how the substance of the field of education is changing–and how it is likely to change in the future–as women create knowledge both from and for their lives. What new or different topics, insights, and ways of knowing are likely to emerge from diverse women's lives? And what will these add to the field? How might such diversity of thought remake the field? We conclude with three conjectures about emergent changes in the field:

We suspect that, with time, the thinking that frames women's lives now, as this grows out of the thinking that framed women's lives in the past, will further infuse educational thought about what it means to educate. Educational thought already reflects the insides of women's lives, and we conjecture that it will continue to do so.

Dorothy Smith, in a classic description of women's perspective as a radical critique of the field of sociology, distinguishes between the "governing" or "conceptual mode" that typically characterizes men's everyday lives and the mode of caring for men's and others' "bodily existences" that characterizes the everyday lives of women who have historically supported males' more worldly endeavors. Smith's assertion is echoed in the writings of other feminists who point out that "intellectualism" has often been defined at some distance from women's everyday lives—that the substance of women's lives, and their thoughts about life, have historically been set apart from intellectual endeavor. This has resulted in the historic exclusion of much of the substance of women's lives from intellectual scrutiny; it has also resulted in women's exclusion from intellectual endeavor, for example, as women's ways of knowing were separated from intellectual ways of knowing.

We suspect that as women assume positions of recognized intellectual leadership in the field of education, and as the thoughts of their lives become more widely accepted as legitimate academic and intellectual concerns, that the very meaning of the term *intellectual* in education will change. Intellectualism will encompass—as it has already begun to do—the personal concerns that comprise the insides of individual women's lives: caring for the young and elderly and caring for oneself as a caregiver (see, for example, Nel Noddings's work); encouraging people's critical awareness and supporting their efforts to articulate what they know and what they seek to learn (see work by Maxine Greene and Ellen Condliffe Lagemann); struggling to unify the efforts of home, community, and school in fostering environments conducive to growth (see work by Concha Delgado-Gaitan, Gloria Ladson-Billings, and Penelope L. Peterson); working to enhance equality, voice, and meaningful educational experiences for diverse children and adults (see studies by Linda F. Winfield, Kathryn H. Au, and Martha Montero-Sieburth); seeking to understand and shape how human beings know themselves and each other and how they connect in human ways to the knowledge of each other's lives (see studies by Patricia J. Gumport and Anna Neumann). We suspect, as well, that women's ways of knowing themselves and the world will permeate and re-form visions of intellectual knowing.

We conjecture that women's struggles to craft meaningful intellectual identities—identities reflective of their lives—will be inscribed, reflexively, in the field. We also expect concerns about intellectual and personal identity and its development to flourish as a topic in educational scholarship.

Several of the women writing for this volume show how they turned their own struggles to become publicly acknowledged intellectuals into topics of intellectual pursuit. Linda Winfield explains how the personal resilience that helped her survive hostile academic environments and family pressures was transposed into her research on African American youth, and how she has centered this topic as a concern for the field. Martha Montero-Sieburth describes how her commitments to the intertwining of teaching and research in the forging of her scholarship grow, in good part, from institutional norms that devalued teaching and relationships with students. Maxine Greene presents herself as contributing to the reconstruction of the field of philosophy of education through what she eventually brought to it by virtue of her early exclusions from the field and unplanned detours through literary and aesthetic studies. We speculate, based on these examples, that at least some of the topics of expertise and interest appearing on the curricula vitae of accomplished academic women may be marks not of choice or initiative but of hardship and exclusion turned, paradoxically, into intellectual accomplishment.

But given the steep barriers, how, in fact, do women, historically removed from socially recognized intellectual circles, assume intellectual status? And how do they do this at the same time that they struggle to redefine what it means to engage in intellectual endeavor–to legitimize, as the subject of intellectual endeavor, that which has historically been set outside its purview? We suspect that responses to these questions will require women to take long and hard looks at their own lives, at their own experiences as learners and professionals in education, and at their own aspirations for educational reform. We surmise that personal searches of this sort will result in turns toward reflexive inquiry in education–indeed, turns already strongly in evidence. We suspect this trend will continue with reflexive attention not only to women's past experiences (as in the form of autobiographical research) but also to their experiences in the present as they strive to remake themselves and their professional practice (as in the form of researcher-practitioners' studies of their own practice). But we do not expect these changes to be limited to women researchers; we expect that more men as well will become engaged in this kind of inquiry. In sum, we anticipate that researchers' personal questions about how they wish to enact intellectualism–given their diverse personal backgrounds–will become topics of the more public discourses of education. We view this volume as part of this trend.

We speculate that just as women's personal efforts to re-present their lives become inscribed in their research, so will these efforts become, in time, inscribed in the shared knowing of the scholarly and professional communities that they join, reform, and lead.

Through this assertion, we theorize that a woman who achieves a position of intellectual leadership inscribes her conceptions of research–and thereby her personal efforts at self re-presentation through her research–in her leadership work in communities of scholars. Maxine Greene built her program, as president of the American Educational Research Association, by drawing on her own well-analyzed conceptions of education and on her views of how education might develop. The values that drive her personally, and the values and understandings that drive her scholarly work, also drove–and continue to drive–her intellectual agenda for the association and for the educational community generally. "Then, as now," she says of her actions as president of AERA, "I was obsessive about connecting the domains of imagination, the arts, social commitment, and cultural transformation." Greene, along with several of these authors, shows how she struggles to bring all of her self to any expression of research–whether her writing, her teaching, her editorial work, or her crafting of a national research program. As such,

Greene brings to her intellectual leadership of the educational community the lessons of her personal home and family life, the lessons of her acceptances into and exclusions from diverse areas of study, and the lessons of her awakenings to new understandings in life and in research.

Working from the examples of this volume's authors, we propose that the field of education will change so long as women–but men as well–bring all that they know and think and wonder about in the contexts of their lives and their research to their work as intellectual leaders. That is, education will change so long as women and men bring their selves–authentically–to their intellectual work.

But what might it mean for a woman to bring her self in this way to research, to teaching, to scholarship cast broadly, and to intellectual leadership? Bringing all of one's self to one's scholarly work means bringing one's personal knowledge and personal ways of knowing to professional tasks, openly and unselfconsciously. For women this means bringing knowledge and knowing–from their lives as unique women–to their scholarship.

Earlier in this section we noted that the subject matters of education are changing–for example, in their growing reflection of the substantive and epistemological insides of women's lives. Historically, intellectuals in education (and in other fields) have viewed the personal concerns of women's lives as inconsistent with intellectual endeavor. Today, however, intellectuals in education purposefully and openly explore subjects derived from women's experiences–and they intentionally incorporate women's ways of knowing their own lives–in scholarly study. We view this volume as an extension of this pattern, moving against the grain of intellectual history.

It would have been all too easy for us to create this book as a collection of "stories" about the personal side of the personal-professional struggle that academic women are assumed to encounter. But it also would have been too easy for us to turn this book into a compilation of abstract analyses quite devoid of personal (and human) content. What we have tried to do here is to illuminate some of the personal-intellectual braidings of women's lives in ways that do not diminish either of these strands and that search intentionally for connections and continuities between them.

We–and now we refer to the collective of women who authored this volume–have tried to speak personally about our intellectual work. We have also tried to "intellectualize" (in the best sense of the word) selected facets of our personal lives–that is, we have tried to legitimate the knowledge of our personal/academic lives, to define such knowledge as worthy of deep intellectual consideration. In doing this, we strive to extend the range of subjects deemed appropriate for research–for questioning, articulation, and reflection–in education. In acknowledging the humanness of the researched, the researcher, the reader of research, and the research experience itself, we also strive to extend the range and depth of education as a field of humanistic study and, more broadly, humanistic endeavor.

NOTES

1. We use the terms *present* and *re-present* in a social constructivist and social reconstructivist (Berger and Luckmann, 1967; Rabinow and Sullivan, 1987) spirit, viewing everyday life as socially created but also as personally (and socially) re-created in reflection, critique, and imagination. We use the term *given* to signify the previously constructed social realities into which one steps and with which one must contend.

2. These, of course, are our own (Anna Neumann's and Penelope Peterson's) re-presentations of the authors' autobiographical accounts. Through them we strive to convey how we have taken these women's lives into our own, given the unique contours of each of our own lives. We hope that in making our own learning from these lives explicit, we may encourage you, our reader, to do the same–though creating your understandings within the contours of your own life.

3. Susan Krieger (1991) explains how more general knowing may be achieved, ironically, through personal (idiosyncratic) connection in this way: "One consequence of being more specific about the self is that, in the end, one becomes more general. One person's idiosyncratic experience speaks to the experience of another. . . . To encourage a social science based on individually different expressions is not, I think, ultimately destructive to the building of joint visions. It is simply a different way to go about developing such visions, and it is potentially a more rich way than others that emphasize likeness, or a common view, or that leave the definition of self unclear" (p. 48).

BIBLIOGRAPHY

Anzaldua, Gloria. 1987. *Borderlands-la Frontera: The New Mestiza*. San Francisco: spinsters/aunt lute.

Berger, Peter L., and Thomas Luckmann. 1967. *The Social Construction of Reality: A Treatise in the Sociology of Knowledge*. New York: Anchor/Doubleday.

Collins, Patricia Hill. 1991. *Black Feminist Thought: Knowledge, Consciousness, and the Politics of Empowerment*. New York: Routledge.

Kondo, Dorinne K. 1990. *Crafting Selves: Power, Gender, and Discourses in a Japanese Workplace*. Chicago: University of Chicago Press.

Krieger, Susan. 1991. *Social Science and the Self: Personal Essays on an Art Form*. New Brunswick, NJ: Rutgers University Press.

Rabinow, Paul, and William M. Sullivan, eds. 1987. *Interpretive Social Science: A Second Look*. Berkeley: University of California Press.

Smith, Dorothy E. 1974. "Women's Perspective as a Radical Critique of Sociology." *Sociological Inquiry* 44(1):7–13.

Smith, Dorothy E. 1987. *The Everyday World as Problematic: A Feminist Sociology*. Boston: Northeastern University Press.

About the Editors and the Contributors

Kathryn H. Au is Associate Professor of Curriculum and Instruction at the University of Hawaii at Manoa. She earned her Ph.D. in educational psychology at the University of Illinois at Urbana-Champaign (1980). Previously, she was an educational psychologist and classroom teacher at the Kamehameha Elementary Education Program (KEEP) in Honolulu. Au conducts teacher education efforts aimed at increasing the number of native Hawaiian teachers in classrooms in their own communities. Her research interest is the school literacy development of students of diverse cultural and linguistic backgrounds. She has published over fifty articles on this topic as well as a textbook, *Literacy Instruction in Multicultural Settings* (1993). Au is president-elect of the National Reading Conference and a vice president of the American Educational Research Association. She is an active member of the International Reading Association, and she drafted that organization's resolution on cultural awareness. Au received the first National Scholar Award presented by the National Association for Asian and Pacific American Education and has been recognized as a Distinguished Scholar by the AERA Standing Committee on the Role and Status of Minorities in Educational Research.

Concha Delgado-Gaitan is Professor in Sociocultural Studies in Education at the University of California, Davis. She holds a Ph.D. in anthropology and education from Stanford University (1983). Delgado-Gaitan has published several books reporting her ethnographic research on education in ethnic and immigrant communities, including *Literacy for Empowerment* (1990), *Crossing Cultural Borders* (with Henry T. Trueba, 1991), and *Protean Literacy: Extending the Discourse on Empowerment* (1996). Numerous articles appearing in journals such as the *Harvard Educational Review*, the *American Educational Research Journal*, and the *Anthropology and Education Quarterly* reflect Delgado-Gaitan's interests in the socialization and educational experiences of immigrant families, connections between home and school in Latino/a communities, and literacy learning among Mexican American children.

Maxine Greene was born and attended school in New York City, where she received her B.A. (1938) from Barnard College and her M.A. (1949) and Ph.D. (1955) degrees in philosophy of education from New York University (NYU). After receiving her doctorate, Greene taught at NYU, Montclair State College, and Brooklyn College. From 1966 to the present, she has been on the faculty of Teachers College, Columbia University, where she has served as editor of the *Teachers College Record*, professor of English education, and professor of philosophy and education. She is now *emerita*, but still teaching. From 1975, Greene held the William F. Russell Chair in the Foundations of Education at Teachers College, becoming *emerita* in 1994. From 1974 to the present, she has been "philosopher-in-residence" at the Lincoln Center Institute for the Arts in Education. Greene is past-president of the Philosophy of Education Society, the American Educational Studies Association, and the American Educational Research Association. She has written more than 150 articles and book chapters on many subjects including educational philosophy, the arts, literature and literary theory, curriculum, critical pedagogy, women's issues, modernism and postmodernism. Her books include *The Public School and the Private Vision* (1965), *Existential Encounters for Teachers* (1967), *Teacher as Stranger* (1973), *Landscapes of Learning* (1978), *The Dialectic of Freedom* (1988), and *Releasing Imagination: Essays on Education, Art, and Social Change* (1995).

Patricia J. Gumport is Associate Professor in the School of Education at Stanford University where she also serves as Director of the Stanford Institute for Higher Education Research and as Director of Higher Education Programs. She earned her Ph.D. in education (higher education/administration and policy analysis) from Stanford University (1987). Gumport has received a postdoctoral fellowship from the Spencer Foundation and two awards from the Association for the Study of Higher Education (ASHE), including the Outstanding Dissertation of the Year Award in 1988 and the Early Career Scholar Award in 1993. She has published several articles and book chapters on the social construction of academic knowledge and academic identities, and she is currently developing a book manuscript on academic restructuring using case studies of research universities.

Gloria Ladson-Billings is Associate Professor of Curriculum and Instruction at the University of Wisconsin-Madison where she specializes in issues of multicultural education and culturally relevant pedagogy. She holds a Ph.D. in curriculum and teacher education from Stanford University (1984). Ladson-Billings has written extensively on successful teachers for African American students, including publishing a book entitled *The Dreamkeepers* (1994). She is a 1989 recipient of the National Academy of Education's Spencer Post-Doctoral Fellowship, the 1995 recipient of the National Association of Multicultural Education's Outstanding Research Award, and the 1995 recipient of the American Educational Research Association's Committee on the Role and Status of Minorities, Early Career Contribution Award. In her latest research, Ladson-Billings focuses on critical race theory and its application to education. At the University of Wisconsin-Madison, she currently teaches courses in multicultural perspectives in education, culturally relevant pedagogy, and social studies methods.

Ellen Condliffe Lagemann is Professor of History and Education and Director of the Center for the Study of American Culture and Education at New York University. A graduate of Smith College (A.B., 1967), Teachers College (M.A., 1968), and Columbia University (Ph.D., 1978), Lagemann taught at Teachers College from 1978 until 1994. She was also a member of the Columbia University Department of History. From 1990 until 1995, she was editor of the *Teachers College Record*. Lagemann is the author or editor of six books, including *Private Power for the Public Good* (1983), which won a Critics' Choice Award from the American Educational Studies Association, and *The Politics of Knowledge* (1989), which won the National Society of Fund Raising Executives Outstanding Research Award. She has also written many articles, book chapters, and reviews. A former president of the History of Education Society, Lagemann was elected to the National Academy of Education in 1990. She is currently co-chair of the Academy's Commission on the Improvement of Education Research as well as a member of the Executive Council and of the final selection committee for the Spencer Post-Doctoral Fellowship program run by the academy. Lagemann is a trustee of Riverdale Country School, the Markle Foundation, the Russell Sage Foundation, and the Center for Advanced Study in the Behavioral Sciences, where she was a fellow in 1991–92.

Martha Montero-Sieburth holds master's degrees in the teaching of social sciences, awarded by Washington University (1969), and in Hispanic language and literature, awarded by the University of the Americas in Puebla, Mexico (1976); she received her Ed.D. in instructional development and administration (with concentration in bilingual education) from Boston University (1981). Montero-Sieburth is currently Associate Professor in the Graduate College of Education at the University of Massachusetts–Boston where she served previously as Director of Educational Research for the Mauricio Gastón Institute for Latino Community Development and Public Policy. She was also project manager for Multicultural Educational Experiences at Harvard Medical School and associate professor at Simmons College; she has held teaching positions at several other institutions of higher education. Drawing on her background in cultural anthropology, Montero-Sieburth has carried out a variety of ethnographic studies in Costa Rica, Honduras, Guatemala, and the United States. She is currently co-editing two books (one with Gary Anderson and another with Francisco Villarruel) reflecting her interests in Latino students and qualitative research.

Anna Neumann (Editor) is Associate Professor of Education at Michigan State University. She earned her Ph.D. in education (higher education) at the University of Michigan in Ann Arbor in 1983 and subsequently worked as an instructor and administrator at Antioch College in Yellow Springs, Ohio, and California State University at Fresno. From 1986 to 1990 she served as a principal researcher for two multi-year, national studies of college and university leadership within the National Center for Postsecondary Governance and Finance at Teachers College, Columbia University. Neumann's analyses of how college presidents, administrators, and faculty learn about and construct campus realities through their interactions with one another have appeared in a series of articles published in journals such as the *American Educational Research Journal*, the *Journal of Higher Education*, and the *Review of Higher Education*, and in a book, *Redesigning Collegiate Leadership: Teams and Teamwork in Higher Education* (with Estela M. Bensimon, 1993). She is currently studying how professors construct their scholarly agendas (and themselves as scholars) in a modern American university and how the university, in turn, shapes professors' scholarly work and identities.

Nel Noddings is Lee Jacks Professor of Child Education at Stanford University. She received her master's degree in mathematics from Rutgers University (1964) and her Ph.D. from Stanford University in education (1973). Noddings's areas of special interest are feminist ethics, moral education, and mathematical problem solving. Noddings is a past-president of the national Philosophy of Education Society and president of the John Dewey Society. She was a Phi Beta Kappa Visiting Scholar for the year 1989–90. She also served as Associate Dean and then Acting Dean of Stanford University's School of Education for four years. Noddings has published nine books—among them are *Caring: A Feminine Approach to Ethics and Moral Education* (1984), *Women and Evil* (1989), *The Challenge to Care in Schools* (1992), and *Educating for Intelligent Belief or Unbelief* (1993). In addition, she is author of more than one hundred articles and chapters on various topics ranging from the ethics of caring to mathematical problem solving.

Penelope L. Peterson (Editor) is University Distinguished Professor of Education at Michigan State University. She received her M.A. and Ph.D. degrees from Stanford University in psychological studies in education (1976). Before assuming her current position, Peterson was Sears-Bascom Professor of Education at the University of Wisconsin-Madison. For six years, Peterson served as editor of the *Review of Educational Research*, a major journal of the American Educational Research Association (AERA); she is currently president of AERA. In her research, Peterson focuses on teaching and learning in schools and classrooms, particularly in mathematics and literacy; and relations among educational research, policy, and practice. She has published more than eighty-five articles and book chapters in these areas and has recently published a book with Richard Elmore and Sarah McCarthey entitled *Teaching, Learning, and School Organization* (1996). In 1980 Peterson received the Palmer O. Johnson Memorial Award given by the American Educational Research Association (AERA) for her article on teachers' decision making during interactive classroom teaching. In 1986, she received the Raymond B.

Cattell Early Career Award from the American Educational Research Association (AERA) for her outstanding programmatic research on effective teaching. In 1992, Peterson was given the Distinguished Research Award by the Association of Teacher Educators.

Linda F. Winfield holds an M.A. in human growth and development (1981) and a Ph.D. in learning and cognition (1982) from the University of Delaware. Until recently, she was Professor of Educational Administration and Policy at the University of Southern California. Formerly at Johns Hopkins University's Center for Research on Effective Schooling for Disadvantaged Students, she was a principal research scientist and former co-director of Special Strategies, a congressionally mandated national study of promising school programs designed to inform the reauthorization of Chapter 1 federal legislation. In 1992, Winfield received the American Educational Research Association's Palmer O. Johnson Memorial Award for distinguished contribution to educational research in the area of educational policy and national assessment. Winfield is the author of *Developing Resilience in Urban Youth* (1994). She has published numerous articles and chapters on urban education and on policies related to the achievement and development of youth in disadvantaged settings.

Index